SYNERGISTIC
GOLF
ONE DAY AT A TIME

SYNERGISTIC GOLF

ONE DAY AT A TIME

*Get Your
Body, Mind and Spirit
Working Together for a Better Game*

Mary Ann Souter and Mindi Boysen

SYNERGISTIC GOLF
One Day at a Time

Get your Body, Mind and Spirit Working Together for a Better Game

M&M Publishing
Phoenix, AZ
www.synergisticgolf.com

WARNING: Not all exercises are suitable for everyone. This or any other exercise program may result in injury. Any user of this program assumes the risk of injury resulting from performing the exercises. To reduce the risk of injury in your case, consult your Doctor before beginning this exercise program. The instructions and advice presented are in no way intended as a substitute for medical counseling. The creators, producers, participants and distributors of this program disclaim any liabilities or loss in connection with the exercises and advice herein.

NOTE: Some of the humor presented in this book is adult only material. The content of the joke/statement may contain information meant for mature adults and may not be suitable for young readers.

ISBN: 0-9767067-0-9

Cover and book design by Robert Aulicino, www.aulicinodesign.com

Printed in the United States of America

ACKNOWLEDGEMENTS

Thanks and appreciation go to our family members and friends who were always willing to give us input, review sections, offer jokes, and provide us with comments to make the book more reader-friendly. We are grateful for their feedback and the interest and support they have shown in this project.

Tom Souter's passion for golf made him Mary Ann's ideal encourager. His knowledge of the game led to valuable suggestions that were incorporated into this book. His clever remarks and humorous observations kept levity in our home during my countless hours spent on the computer. He was and is "the wind beneath my wings."

Brian Quackenbush, golf professional, not only offered golf tips but also provided much needed information technology support. In addition, Brian took a substantial number of the photos used to demonstrate exercises.

We are lucky to have family members who believed in us from the beginning of the project all along the way. They assisted us through research, editing, website development and much-needed honest recommendations. They are Richard and Linda Griffith (Mindi's parents); Jessica Plichta, RNC, BSN (Mary Ann's daughter and friend); Ned Griffith, owner of QUIK Internet of Virginia Beach (Mindi's brother); and Linda Souter, law student (Mary Ann's new daughter).

We would also like to thank the "models" who posed for the exercises. All of the models are golfers. It was our intent to demonstrate that these exercises can be performed by anyone, no matter what physical shape you're in or how old you are. So, included in the photos are young and not-so-young; active and less active; physically fit and those needing a little help; and athletes who work out regularly.

Special thanks go to the management at Tatum Ranch Golf Club in Cave Creek, Arizona for their cooperation in allowing us to use their facility for most of the photos. Many of the people in the photos are members of Tatum Ranch Golf Club.

MODELS FOR EXERCISE PHOTOS
(OTHER THAN THE AUTHORS)

Brian Quackenbush: Professional golfer; golfed for University of Virginia; Mini-Tour player; in the process of designing a technologically-advanced putter with exact direction control; www.brianquackenbush.com

Tom Souter: Low-handicap golfer; Project Manager for commercial contractor; believes in the value of a pre-game warm-up routine, especially flexibility exercises

Kay Betz: Grandmother, retired school nurse; works out and does Pilates twice a week

Richard Dirmantas: Golf Shop Operations Manager at Tatum Ranch Golf Course in Cave Creek, Arizona; avid golfer

Garrett Durkin: Senior in high school; learning now that exercise, focus, and a positive attitude help restore energy in all areas of life

Kit Grove: Professional golfer; golfed for University of Kansas, currently on Gateway Tour; works out consistently using weighted ball exercises

Helen Gruener: Pharmacist; avid runner of 5k distance; works out with weights 2 times a week

Alan Hunter: Producer of Golf Southwest TV show aired in Arizona, Nevada, and California; recreational golfer

Carolyn Jarvis: Retired training consultant; grandmother; started golfing in her forties; motivated to play her best game incorporating a weekly physical fitness program into her routine

Mike Kalsched: Triathlete — swim, bike, run; believes there is no magic bullet, success takes hard work, perseverance, and a love for what you are doing so that it is fun

John Loleit: Pinnacle Peak Park Coordinator in Scottsdale, Arizona; avid mountain runner; backpacker; fly fisherman; worked 25 years in outdoor recreation field.

Kristoffer Marshall: Professional golfer currently playing on the Gateway Tour; golfed for University of Kansas 2000-2004, two-time All American; work outs focus on intense cardio and core with particular attention to diet

Todd Rakotz: Professional golfer currently playing on the Gateway Tour; played baseball for East Carolina University; married and father of two

Jeff Seabaugh: Account Manager for Network Product company, plays golf two times a week; believes work outs are all about intensity

Jack Thompson: 88 years old; playing golf for more than 70 years; believes golf and all movement helps your health and overall happiness; only wears knickers when playing golf — helps keep him warm in the winter and cool in the hot Arizona summer

INTRODUCTION

WHAT IS SYNERGISTIC GOLF?

The idea that "golf is more than swinging a club" is not a new concept to most players. Although technique, club selection, and experience are all vital elements that lead to success, you will never reach your maximum potential without involving your whole being into the game. Each unique facet of your "self" must be nurtured to create a totally positive result. Your best game is not simply the function of learning the perfect swing. It's a combination of many skills (some not even directly related to the play itself), including exercise, proper nutrition, a positive attitude, an understanding of the complete game of golf, and a sense of humor.

So then, what is Synergistic Golf? Synergistic Golf is a brand new term — in fact, we made it up. But it actually describes a "complete" approach to the game of golf, one that integrates — simultaneously — the physical, mental/emotional, and spiritual elements of a player's being to produce results that are more productive than the sum of all these elements individually.

Synergy in golf is the combination of the relationship between the following:

1. Body—which encompasses the technique of the swing, physical fitness of the muscle groups involved, and the overall health of the body through nutrition;
2. Mind—which includes the ability to maintain the focus required to achieve better swing techniques as well as motivation to succeed in the game;
3. Spirit—the inner "self" of each of us that incorporates humor and a proper attitude (including golf etiquette) for success on the course and in life, the force that also keeps us continuously aware of our surroundings through our senses. The visual aesthetics associated with the game of golf are an integral part of the enjoyment and positive experience that all golfers want to perceive as they play.

To play your best golf, you must incorporate all three of these components into your game. This book gives you the tools with which to do it, easily, one day at a time, at whatever comfort level you find most helpful.

And where in the world could you find a better opportunity to do just that for yourself? The game of golf itself, simply by being played outdoors on beautifully landscaped terrain, stimulates the use of our senses, our bodies, and our imaginations. By taking those remarkable stimulants into other parts of your life, you can make much of what you think, say, and do contribute tremendously to the improvement of your game. It's about attention — and intention.

HOW THIS BOOK WILL HELP YOU

You must learn to be aware of the way each of these components work together in your life to produce positive overall results. No one section stands alone to offer all the answers, so we are encouraging you to strengthen the parts of your being that need attention. If your body is not fit, then taking the time each day to perform the exercise is imperative. We must have strong and healthy bodies to enjoy the game of golf and life in general.

But, if you are currently participating in a fitness program and paying close attention to your diet and nutrition, then focus your attention on the sections that nurture your mind and spirit. Maybe you need to have a more positive outlook, in which case the motivational quotes will bring that area to the forefront of your mind each day. Perhaps you are not appreciating the beauty of the outdoors or daily interaction with others. The quotes that stress the spiritual elements will help you to become more aware of those qualities. And last, but certainly not least, cultivating your sense of humor can only be a constructive act that will influence your entire life.

Humor has often been touted as one of the most effective ways to judge the quality of a relationship. If laughter is part of any relationship, it is probably a healthy one. Therefore, to have a more enjoyable time on the course and with your fellow players, it is imperative to develop your sense of humor. And, in case you didn't know, you are not born with a good sense of humor; it is learned. This is definitely an area that you have the power to sharpen, and you will absolutely reap the benefits if you do. By enjoying the natural highs associated with a good sense of humor, you will intentionally find the happiness and euphoria that leads to a more content life.

Exercises with Explanations and Goals

Golf is the ideal sport for almost anyone. Unlike most other sports, it's a sport that individuals can enjoy playing at different levels for almost all their lives. And unlike other sports, there's no grueling training required. But in order to get the most from the game, it's a good idea to be in the best physical shape you can be. As an individual sport, golf relates only to the player involved. It's not like team sports where each person has to contribute in order to win the game. In golf, it's the player against the course. It's a challenge at whatever age or skill level you can play. That's probably why over 26 million people play golf in the U.S. today.

Most non-professional golfers spend each day at a fairly sedentary job and look to the golf course as their little bit of exercise for the week. They throw their bags on a motorized cart, get to the tee and start swinging hard. Ouch! Ouch! Ouch! With the amount of force that goes into each swing, the undue stress on an imbalanced and inefficient body, repeated over and over, can cause IRREVERSIBLE damage! Golf is definitely a sport most people can enjoy, but only regular practice and correct exercise techniques will help to prevent injury and promote a better swing.

Many golfers (maybe even you?) believe that hitting a few dozen balls at the driving range is all the warm-up you need to loosen up your muscles and to practice that "perfect" swing to improve your scores. Yes, practice does make perfect—*well, actually, perfect practice makes perfect.* Practice will improve consistency, but what we all want is to maximize our skills while preventing injuries.

Back injuries and joint damage are fairly common among golfers, even though the game of golf is considered to be a sport that is fairly easy on the body. Knowing which muscles we use and how to strengthen them is essential to a good golf swing.

So if you want to add more control and power to your swing, complete a backswing with an extended follow-through, have more energy and stamina to enjoy even the last holes, and finish the game without having aches and pains the next day, then the fitness section of this book will help you.

The exercises in this book can be categorized into three themes:

1) Dynamic and static flexibility
2) Strength training for the major muscle groups
3) Stabilization techniques to improve your balance and posture

Start all movements slowly and in a controlled manner. Do not "throw" your limbs into position. Start with a small range of motion and gradually increase it as you get warmer. Breathe! Never hold your breath. Breathing allows oxygen to get to the muscles and relieves stress.
Visualize longer and taller posture throughout each movement. Evenly disperse

your body weight. Move from side to side until you feel balanced. READ YOUR BODY SIGNS! Make sure the movement does not cause pain. A slight pulling or stretching sensation is fine. Repeat each exercise approximately 10 times.

The one fitness component that has only a minor presence in this book is cardiovascular endurance. There are a number of exercises designed specifically for cardio fitness. Use these more often and include them on a daily basis. However, they won't be enough. On your own, try to walk, run, bike, or swim to work on the most important muscle in your body—your heart. In fact, if you put as much spirit into your daily fitness routine as you put into your game, a great game and healthier lifestyle are just around the corner.

Nutrition Tips

Some of you may be quite attentive to your nutrition, making this section of each page less appealing. On the other hand, if you really should be learning more about the necessity of a healthy diet, then absorbing one of these Nutrition Tips each day will help you to understand the value of certain foods and their purpose in your diet. Perhaps you'll even hear of a fruit or vegetable you didn't know existed. Keeping your body healthy by being conscious of what goes into your mouth is an important aspect of the synergy we are describing. If you are overweight or don't drink enough water, you will definitely notice it in your game. However, if your body is well nourished with the right mix of foods, it will show in your performance on the course. Since nutrition is in the spotlight today with many best seller books available, many of you may already be making a concentrated effort in the area of eating healthier. If that is the case, focus your attention more on the other elements. The more of these tips to build a healthy body, mind, and spirit you incorporate into your everyday life, the less you will have to make an effort to learn to use on a daily basis.

So far we have discussed the importance of the two physical elements of this book, exercise and nutrition, both essential parts of maintaining a fit body. They go hand in hand keeping the body in shape and healthy. Now let's move on to the other sections of the book, the ones that deal with your mind and spirit.

Experience Good Thoughts

Our thoughts literally define who we are. Since we can choose our thoughts, we can choose the direction of our lives. The idea that what goes into our minds is also what shows itself in our disposition, our character, our values, our interpretation of events, our performance and our interaction with others is a dramatic window to our inner selves. You may have heard some of these quotes many times before, but have you incorporated them into your daily thinking pattern to reinforce positive results? You have to do more than just read the daily quote. Each one was chosen because of the impact it could have on your thinking and therefore, your actions. Open your mind. Be flexible. Read it more than once. Think about it while you're getting ready in the morning. Process its meaning and absorb its message into your mind. Think about it in all you do until you feel that it has become part of your psyche. Be conscious about what goes into your thoughts for it will most assuredly manifest itself in what comes out.

If you have a tendency to be one who sees the cup half empty or who projects the worst possible scenario (most of which never come to pass), then the motivational and inspirational quotes in *Experience Good Thoughts* may be the section that serves you best. Included are quotes from recognized authorities in all areas of the mind and spirit. Quotes from the Bible to The Buddha and The Dalai Lama to Mother Teresa reinforce the spiritual component of this book. Thinking positive thoughts is an essential factor for success, but the inclusion of these quotes adds a more complex dimension to this section. The element of "love" is referred to frequently; the message of compassion is repeated often; the definition of "wisdom" is described in various forms; and belief, trust, giving, kindness and friendship are also mentioned. These qualities are vital attributes of a healthy mind and spirit and can be formed or reinforced through repetition. Incorporating these traits into our daily lives has the potential of redefining who we are. Every time we repeat an act, we strengthen its hold on us, for good or bad. To act in a more compassionate, concerned and involved way by consciously thinking about these attributes will generate more and more of the same actions. Even feelings can be created, learned and molded.

So what does this have to do with your golf game? Thinking positive thoughts will produce positive results. Processes such as visualization (using your mind's eye to see yourself perform positively and successfully in all situations) and imagery (purposefully using your imagination incorporating all of your senses to project the best scenarios possible such as, imagining yourself hitting long and straight drives or holing thirty foot putts) are instrumental. Combining these techniques with the intention of absorbing beneficial characteristics from the quotes, your game will start to improve and you'll have more fun on the course. When anger and frustration can be diffused into congenial interaction, you'll not only enjoy the game more but so will the people in your group.

Think Golf

Maybe you're a novice golfer who can really benefit from a swing tip or one of the Rules of Golf made a little easier to understand. To this end, you can incorporate one tip at a time, digesting it and making it part of your store of golf knowledge. At the end of a week, you'll have several tips that over time will help your score. Some simple questions that you may not want to ask an experienced golfer for fear of being teased may be answered in the Think Golf section.

Some insertions are merely interesting facts about golf. They give some relief from swing and play tips and offer a respite to read a piece of golf trivia. The more experienced golfers may find these additions appealing. There are some golf statistics interspersed with tips from golfing greats. So don't write off this section if you're an avid golfer. There may be a hidden jewel in this group that you may find helpful and useful. It may offer a tip that you have heard in many other ways but this time it becomes an epiphany and you understand it for the first time. However, this isn't a book about teaching the best swing techniques or how to get out of difficult lies. It's about incorporating your golf knowledge with the other physical and mental components to enhance your game.

Make Me Smile

Everyone loves to laugh. And it has been noted by experts worldwide that "laughter is the best medicine," whether you're going through worrisome health issues or dealing with a bout of the blues. This section has more of an influence than you may think and will have a great effect on your game and your overall outlook on life.

Although most of the jokes center around golfers, the topic to recognize is that we must learn to laugh at ourselves. As human beings, we are not perfect. We will never be perfect. And we often make mistakes that are incredibly funny, but we are too insecure to laugh at ourselves. We are afraid to look foolish in the eyes of others. Life offers one opportunity after another for major blunders, often showing our weaknesses to the whole world. When we laugh at ourselves, they become trivial. When we take ourselves too seriously, it can feel like everything we do is a major effort — even playing a game of golf. The effect of a heart-felt laugh out loud or even a tiny little snicker is a mighty force. Once we allow ourselves to laugh, we break down the walls of pressure, negativity, and seriousness. We awaken the lighter side of our emotions and arouse a brighter point of view for our future. Cultivating an atmosphere of humor and laughter will ensure a richer and more satisfying life.

If you had the option, would you choose to be in the company of a totally serious person who is always anxious about the future OR a person who makes you laugh and who lives in the present — one day at a time? We would make an educated guess (basing it on our own choices) that most people like to be around a good-natured person. If that's the type of person you'd like to be with, then that's the type of person you should strive to be. Of course, we can't all be stand-up comedians and that's not the goal in developing a good sense of humor. But if we learn to value the power of levity, we'll begin to see life in a completely different light — yes, we'll begin to see the lighter side of life.

GETTING STARTED — HOW TO USE THIS BOOK

This book is for everyone who loves the game of golf. Whether you're a beginner, a weekend amateur, or a tournament player, Synergistic Golf will be an increasingly valuable tool for you to improve your game.

The exercises can be done by golfers of all ages and all body types. The people demonstrating the exercises in our photos are all golfers — but not all of them are golfers in good shape. So don't worry about your athletic ability. Jump in with both feet and get started.

Golf is also known to be a mental sport. As we've been discussing, a good attitude is vital to success on the course, so feel free to laugh at yourself when you lose your balance or can't do the exercise the way it looks in the book. Nurturing all elements of your being is essential to both playing well and living well.

The book is designed to be used on five consecutive days each week — reading and exercising Monday through Friday. The weekend is reserved to enjoy the time playing golf.

You may find that some of the exercises just don't work for you. Simply move on. But when you discover an exercise that stimulates and stretches you, mark on the page designated for your notes at the end of the week. These are the exercises you will later incorporate into a totally unique, totally personal fitness program that will raise your level of play and keep it there. Use this concept for the rest of the sections as well. Mark down your favorite quotes or jokes for later use.

A page is inserted between each week to record your golf scores, how your body is improving, changes in your eating habits, observations about your mental attitude, motivation, sense of humor and any other thoughts or feelings you think would be helpful in shaping your lifestyle. Write down the pages that had an impact on you, no matter which section it involved.

Working on the whole "you" will help to improve your game and your way of life. With practical hints for your body and positive messages for your mind, you'll notice your body getting healthier and your mind becoming more focused and relaxed.

HOW THE PAGES WORK

Each page is intended to provide nourishment for body, mind, and spirit. At the top of each page is the name of an exercise or stretch, along with its goal. A photo or set of photos demonstrate the motion involved, and the accompanying text provides an explanation of the body movements required making it easy to perform the exercise. Almost no equipment is needed for most exercises. A fitness ball is required for some.

The bottom part of each page is devoted to fueling our physical, mental and emotional beings. A daily nutrition tip, a motivational quote, a golf tip or interesting fact, and a little bit of humor to start your day with a smile, complete the effort to bring about an all-inclusive plan for a better you and a better golf score.

By following this simple weekly program, you can add years to your golfing life and life to your golfing years!

THE TIME IS NOW

Over the years, we have learned that "golfers want to golf." They don't want to work out or spend time studying mental techniques. Of course you want to play better golf today, but it's just as important to be able to play better golf tomorrow and in the years ahead. So get out of your comfort zone, put out a tiny bit of physical effort, and fill your mind with some healthy tips. Be part of the cutting edge of fitness for your whole being.

Here it is — in a compact edition ready for a quick read each day. By following this simple program of combining an exercise or stretch with better nutrition, a positive attitude, practice on the course, and a sense of humor, you'll come out on the up-side of being fit for golf — and — fit for life. Whether you're 18 or 81 years old, the basics in this book will guide you to a more balanced life and a lower golf score in just a few minutes a day. When you get right down to the root of the meaning of the word "succeed," you'll find that it simply means to *follow through*.

So let's get going. Open to the first page of exercises. You can start any month, any day. It is designed to be used Monday through Friday with two days for rest and recreation. Whether it's April or October, start feeding your body, mind, and spirit with the nourishment that will improve your golf game and your lifestyle. Isn't that worth about 10 minutes a day of your time?

MONDAY

Name: DYNAMIC STRETCH: MERRY-GO-ROUND
Goal: Increase flexibility and spinal rotation while maintaining balance through backswing and follow-through.

Explanation:

Stand with your feet firmly planted a little wider than hip distance apart and extend your arms shoulder height to your sides. Rotate 180 degrees facing behind you keeping your arms straight out at your sides and maintain weight centered between both feet. Focus on lifting through the spine and be sure to lift your trailing heel for easier rotation. Repeat 5 times each direction.

Nutrition Tip:
Eat Nuts when you need a snack. Nuts have unsaturated fats that actually help to lower cholesterol and they're loaded with protein, fiber and vitamins. Choose Almonds, Pecans, Walnuts and Hazelnuts. Almonds are also rich in calcium.

Experience Good Thoughts:
"Life is a great big canvas, and you should throw all the paint you can on it."
—Danny Kaye, Entertainer

Think Golf:
Did you know there are 336 dimples on a regulation golf ball? You say, "What difference does that make?" A big difference in the speed and distance your ball will travel. Their purpose is to reduce drag by creating turbulence as the ball flies through the air.

Make Me Smile:
A fan was talking to Jack Nicklaus and applauded his name as being synonymous with the game of golf. "You really know your way around the course. What's your secret?" he asked. Jack replied, "The holes are numbered!"

TUESDAY

Name: STRENGTH: PUSH UP HOLD WITH ROTATION

Goal: Promote shoulder girdle strength and stability to prevent overuse of arms during swing, especially for women.

Explanation:

Hold a pushup position for 30 seconds. Watch in a mirror to ensure straight alignment of shoulders, hips, knees and ankles. Do not lift buttocks up or let them sag (which compresses low back). Once 30 seconds can be held comfortably, move on to level two by lifting one arm and rotate.

Nutrition Tip:
Green tea has been known to be beneficial to your health since the 12th century when the Chinese noticed its great powers. Now green tea is believed to reduce the risk for some cancers and heart disease. It contains the antioxidant polyphenol, a cancer fighter.

Experience Good Thoughts:
"You can't wait for inspiration. You have to go after it with a club."

—Jack London

Think Golf:
Having trouble with "golfer's elbow"? Medial epicondylitis is an inflammation of the tendons around the elbow. Its main cause is holding the grip too tightly and pronating the forearm excessively (stronger grip). Try lessening your grip slightly. The best remedy for pain: Rest, Ice, Compression, and Elevation of the area daily!

Make Me Smile:
One golfer asked his friend why he was so late getting to the tee. His friend said that it was Sunday so he had to toss a coin between going to church or playing golf. "But that still doesn't tell me why you're so late." "Well," said the golfer, "It took me over 25 tosses to get it right!"

WEDNESDAY

Name: PILATES: OBLIQUE CROSS/BICYCLE
Goal: Strengthen core and rotating muscle strength during swing.

Explanation:

Lie on your back with both knees hugged into chest and fingertips lightly behind ears with elbows open. Bend one knee toward chest while other leg extends out parallel with floor. Use your abdominals to keep a flat back to the floor and switch legs while rotating opposite elbow toward opposite knee. Repeat 10 times.

Nutrition Tip:
Red kidney beans, artichokes, and russet potatoes are among some of the best food sources of antioxidants. Antioxidants help guard against cell damage that can lead to cancer, heart disease, and aging. Sweet cherries, pinto beans, gala apples, plums, and pecans are good choices as well.

Experience Good Thoughts:
"If wrinkles must be written upon our brows, let them not be written upon the heart. The spirit should never grow old."

—James Garfield, 20th President

Think Golf:
Did you know? There are at least 32 major muscles involved in a full golf swing. That's why it is in your best interest to stay fit.

Make Me Smile:
John and Brian were enjoying a round of golf one Saturday morning. About the fifth hole John had a heart attack and died. Later that day in the Clubhouse, Brian was talking to some friends and told them that John had died on the course. "That must have been terrible," they all said compassionately. "Yes, it was," said Brian. "All day long it was hit the ball, drag John, hit the ball, drag John . . . "

THURSDAY

Name: PRE-ROUND WARMUP: LAT/HAMSTRING STRETCH
Goal: Open muscles under arms and throughout back as well as back of legs.

Explanation:

> Place both hands on cart or on platform waist high. Keep feet hip width apart and walk feet backward far enough to allow head to hang between arms. Focus on muscles around sides pushing hips back and weight in heels.

Nutrition Tip:
Try to eat 5 mini-meals a day. Eating two or three meals simply isn't often enough. Your blood sugar levels will be controlled, you'll get protein in small amounts throughout your day to support growth and recovery, and (most importantly) the enzymes that store fat will no longer be produced, making you biochemically incapable of storing fat!

Experience Good Thoughts:
"There are no secrets to success. It is the result of preparation, hard work, and learning from failure."

—Colin Powell

Think Golf:
"You miss 100% of the shots you don't take."

—Wayne Gretsky

Make Me Smile:
The doctor gave the golfer his bad news. "I'm sorry I have to tell you that you have both cancer and Alzheimer's." "Oh, no!" said the golfer. "At least I don't have cancer!"

FRIDAY

Name: **YOGA/STRETCH: UPWARD FACING DOG**

Goal: Open tight chest muscles to reduce rounded shoulder syndrome as well as tight hip flexors, which lessen ability to turn.

Explanation:

Lying face down with palms on floor directly under shoulders, lead with head and peel upper body off floor down to belly button. Take deep breaths and feel the lifting effect of ribcage bringing shoulders back and down while spine lifts.

Nutrition Tip:
Whether you are trying to lose fat or adding lean muscle, remember to "zigzag" your calorie intake. For example, if you are dieting, reduce your calories during the week, but have a "free" day on Saturday or Sunday. This will readjust your metabolic rate upwards, support your lean tissue building and give you a psychological lift. YES! You CAN do this ONCE in awhile!

Experience Good Thoughts:
"No one keeps up his enthusiasm automatically. Enthusiasm must be nourished with new actions, new aspirations, new efforts and new vision. It is one's own fault if his enthusiasm is gone; he has failed to feed it."

—Papyrus

Think Golf:
"You hear and you forget. You see and you remember. You do and you understand. What's that spell? Practice!"

—Golf Proverb

Make Me Smile:
The advantage of exercising everyday is that you die a healthier person.

SATURDAY/SUNDAY

GOLFING DAYS ARE GOOD FOR YOUR HEALTH

REFLECTING ON THE PAST WEEK:

What was your basic attitude? Were you a positive thinker or did you need an "attitude adjustment?" Are you having success with eating healthier and doing your exercise program? How do you feel physically? If you went golfing, write down any comments that might be helpful later in improving your game. Remember, that laughter is the best medicine in the face of adversity. Are you seeing the lighter side of life?

The exercise that helped me the most this week was on page:

_____

My nutritional habits this week were:

_____

What made me smile this week?

_____

_____

Looking back at my golf week:
     My Score: _____ What did I do right? _____

_____

_____

     What could I do to improve?

_____

_____

Goals for next week: _____

_____

_____

MONDAY

Name: BIG BALL: WALK-OUTS

Goal: Reinforce trunk musculature promoting stability and power through swing.

Explanation:

Lie over big ball with hands on floor and legs squeezed together parallel to the floor and top of ball. Maintain strong plank position and slowly "walk" hands out away from ball while ball rolls down legs. The farther you go, the more difficult it is to balance. Can you walk out the whole way to your toes? Be aware of back position. Keep it straight and abdominals tight. Walk back in and repeat 5 times.

Nutrition Tip:
Apple skins are your friend! According to French researchers procyanidins, a type of antioxidant found in apple skins, may protect against colon cancer. So just maybe the old cliché, an apple a day keeps the doctor away, has some truth to it.

Experience Good Thoughts:
"What would you do if you knew that you could not fail?"
—Robert Schuller, Minister & Author

Think Golf:
To develop a more consistent swing, take practice shots with the sun at your back and the shadow of your head covering the ball. If the shadow moves off the ball during your swing, then your upper body has shifted out of the proper position. By keeping the shadow over the ball, you'll learn the feeling of a well-centered swing.

Make Me Smile:
"The older you get, the stronger the wind gets — and it's always in your face."
—Jack Nicklaus

TUESDAY

Name: HEAVY BALL: AROUND THE WORLD (AND DOWN)

Goal: Promote coordination, timing and rhythm during swing as well as finger/wrist/forearm strength for club control.

Explanation:

Stand with feet in address position. Circle heavy ball around waist 10 times each direction while rotating hips as if using a hula hoop. Maintain abdominals tight and focus on good posture. As an advanced move, circle the ball both ways down the hips, legs, ankles, and back up.

Nutrition Tip:

Pineapples are rich in one of the trace minerals we all need — manganese. Manganese is needed to metabolize protein and carbohydrates.

Experience Good Thoughts:

"No matter what you've done for yourself or for humanity, if you can't look back on having given love and attention to your own family, what have you really accomplished?"

—Lee Iacocca

Think Golf:

The first person to hole out is responsible for replacing the flagstick. It is courteous and well-known etiquette.

Make Me Smile:

There was a guy who went golfing every Saturday and Sunday. The weather usually didn't matter because he was hooked. One Saturday he left the house early heading for the golf course but it was so bitter cold that he decided to go back home. His wife was still in bed when he got there, so he took off his clothes, snuggled up to his wife and said, "It's so cold out there. It's so nice being here with you." She answered, "Can you believe my stupid husband went golfing this morning?"

WEDNESDAY

Name: PRE-ROUND WARMUP: TOE/HEEL

Goal: Increase blood flow in ankles to prepare them for unlevel lies while swinging.

Explanation:

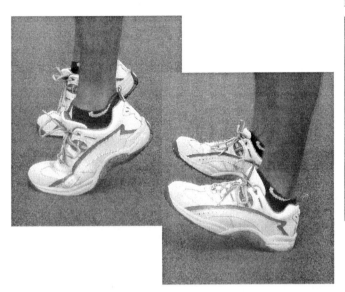

Stand with feet in address position. Hands on hips. Lean, shift weight, and stand on toes, lifting heels. Then switch weight to heels and lift toes. Keep knees slightly unlocked. Repeat back and forth shifting weight 20 times. You should feel a stretch on the bottom of feet as well as back and front of lower legs.

Nutrition Tip:
Protein's main purpose is to build and repair body tissues including muscles, scars, scabs, bumps, bruises, broken bones, tendons, ligaments, etc. The best sources of protein are: red meat, fish, poultry, eggs, legumes, dairy products, nuts, soy, tofu, and protein bars.

Experience Good Thoughts:
"My mother said to me, "If you become a soldier, you'll be a general; if you become a monk, you'll end up as the pope." Instead, I became a painter and wound up as Picasso."

—Pablo Picasso

Think Golf:
The arm muscles (biceps, triceps, and forearm flexors/extensors) are responsible for club control and largely determine clubhead accuracy. So work on your strength and flexibility for a better stroke.

Make Me Smile:
A local attorney sent golf balls inscribed with his name as gifts to many of his clients. Thinking this was an opportunity he couldn't pass up, one of the recipients sent him a Thank You note saying, "This was the first time I've ever had a lawyer buy the balls."

THURSDAY

Name: DYNAMIC STRETCH: OPPOSITE HAND AND TOE REACH

Goal: Enhance flexibility of hamstrings and lower back with focus on posture and trunk stability.

Explanation:

Stand tall with feet together and arms overhead and fingers clasped together. Lengthen right arm forward while lifting left leg and try to touch toward toe. Return leg and arm and repeat with other side. Exhale during reach forward and try not to hunch over. Maintain posture and keep abdominals tight.

Nutrition Tip:

Sugar is hidden in many foods we might not expect such as bread, crackers, peanut butter, frozen dinners and ketchup. It is also disguised in many names including molasses, corn syrup, fructose, dextrose, maltose, honey, and maple syrup.

Experience Good Thoughts:

"You can do what you think you can do AND you cannot do what you think you cannot do."

—Ben Stein

Think Golf:

When the ball rests above your feet, the tendency is to catch the ball on the toe and pull hook the ball. So, to offset this, there are several adjustments you need to make. First level your hips to create a position of balance – not level to the slope but level to a flat surface. To neutralize the tendency to fall downhill, flex your knees into the hill with weight toward the balls of your feet. Also, your weight needs to be on the inside of the back foot to help anchor your swing.

Make Me Smile:

One sign that you're too old for even the Senior Tour: Your foursome tells you to be quiet but you can't because it's just your bones creaking every time you move!

FRIDAY

Name: DB STRENGTH: OVERHEAD PUNCHES

Goal: Increase upper body strength and power; reinforce stabilization of shoulder girdle as well as total back for consistent swing.

Explanation:

Stand with feet hip distance apart holding 3-5-8lb dumbbells directly in front of shoulders with palms facing inward toward each other. Inhale to prepare. Exhale alternating controlled "punches" or lifts with arms overhead keeping palms facing each other. Complete 20 repetitions (10x each side). Focus on breathing and strong back and posture throughout exercise.

Nutrition Tip:
How much is enough water to drink every day? Determine the amount of water your body needs by taking your body weight and dividing it by two. That's the minimum amount of ounces a person should drink daily.

Experience Good Thoughts:
"Try not to become a man of success but rather try to become a man of value."
—Albert Einstein

Think Golf:
Remember, the higher the elevation, the thinner the air, and thin air allows the ball to carry further. To compensate for this, take 10% of the total yardage and subtract it from the total distance.   That gives you the effective yardage. Usually in thin air most golfers can use almost two clubs less.

Make Me Smile:
It is well documented that for every mile you jog, you add one minute to your life. This enables you to, at 85 years old, spend an additional 5 months in a nursing home at $5,000 per month!

SATURDAY/SUNDAY

GOLFING DAYS ARE GOOD FOR YOUR HEALTH

REFLECTING ON THE PAST WEEK:

What was your basic attitude? Were you a positive thinker or did you need an "attitude adjustment?" Are you having success with eating healthier and doing your exercise program? How do you feel physically? If you went golfing, write down any comments that might be helpful later in improving your game. Remember, that laughter is the best medicine in the face of adversity. Are you seeing the lighter side of life?

The exercise that helped me the most this week was on page: _____
_____

My nutritional habits this week were: _____
_____

What made me smile this week?
_____
_____

Looking back at my golf week:
    My Score: _____ What did I do right? _____
_____
_____
    What could I do to improve? _____
_____
_____

Goals for next week: _____
_____
_____
_____

MONDAY

Name: BIG BALL: BODY BRIDGE

Goal: Develop stability in leg muscles and promote body awareness.

Explanation:

Sit on big ball. Walk yourself forward and lean back until only your head and shoulders are on top of the ball. Legs should be hip width apart with knees directly over heels. Squeeze your gluteals and lift your hips as to form a plank or bridge with your body from your knees to your shoulders. Can you balance? Challenge yourself by closing your eyes or walk your feet closer together. Arms should be reaching straight toward the sky.

Nutrition Tip:

Corn has been thought to have little nutrition but it just isn't true. It is a respectable source of iron, zinc, and potassium and very low in sodium. Research has also shown that its protein quality is better than nutritionists originally thought.

Experience Good Thoughts:

"All that we are is the result of what we have thought. If a man speaks or acts with an evil thought, pain follows him. If a man speaks or acts with a pure thought, happiness follows him, like a shadow that never leaves him."

—The Buddha

Think Golf:

The "yips" are convulsive-like twitches that occur mostly during putting and affect nearly 12% of all golfers. They are involuntary movements due to extreme concentration and using finely controlled motor behavior.

Make Me Smile:

If God meant for us to touch our toes, he would have put them on our knees!

TUESDAY

Name: CARDIO: MOUNTAIN CLIMBERS

Goal: Increase total body power and endurance with focus on breath and rhythm.

Explanation:

Start with hands on floor and one leg extended back in lunge position. Rapidly alternate feet jumping forward and back. Allow hips to go up and down in air as feet jump. Work quickly and generate power and momentum. Repeat 20-30x.

Nutrition Tip:

When lowering fat intake, don't fry foods. Instead, try baking, broiling, steaming, or grilling. And try to avoid butter. Flavor your foods with spices or lemon.

Experience Good Thoughts:

"Stop acting as if life is a rehearsal. Live this day as if it were your last. The past is over and gone. The future is not guaranteed."

—Dr. Wayne Dyer, Psychologist

Think Golf:

The Four Main Causes of Golf Related Injuries:

a) overuse/repetitive swings

b) technical errors during swing

c) physical fitness deficiencies

d) no pre-game warm-up.

Make Me Smile:

"Pressure is when you have thirty-five bucks riding on a four-foot putt and you've only got five dollars in your pocket."

—Lee Trevino

WEDNESDAY

Name: PRE-ROUND WARM UP: SUPPORTED LUNGE

Goal: Lengthen muscles in hips and legs allowing more extension and ability to generate more power.

Explanation:

Supported with club or cart, bring right foot forward with weight remaining in heel. Reach left leg back far enough so heel is unable to touch down. Keep center of gravity between both legs and dip back knee down toward the floor. Focus on tall posture and navel pulled to spine.

Nutrition Tip:
Peaches are diuretic and detoxifying so they are good to eat when you're trying to diet. Peaches have been known to help lung debility, liver infections, hypertension, and anemia.

Experience Good Thoughts:
"The will to win, the desire to succeed, the urge to reach your full potential . . . these are the keys that will unlock the door to personal excellence."
—Confucius

Think Golf:
Etiquette to remember: Remain QUIET while others are swinging. It is a common courtesy. Be aware of the fairways around you as well. Talking, coughing, laughing and other loud noises can be very distracting to the player.

Make Me Smile:
Two golfing buddies were standing by the river getting ready to hit their shots. One golfer looked to the other shaking his head and commented, "Look at those idiots fishing in the rain."

THURSDAY

Name: PILATES: CORKSCREW
Goal: Promote abdominal strength and ability to control and activate right and left sides of spine at different times while stabilizing with opposing muscles.

Explanation:

Lie on back with legs together extended in the air at an angle while back is imprinted flat on floor. Send legs overhead while spine flexes. Inhale and hold. Exhale and roll down one side of spine with feet over that same shoulder. Once tailbone reaches floor, circle legs around to other side and roll off again on that side. Reverse and repeat 5 time each side.

Nutrition Tip:
It takes an energy deficit (less) of 3,500 calories to lose one pound of stored fat.

Experience Good Thoughts:
No one can go back and make a brand new start. But anyone can start from now and make a brand new ending.

Think Golf:
As a golfer's long game starts to fade, the short game becomes so important. It is not always easy to hit the green on the second shot. That's where the chip shot comes in. The chip shot is used up to five yards away from the green. It is a low running shot that lands on the green and rolls to the hole like a putt. If hit correctly, it has minimum air time and maximum roll. It is merely an extension of the putting stroke, a controlled pendulum motion with no lower body movement or wrist action. Practice chipping. It will serve you well!

Make Me Smile:
Golfer: Would you mind going into the pond to get my ball?
Caddie: Why?
Golfer: Because it's my "lucky" ball.

FRIDAY

Name: DYNAMIC STRETCH: OUTER THIGH/EAR SWIPE
Goal: Increase range of motion of knees, hips, shoulders, and low back.

Explanation:

Stand tall with feet together and arms overhead with elbows as close to ears as possible. Inhale to prepare. Exhale and allow arms to "swipe" down on either side of thighs or shins, then inhale stand back up with arms overhead. Focus on reaching and stretching up and down. Repeat 10x.

Nutrition Tip:
Vitamin A is good for your eyes, skin and helps you to resist infection. A couple of foods rich in Vitamin A are carrots, spinach, sweet potatoes, and cantaloupe.

Experience Good Thoughts:
You may be only ONE person in the world, but you may also be the WORLD to one person.

Think Golf:
Play Ready-Golf as long as you do not verbally agree to it as you begin your round since that would be breaking Rule 1-3. Efficiency is key for those behind you. Let others play through if they are playing faster than your group. Better yet, be prepared to take your shot when it is your turn and start walking toward your ball instead of waiting for your cart partner has played. Speeding up pace of play in accordance with the Rules of Golf is best but being courteous to those playing behind you is just as important.

Make Me Smile:
At the US Masters in Augusta, Lee Trevino was asked by a spectator why he took a 5 on that easy par-three hole. Trevino replied, "Because I missed my putt for a 4!"

SATURDAY/SUNDAY

GOLFING DAYS ARE GOOD FOR YOUR HEALTH

REFLECTING ON THE PAST WEEK:

What was your basic attitude? Were you a positive thinker or did you need an "attitude adjustment?" Are you having success with eating healthier and doing your exercise program? How do you feel physically? If you went golfing, write down any comments that might be helpful later in improving your game. Remember, that laughter is the best medicine in the face of adversity. Are you seeing the lighter side of life?

The exercise that helped me the most this week was on page:

_____

My nutritional habits this week were:

_____

What made me smile this week?

_____

_____

Looking back at my golf week:
       My Score: _____ What did I do right? _____

_____

_____

       What could I do to improve?

_____

_____

Goals for next week: _____

_____

_____

MONDAY

Name: BIG BALL: HIP RAISES
Goal: Increase structural integrity of back of body to help prepare body for repetitive stress of swing.

Explanation:

Lie on your back with arms down by your sides, palms down. Place big ball under feet with legs straight. Pull abdominals in and squeeze your gluteals tight. Lift hips up off the floor while maintaining neutral spine. Try not to allow the ball to move. Focus on strong trunk. For extra challenge, lift one leg to sky and repeat exercise with other leg 10 times.

Nutrition Tip:
Selenium is essential to the health of the heart muscle. It also helps maintain healthy hair, nails, muscles, and blood cells. Good sources for this mineral are beef, garlic, asparagus, and mushrooms.

Experience Good Thoughts:
"As the family goes, so goes the nation and so goes the whole world in which we live."
—Pope John Paul II

Think Golf:
A player may change a ball in play if it is visibly cut, cracked, or out of shape. It cannot be changed solely because of any of the following:
1) mud or other materials adhering to it
2) its surface is scratched or scraped
3) its paint is damaged or discolored.

Make Me Smile:
Why is it that you can hit a two-acre fairway only about 10% of the time and hit smack into a small, newly-planted tree about 90% of the time? Maybe you should try aiming for the small, newly-planted tree instead!

TUESDAY

Name: **HEAVY BALL: ROCKY BOUNCES**

Goal: Enhance strength and power during rotation during downswing through impact.

Explanation:

Sit with bent knees keeping toes on the floor. Lean back with a rounded back continually drawing in belly button to spine. Hold heavy ball in center and rotate left and right lightly tapping ball to the floor on either side. Repeat 30 times. Exhale each side.

Nutrition Tip:
Lifting weights builds lean muscle. Fat burns about 3 to 5 calories an hour but muscle burns 20 to 30 calories and hour – and that's even if you're just sitting down. Message in this statement – if you do your work to build muscles, it'll be easier to maintain a healthy weight.

Experience Good Thoughts:
Today stretches ahead of you waiting to be shaped. And YOU are the sculptor who gets to do the shaping. Be thoughtful about what you do today!

Think Golf:
When talking about practice, Gary Player said, "The harder I practice, the luckier I get."

Make Me Smile:
I was ready to begin a round of golf when an old man came up to me and asked if I would like him to caddie. Reluctantly, I said, "OK," and he picked up my bag, threw it over his shoulder, and ran over to the tee. "How old are you?" I asked him. "I'm turning 90 soon and I'm in great shape," he answered. "As a matter of fact, I'm getting married in a couple of weeks." "Why would you want to get married at your age?" I asked. He quickly replied with a little grin on his face, "Who said I want to?"

WEDNESDAY

Name: PILATES: SINGLE LEG STRETCH
Goal: Strengthen abdominals and hips for power production.

Explanation:

Begin on your back with belly button to spine. Exhale and pull your right knee to your chest as you lift your shoulders off the mat and "try to kiss your knee". Extend you leg outward. Maintain a rounded upper back and ribs flat to ground. Keep belly button to spine as you switch sides. Repeat 10 times.

Nutrition Tip:
Drink your water! 75% of Americans are chronically dehydrated. In 37% of Americans, the thirst mechanism is so weak that it is often mistaken for hunger.

Experience Good Thoughts:
"It is better to have wise people reprimand you than to have stupid people sing your praises."

—Ecclesiastes 7:5

Think Golf:
Consider the time and money spent practicing and playing golf. Maximize your investment by setting aside 30 minutes of your time 2-3 times a week prior to the start of your golf season to participate in a golf fitness program. You'll feel better and you'll play better.

Make Me Smile:
Two golfers at the first tee are talking: "Hey, guess what?" said the first golfer. "I just got a set of golf clubs for my wife." His friend replied: "Great trade!"

THURSDAY

Name: YOGA/STRETCH: LETTER T STRETCH

Goal: Increase flexibility in low back and ease tension post-round due to force weight shifting and torque during swing.

Explanation:

Lie on floor with arms straight out to sides in a letter T position. Lift left leg straight up to sky and cross over body so that left foot almost touches right hand. Can you keep both shoulder blades and hands on the floor? Hold for 10 seconds then alternate legs 5 times.

Nutrition Tip:
If you spend a lot of time on the computer, you could end up with many symptoms including dry eyes, headaches, and blurry or double vision. Take vitamins and supplements that help protect your vision. Include those that contain bilberry extract, which has been shown to improve night vision.

Experience Good Thoughts:
"Focus on remedies, not faults."

—Jack Nicklaus

Think Golf:
Etiquette to remember: NEVER bang or throw your clubs! Show your good sportsmanship at all times. Besides, they could damage the green or interfere with another player's shot.

Make Me Smile:
During the weekly Lamaze class the instructor stressed the importance of exercise for the mother-to-be, hinting strongly that husbands need to start walking with their wives. From the back of the room one expectant father asked, "Would it be OK if she carries a bag of golf clubs while she walks?"

FRIDAY

Name: STRENGTH: ABDOMINAL CRUNCH

Goal: Facilitate trunk and core strength for better rotation and power during downswing through impact — Support spine angle.

Explanation:

Lie on the floor with knees bent and feet flat on the floor hip distance apart and 12 inches from hips. Lightly place fingertips behind ears for slight support of the neck and head. Inhale and prepare for the movement. As you exhale, pull your belly button to your spine and ribs rotate toward hips. Chin and head point toward thighs. Release down slowly and repeat 10 times slowly with focus on abdominals.

Nutrition Tip:
Eating fish is good for your brain! The connection between fish and brainpower is due to the presence of omega-3 fatty acids found in salmon, herring, and mackerel. This appears to offer protection against Alzheimer's disease and depression and is important for normal brain development.

Experience Good Thoughts:
"The one without dreams is the one without wings."

—Muhammed Ali

Think Golf:
Did you know? During a backswing, the average range of motion for the shoulders is a 102 degree rotation. For the hips, it is only 47 degrees.

Make Me Smile:
A foursome of senior golfers went out to play a round. The first one complained that the hills just keep getting steeper as they get older. The second one added that they seem to get longer too. He said, "The walk seems so much farther now." The third one noted that the bunkers are bigger than they used to be. After listening to all these comments, the oldest and wisest of the group got their attention and proclaimed, "Quit your complaining and just be glad we're on this side of the grass."

SATURDAY/SUNDAY

GOLFING DAYS ARE GOOD FOR YOUR HEALTH

REFLECTING ON THE PAST WEEK:

What was your basic attitude? Were you a positive thinker or did you need an "attitude adjustment?" Are you having success with eating healthier and doing your exercise program? How do you feel physically? If you went golfing, write down any comments that might be helpful later in improving your game. Remember, that laughter is the best medicine in the face of adversity. Are you seeing the lighter side of life?

The exercise that helped me the most this week was on page:

_____

My nutritional habits this week were:

_____

What made me smile this week?

_____

_____

Looking back at my golf week:
    My Score: _____ What did I do right? _____

_____

_____

    What could I do to improve?

_____

_____

Goals for next week: _____

_____

_____

MONDAY

Name: TOWEL: LYING INNER THIGH

Goal: Prevent injury to stabilizing inner thigh muscles by warming up area for swing.

Explanation:

Lie on back with right leg extended toward sky. Wrap towel around bottom of foot and hold ends of towel in right hand only. Left arm extends out to left for support while left leg stays straight on floor. Lower right leg 90 degrees straight out to right side keeping leg straight. Stretch will be felt down inside of leg. Exhale while reaching through stretch. Return back to start. Repeat 5x one leg then switch. Challenge: Keep hips stable on floor while stretching leg.

Nutrition Tip:
Smoking increases the need for Vitamin C and damages the digestive tract as well as decreases the immune system. It causes depletion of Vitamin C up to 100 milligrams per cigarette.

Experience Good Thoughts:
The happiest of people don't necessarily have the best of everything; they just make the most of everything that comes along their way.

Think Golf:
Taking lessons I heard my instructor say over and over, "Be one with the ball." At the time I didn't realize the importance of that statement but after playing for awhile, I began to see the gravity of it. The mind has a phenomenal effect on the golf game. A player must learn how to control his thoughts, emotions, and attention to play your best game. Only then can you elevate your game to the potential that is possible.

Make Me Smile:
What's the definition of a handicapped golfer — a golfer who is playing with the boss!

TUESDAY

Name: HEAVY BALL: POWER GOLF SWING

Goal: Promote power while maintaining spine angle through swing.

Explanation:

Stand with your body in address position holding a heavy ball in both hands instead of a club. Perform a slow smooth controlled takeaway and downswing. Remember to keep head still throughout movement and maintain normal swing angle. Focus on rotating shoulders away from target with minimal hip rotation. Repeat 10 times one side then switch to opposite handed backswing to promote symmetry.

Nutrition Tip:
Alcohol damages organs essential to digestion and metabolism of nutrients. Alcohol also increases the need for B-complex vitamins as well as Vitamins A and C. It stimulates the kidneys to excrete more fluid than you take in, which can create a relative state of dehydration that's dangerous.

Experience Good Thoughts:
"My dad has always taught me these words: care and share. That's why we put on clinics. The only thing I can do is try to give back. If it works, it works."
—Tiger Woods

Think Golf:
The Vardon grip, named after Harry Vardon, is by far the most popular in golf today. It is accomplished by overlapping the last finger of the right hand between the second and third fingers of the left hand. Two other types of grips are the interlocking and the 10-finger.

Make Me Smile:
Why is using a golf cart better than having a caddie? Because golf carts can't count your strokes or laugh at you.

WEDNESDAY

Name: PILATES: TEASER III

Goal: Increase complete core stabilization, trunk control and balance so crucial for generating clubhead speed while maintaining balance.

Explanation:

Lie on back with legs extended together on mat, toes pointed and arms overhead by ears. Inhale sliding scapulae down back reaching arms to ceiling, then roll up sequentially one vertebrae at a time. Focus on engaging the lower abdominal area which flexes hips and lifts legs off mat. Spine should be slightly rounded at top with arms reaching toward feet and legs in "V" position. Exhale roll down with control. Repeat movement 5x.

Nutrition Tip:

Potatoes have long been on the nutritional blacklist with a reputation for spiking blood sugar. However, the USDA is now reporting that regular white potatoes have as much antioxidant activity as other reputable disease-fighting vegetables. They noted that a 10.5 ounce baked potato delivers as much antioxidant clout as two cups of cooked broccoli or one and a half cups of cooked asparagus.

Experience Good Thoughts:

"If you want a rainbow, you've got to put up with the rain."

—Jimmy Durante

Think Golf:

If on a drive or approach shot, a ball strikes a cat, snake, bird, etc., it is considered to have been "deflected by an outside agency" and is played where it lies. But if the dog takes the ball and runs, the player receives no penalty and can place another ball as near as possible to the point of the offense and continue the round. USGA #19

Make Me Smile:

What's the best way to get eagles and birdies when golfing? Put a little birdseed on the course.

THURSDAY

Name: PRE-ROUND WARMUP: LATERAL SPINE STRETCH
Goal: Help to stretch rib cage, promoting better range of motion.

Explanation:

Stand tall holding club overhead with hands wide on grip and close to clubhead. Slowly bend from side to side with intention of lengthening spine and adding space between each vertebrae.

Nutrition Tip:
Stress, aging, lack of sunlight, junk food, carbonated beverages and high levels of physical activity are factors that increase the need for extra vitamins and minerals. "Empty" foods low in nutrition force the body to "borrow" nutrient reserves in order to digest junk.

Experience Good Thoughts:
The successful person has a habit of doing the things failures don't like to do. Successful people don't necessarily like to do them either, but their disliking takes a back seat to the goal that's been set. They continue to move forward.

Think Golf:
During a follow through, the reverse "C" or modern golf swing position may cause excessive lumbar (low back) strain. An upright follow through posture or classic golf swing results from releasing the upper body, causing less lumbar strain. Which do YOU do?

Make Me Smile:
My 6 year-old grandson wanted to caddie for me one Saturday morning. "You have to be able to count and add," I said. "How much is 4 plus 5 plus 7?" My little grandson very proudly said, "12." "OK, you're just the kind of caddie I need."

FRIDAY

Name: BIG BALL: THE 4 POINTER
Goal: Stretch and open up front of the body while promoting balance and spine flexibility for ease of full follow-through.

Explanation:

Sit on Big ball and slowly walk feet forward to bridge position with head and shoulders on ball. Reach arms overhead as feet walk back toward ball. Allow your spine to form to the ball reaching back to touch floor. Reverse it. Walk feet back out to bridge then back in to a seated position without using hands.

Nutrition Tip:
Eat breakfast! It is important to stock your kitchen or pantry ahead of time with healthy ingredients you can prepare quickly for a nutritious meal in the morning (or anytime). Great foods for breakfast are oatmeal, whole-wheat toast, wheat germ, nuts, egg substitutes or egg whites. Additionally, low fat cheeses, low carbohydrate fruits, yogurt and protein shakes or bars are excellent choices.

Experience Good Thoughts:
Have a GREAT DAY!   Unless you have other plans.

Think Golf:
In her book, A Trust Walk: Mindful Golf, Dr. Paula King, Sports Psychologist, teaches golfers to approach each shot actively choosing to focus your imaginative mind on the process of creating the experience you want. "A well-imagined shot," she says, "is experienced by the mind/body just like a shot executed in reality, and therefore has a powerful practice effect." Take note. She practices what she preaches and is a skilled golfer.

Make Me Smile:
If you think it's hard to meet new people, pick up the wrong golf ball on the course sometime.

SATURDAY/SUNDAY

GOLFING DAYS ARE GOOD FOR YOUR HEALTH

REFLECTING ON THE PAST WEEK:

What was your basic attitude? Were you a positive thinker or did you need an "attitude adjustment?" Are you having success with eating healthier and doing your exercise program? How do you feel physically? If you went golfing, write down any comments that might be helpful later in improving your game. Remember, that laughter is the best medicine in the face of adversity. Are you seeing the lighter side of life?

The exercise that helped me the most this week was on page:

_____

My nutritional habits this week were:

_____

What made me smile this week?

_____

_____

Looking back at my golf week:
     My Score: _____ What did I do right? _____

_____

_____

     What could I do to improve?

_____

_____

Goals for next week: _____

_____

_____

MONDAY

Name: YOGA/STRETCH: PIGEON POSE
Goal: Stretch hips and abdomen while lengthening spine.

Explanation:

Begin on your hands and knees. Take your left knee forward resting the entire outside of the leg on the ground. Keep your knee and thigh facing forward as your foot crossing over the center line toward your right hip. Try to keep your hips level. To intensify the stretch, lift through and bend forward.

Nutrition Tip:
Lentils have more protein than beef and less fat — actually they are fat free — a claim that no hamburger could ever make. Make soup with them adding onions, carrots and celery and you have a meal composed of protein and vegetables. Add rice and it's complete.

Experience Good Thoughts:
"A woman is like a tea bag —you can't tell how strong she is until you put her in hot water."

— Nancy Reagan, Former First Lady

Think Golf:
If you expect to play well, get to the course at least a half hour before your tee time instead of at the minute you're scheduled to start. Give yourself plenty of time to warm up your muscles, hit some drives and chip shots and get the feel of the grass on the putting green.

Make Me Smile:
Little known Rule of Golf: Hazards attract — Fairways repel. This is one Rule that most golfers find easy to follow.

TUESDAY

Name: DB STRENGTH: BENT OVER FLY
Goal: Increase upper back and trunk strength; reinforce stabilization of shoulder girdle for consistent swing.

Explanation:

Stand with feet slightly wider than hips. Unlock knees and hinge from waist so back is flat and parallel with floor. Arms are hanging straight down from chest holding 3-5-8lb dumbbells facing each other. Inhale prepare. Exhale lifting and "flying" dumbbells out to sides so arms spread like wings parallel to floor. Inhale as arms slowly return to start. Focus on strong back and good posture. Abdominals held in to support back. Repeat 10-15 repetitions.

Nutrition Tip:
On a diet? Hearts of palm, usually sold canned, contain only 21 calories per cup, are considered a gourmet food, and a one-cup serving provides 100% of the RDA for Vitamin A.

Experience Good Thoughts:
"Electric communication will never be a substitute for the face of someone who with their soul encourages another person to be brave and true."
—Charles Dickens, Author

Think Golf:
Watch your friends' shot from your ball position when they hit. That will help you locate a stray ball and will also give you a better sense of wind speed and direction at the time. Their disadvantage of playing first can turn out to be an advantage for you.

Make Me Smile:
"The reason the Pro tells you to keep your head down is so you can't see him laughing."
—Phyllis Diller

WEDNESDAY

Name: PILATES: BRIDGE W/FOOT LIFTS

Goal: Lengthen spine while strengthening muscles in back of body for stabilization and control.

Explanation:

Lie on back with both knees bent and feet hip distance apart. Place arms face down at sides. Inhale. As you exhale, imprint your spine flat to the floor as you tuck your pelvis and roll your spine one vertebrae at a time off the floor up into a straight bridge. Inhale at the top then exhale as you roll your spine back down to the floor pulling your hips toward your heels. Variations; at top, lift one foot off floor at a time without moving pelvis.

Nutrition Tip:
Always buy tuna packed in water instead of tuna packed in oil. It tastes better and is a healthier choice as well.

Experience Good Thoughts:
"Opportunity is missed by most people because it is dressed in overalls and looks like work."

—Thomas A. Edison

Think Golf:
As you approach the green, make it a point to leave your bag on the side of the green that is closest to the next tee. That will save time and steps, which will keep the game moving at a faster pace.

Make Me Smile:
An avid golfer goes to see a fortune teller to see if there are golf courses in heaven. "I have good news and bad news," she tells him. "The good news is that there are plenty of courses in heaven and they are spectacular — better than any you have ever seen before." So he sheepishly asks, "What's the bad news then?" She smiles and says, "You have a tee time at 7:00 tomorrow morning."

THURSDAY

Name: YOGA/STRETCH: EXTENDED TABLE

Goal: Balance and trunk stability while maintaining proper spine angle and stable base for swing.

Explanation:

On hands and knees, keep your back flat and abdominals supporting spine. Lengthen your left leg behind you while squeezing the gluteal. When you feel balanced. Lengthen the right arm in front of you. You want your extended arm, leg, and spine to be horizontal to the floor. Hold up to 30 seconds. Focus on your breathing and relaxation.

Nutrition Tip:

Whole grains are a rich source of phyto-chemicals, health-protective substances that occur naturally in all plant foods. When shopping for whole grains, choose products that list "whole grain" or "whole wheat" as the first item in the ingredients. Make sure the list also says the product contains at least 3 grams of fiber per serving.

Experience Good Thoughts:

"Do not let your fears hold you back from pursuing your hopes."

—John F. Kennedy, 35th President

Think Golf:

"Fifteen years ago the average American male golfer's handicap was 16.2. The average female golfer's handicap was 29. Today the average American male golfer's handicap is 16.2 and the average female golfer's handicap is 29!"

—Bob Rotella, Ph. D.

Make Me Smile:

"I'll shoot my age if I have to live to be 105."

—Bob Hope

FRIDAY

Name: BIG BALL: LYING HAMSTRING CURL

Goal: Develop and strengthen hamstrings, gluteals and low back while promoting balance.

Explanation:

Lie on floor with legs straight and heels on ball. Place hands on floor at sides. Squeeze gluteals, digging heels into ball and tilt pelvis off floor. Bend knees and pull ball into buttocks.
Straighten legs slowly then lower hips. Keep abdominals tight and repeat 10 times.
Advanced: try with arms in the air or try one leg at a time

Nutrition Tip:
Did you know that lamb provides something that most of us fall short on — the mineral "iron." Some of the iron in lamb is the "heme" type that is most easily absorbed by the body and in addition, helps us to absorb more of the iron in other foods.

Experience Good Thoughts:
"You've got to get to the stage in life where going for it is more important than winning or losing."
—Arthur Ashe

Think Golf:
Before making a shot from a bunker, a player may NOT smooth the sand, remove loose impediments, or touch a loose impediment with his club at address or on his backswing.

Make Me Smile:
"I like golf because you can be really terrible at it and still not look much dorkier than anybody else."
—Dave Barry, Humorist

SATURDAY/SUNDAY

GOLFING DAYS ARE GOOD FOR YOUR HEALTH

REFLECTING ON THE PAST WEEK:

What was your basic attitude? Were you a positive thinker or did you need an "attitude adjustment?" Are you having success with eating healthier and doing your exercise program? How do you feel physically? If you went golfing, write down any comments that might be helpful later in improving your game. Remember, that laughter is the best medicine in the face of adversity. Are you seeing the lighter side of life?

The exercise that helped me the most this week was on page:

_____

My nutritional habits this week were:

_____

What made me smile this week?

_____

_____

Looking back at my golf week:
    My Score: ——————— What did I do right? ——————

_____

_____

    What could I do to improve?

_____

_____

Goals for next week: ————————————————

_____

_____

MONDAY

Name: HEAVY BALL: MERRY GO ROUND
Goal: Increase spinal flexibility as well as stability and strength while promoting upright posture.

Explanation:

Stand with your feet firmly planted a little wider than hip distance apart and extend your arms in front of you while holding heavy ball. Rotate 180 degrees facing behind you keeping your arms straight out in front of you and maintain weight centered between both feet. Focus on lifting through the spine and be sure to lift your trailing heel for easier rotation. Repeat 5 times each direction. Ribcage and spine stay lifted with shoulders back and chin up.

Nutrition Tip:
According to the government's 2005 Dietary Guidelines, we should be eating more fiber-rich fruits, vegetables and whole grains. Fiber, a carbohydrate produced only by plants, passes through the digestive system unchanged. Soluble fiber, which dissolves in the body, offers many benefits for body chemistry. Insoluble fiber doesn't dissolve and acts as a laxative. Both types are valuable and lower the risk of cancer and heart disease.

Experience Good Thoughts:
"Money was never a big motivator for me, except as a way to keep score. The real excitement is playing the game."
—Donald Trump, American Businessman

Think Golf:
Playing golf should not be used as the sole means of cardiovascular exercise. Why? The average heart rate of a golfer — even walking 18 holes — is only 108 beats per minute. Cardio exercise should be part of your daily routine to build and maintain a strong and healthy heart.

Make Me Smile:
"If the sun is up, why aren't you playing golf?"
—Lee Trevino

TUESDAY

Name: PILATES: ROLLING LIKE A BALL

Goal: Abdominal control during movement of swing as well as spinal massage to loosen back musculature.

Explanation:

Sit just back of your sit bones with knees flexed toward chest. Maintain balance with feet off the ground. Remain in C-curve and rock back and forth on spine. Inhale while rolling back one vertebrae at a time. Exhale while rocking spine back to seated position balancing behind sit bones constantly keeping the abdominals pulled in tight. Repeat 10 times.

Nutrition Tip:
Grapefruit is high in potassium (which is good for your heart) and meets the entire Vitamin C allowance in one serving. A medium grapefruit provides 50% more than the RDA for Vitamin C.

Experience Good Thoughts:
"In the sweetness of friendship let there be laughter and sharing of pleasures. For in the dew of little things, the heart finds its morning and is refreshed."
—Kahlil Gibran

Think Golf:
Most golfers are aware that they should not step in the line of their partners' putt. Did you know that professional golfers are also very conscious of avoiding the through line of their partners' putt? The through line is the line extending beyond the hole approximately 3 feet and is where a well-struck putt could finish if it misses the hole.

Make Me Smile:
"If you are stupid enough to whiff, you should be smart enough to forget it."
—Arnold Palmer

WEDNESDAY

Name: CARDIO: POWERWALKING

Goal: Increase cardiovascular endurance and stamina for the 4+ hours of golf; enhance concentration and focus; improve coordination, balance and rhythm.

Explanation:

Power walking is walking at a pace that gets your heart rate and breathing rate up. It is a faster paced walk than a stroll, but with a slightly longer stride. The longer stride is possible by using the arms to pump back and forth. Start walking outside or on a treadmill. The Goal is to be able to walk a 15 minute mile (4mph). Try walking 5x per week for 30 minutes. Focus on deep breathing and positive thinking.

Nutrition Tip:

Hubbard and butternut squashes have more than a day's recommended allowance of the anticancer nutrient, carotene, in a single serving. Although these are not well known vegetables, it would be beneficial to get out of the familiar vegetable rut and try some new ones for a fresh taste and additional source of nutrients.

Experience Good Thoughts:

"Take action. Seize the moment. Man was never intended to become an oyster."
—Theodore Roosevelt, 26th President

Think Golf:

"Here is a simple guideline to follow when catching the driver solidly. Think — the direction of your weight shift and the direction your clubhead is moving should be the same. When your clubhead is moving away from the target, your weight should be flowing into your right hip joint. When your clubhead is moving toward the target, weight should be flowing into your left hip joint."
—T.J. Tomasi

Make Me Smile:

For men only: You know you're obsessed with golf when — you stand at the urinal and you use the overlapping grip.

THURSDAY

Name: **DYNAMIC STRETCH: HEAD TURNS**

Goal: Increase flexibility of cervical spine (neck) and ability to keep head still as shoulders turn in backswing.

Explanation:

Stand tall with arms hanging to sides and shoulders relaxed. Picture a string pulling the top of your head to the sky and rotate head looking to the right then to the left. Allow approximately 4 seconds to rotate from one side to the other. Keep chin elevated and focus on lengthening. Inhale in center and exhale on turn. Repeat 5 times in each direction.

Nutrition Tip:
Kiwifruit is great for blood pressure. It's rich in potassium and has almost no sodium and fat. It's delicious and can be a refreshing change of pace for an afternoon snack.

Experience Good Thoughts:
The ability to discipline yourself to delay gratification in the short term in order to enjoy greater rewards in the long term is a prerequisite for success.

Think Golf:
Refrain from making negative comments about your game or your playing partners' game. For example, if your playing partner is preparing to hit a shot, you shouldn't say: "Do you ever shank these? I shank these a lot?" Those remarks carry a great deal of weight in upcoming strokes.

Make Me Smile:
Every avid golfer needs an "excuse" to play golf sometimes. Here are a few that sound credible if you need one.
1) I've been practicing putting on my carpet. It's time to see if practice makes perfect.
2) I've never eagled a hole before and I feel lucky today.
3) After watching the golf channel for 24 hours straight, I am really psyched up.

FRIDAY

Name: TOWEL: FIGURE 8 BEHIND BACK

Goal: Increase circulation and blood flow around shoulders; help facilitate more fluid range of motion throughout swing.

Explanation:

Stand tall holding towel from ends with both hands over head. Bend from elbows bringing towel parallel behind head at ear level. Slowly, try to straighten one arm out behind back then the other so arms hold towel behind hips. If possible, return each arm one at a time back up behind ears and return to start position. Try to complete 5 repetitions. Do not force the stretch.

Nutrition Tip:
Oat bran and beans are two powerful foods that bring down cholesterol. Oat bran muffins and soups or side dishes with kidney or pinto beans contain soluble fiber, which is proven to be a fat-buster.

Experience Good Thoughts:
"Like music and art, love of nature is a common language that can transcend political or social boundaries."

—Jimmy Carter, 39th President (Golf promotes this statement.)

Think Golf:
If one of your playing partners gets on a hot streak, take a tip from baseball players who avoid talking to a pitcher during a "no-hitter". Don't talk to the player, but if you have to, refrain from saying how well they're playing. For example, if the player is making a lot of putts, avoid remarks like "Wow, you're really making everything happen today!" Whether you're superstitious or not, better safe than sorry.

Make Me Smile:
What are the four worst words you could hear during a game of golf? It's still your turn!

SATURDAY/SUNDAY

GOLFING DAYS ARE GOOD FOR YOUR HEALTH

REFLECTING ON THE PAST WEEK:

What was your basic attitude? Were you a positive thinker or did you need an "attitude adjustment?" Are you having success with eating healthier and doing your exercise program? How do you feel physically? If you went golfing, write down any comments that might be helpful later in improving your game. Remember, that laughter is the best medicine in the face of adversity. Are you seeing the lighter side of life?

The exercise that helped me the most this week was on page:

_____

My nutritional habits this week were:

_____

What made me smile this week?

_____

_____

Looking back at my golf week:
        My Score: _____ What did I do right? _____

_____

_____

        What could I do to improve?

_____

_____

Goals for next week: _____

_____

_____

MONDAY

Name: DB STRENGTH: BENT OVER "LAWNMOWER" PULLS

Goal: Increase upper back and trunk strength and rotational power for swing; reinforce stabilization of shoulder girdle for consistent swing.

Explanation:

Stand with feet slightly wider than hips. Unlock knees and hinge from waist so back is flat and parallel with floor. Arms are hanging straight down from chest holding 3-5-8lb dumbbells facing each other. Inhale pulling one arm up as other reaches farther to floor then exhale switch with slight rotation of torso with each pull and reach. Focus on control and abdominal support for back. Repeat 20x alternating pulls.

Nutrition Tip:
Eating Yogurt offers so many rewards. Among them are: high in calcium; anti-inflammatory benefits especially for people with arthritis; cuts the risk of colon cancer; fights bacteria such as H. pylori infections; benefits the gastrointestinal system reducing the symptoms of lactose intolerance, constipation, diarrhea, and inflammatory bowel disease. So eat some yogurt several times a week.

Experience Good Thoughts:
"You cannot open a book without learning SOMETHING."

—Confucius

Think Golf:
Middle to high handicap golfers often dread the fairway bunker shot. It's important to remember to keep your spine angle constant while you swing. Too many golfers try to lift the ball out of the sand by dipping their body down toward the ground, a sure way to catch the sand first and leave your shot well short of your target.

Make Me Smile:
Just about the time a man finally gets mature enough to control his temper, he takes up golf!

TUESDAY

Name: PRE-ROUND WARMUP: PEC/SHOULDER STRETCH

Goal: Open your chest for better rotation and help prevent shoulder pain from fast action during swing.

Explanation:

Hold the hozzle end of a golf club behind your neck with your right hand. Align the club down the back vertically and hold the grip end near your glutes, palm facing out. Pull the grip down to stretch triceps, and push elbows out to stretch chest and front of shoulders. Hold for 10-30 seconds.

Nutrition Tip:
Research has shown that the juice from garlic inhibits the growth of many bacteria and fungi.

Experience Good Thoughts:
"If you advance confidently in the direction of your dreams, and endeavor to live the life you have imagined, you will meet with a success unexpected in common hours."
—Henry David Thoreau

Think Golf:
Learn to stay out of the trees off the tee. Instead of hitting the driver, it's a good idea to play safe using a club you know you can control. One alternative is to use a fairway wood, a three or even a five wood off the grass. Create a grass tee by giving the ground a little whack with your club head to raise a small divot, then place the ball on the back of the divot so it sits up on a small mound of grass. Just sweep the ball off the grass by shifting your weight to the front foot on the downswing, which will help to avoid topping your shot.

Make Me Smile:
If it ever starts to storm on the golf course just be calm and hold up your two iron. Why? Because even God can't hit a two iron!

WEDNESDAY

Name: YOGA/STRETCH: DOWNWARD DOG
Goal: Elongate entire body and open shoulder girdle to support better posture at address and throughout entire swing.

Explanation:

Begin on all fours. Evenly disperse weight between all fingers and palm of hand. Slowly lift knees off floor and push hips up and back to straighten legs as much as possible. Heels will be slightly off floor at all times. Lengthen through spine and stretch head and chest toward floor. Breathe and hold 10 seconds. Repeat 5 times.

Nutrition Tip:
When you sit down to eat, ask yourself, "What am I going to be doing in the next three hours?" Then, if you're taking a nap, eat less carbohydrate foods; if you're planning on a golf fitness session, eat more carbohydrates!

Experience Good Thoughts:
"You must have courage to bet on your ideals, to take calculated risks, and act on them. Everyday living requires courage if life is to be effective and bring happiness."
—Maxwell Maltz

Think Golf:
When you get right down to the root of the meaning of the word "succeed", you find that it simply means to "follow through". If you can do that with your swing, you can consistently enjoy a respectable golf score. Follow through and stay in a balanced position.

Make Me Smile:
Overheard on a golf course: "I don't exercise because it makes the ice jump out of my glass."

THURSDAY

Name: STRENGTH: FORWARD LUNGES
Goal: Strengthen legs for stability and driving power.

Explanation:

Stand tall with feet together. Hands on hips. Reach out with heel of right leg and lower left knee down toward floor. Weight remains centered between both feet with spine erect. Push off right heel with power and return to standing. Repeat and alternate legs 10 times.

Nutrition Tip:
Be cautious with Vitamin A. Too much can promote cancer and bone loss and too little can put you at risk for vision problems, infections and bone loss. Beta carotene converts into Vitamin A, but avoid high doses of 30 mg or more of beta carotene supplements. Consult a nutrition professional before taking these.

Experience Good Thoughts:
"It takes a lot of courage to show your dreams to someone else."
—Erma Bombeck

Think Golf:
"Golf is deceptively simple and endlessly complicated. It satisfies the soul and frustrates the intellect. It is at the same time rewarding and maddening. It is without a doubt the greatest game mankind has ever invented."
—Arnold Palmer

Make Me Smile:
"How can I get my score down?" asked the really bad golfer to the pro. "Try skipping the last two holes."

FRIDAY

Name: BIG BALL: WOODCHOP
Goal: Increase circulation and body heat in preparation for game.

Explanation:

Stand with feel wider than hips. Hold big ball over head while maintaining good posture (shoulders down, ribs lifted, belly button pulled in). Bend knees to squat position while bringing ball down to touch floor, then stand and bring ball back up overhead. Resembles a woodchop motion. Inhale up and exhale down. Repeat 10 times.

Nutrition Tip:
No matter how hard you try, or how good you cook, or where you buy your food:
1) You can't always eat perfectly balanced meals
2) You can't always eat 5 or 6 times a day
So help your body's needs with supplements on the "not so great" days. Be prepared with vitamins/minerals, protein bars and drinks.

Experience Good Thoughts:
"Don't bother just to be better than your contemporaries or predecessors. Try to be better than yourself."

—William Faulkner

Think Golf:
Golfers who try to do something new and fail are infinitely better than those who try to do nothing and succeed.

Make Me Smile:
Student to Logics professor, "Can cardiovascular exercise really prolong life?" "The answer is simple," responds the professor. "The heart is only good for so many beats. Don't waste them on exercise! Everything wears out eventually. Speeding up your heart will not make you live longer. That's like saying a car will last longer if you drive it faster. I'd say if you want to live longer — take a nap!"

SATURDAY/SUNDAY

GOLFING DAYS ARE GOOD FOR YOUR HEALTH

REFLECTING ON THE PAST WEEK:

What was your basic attitude? Were you a positive thinker or did you need an "attitude adjustment?" Are you having success with eating healthier and doing your exercise program? How do you feel physically? If you went golfing, write down any comments that might be helpful later in improving your game. Remember, that laughter is the best medicine in the face of adversity. Are you seeing the lighter side of life?

The exercise that helped me the most this week was on page:

_____

My nutritional habits this week were:

_____

What made me smile this week?

_____

_____

Looking back at my golf week:
    My Score: _____ What did I do right? _____

_____

_____

    What could I do to improve?

_____

_____

Goals for next week: _____

_____

_____

MONDAY

Name: YOGA/STRETCH: EAGLE POSE
Goal: Stretch hips, knees, and ankles while challenging balance and mental focus.

Explanation:

Stand with your feet together. Bend your knees and shift your weight to the right foot. Lift your left leg and place it over your right so the left thigh is on top. Wrap your left foot around the outside of the right calf. Cross your arms in front of you with the left arm under the right. Bend the elbows and wind your left hand around to meet the right. Press your palms together. Keep shoulders down and focus on your breath. Hold 30 seconds. Repeat other side.

Nutrition Tip:
No matter what your diet is -- here are some things to keep in mind. Go easy on processed foods, salty snacks, and cured meats. Eat less calories. Eat more fruits and vegetables. This will help both your weight and your blood pressure.

Experience Good Thoughts:
Christopher Dorris, Performance Psychologist, in his book, *Creating Your Dream: How To Get What You Want Through Disciplined Action*, notes, "You can only pursue what you want if you know what you want." Think seriously about your goals. What do you really want to do?

Think Golf:
Golf has recently become one of America's favorite pastimes. There are now over 26 million people, almost 20% of our population, playing golf yearly. According to the National Golf Foundation, 5.7 million are women and that number is steadily increasing. Women golfers represent the largest growing segment of new players in the industry.

Make Me Smile:
I was told that joining a health club would be good for my golf game. So I joined one that cost about 400 bucks. Haven't seen any difference yet. Apparently you have to actually go there!

TUESDAY

Name: HEAVY BALL: PUSHUPS

Goal: Increase range of motion of each shoulder while strengthening chest and trunk for increased power and speed of swing.

Explanation:

On hands and knees, place heavy ball under one hand. Body should be in one line from knees, through hips to shoulders. Perform pushup with one ball on hand while maintain straight line of body. Hold abdominal wall in tightly. Keep chest in alignment with hands. For more challenge, lift knees to straight leg plank position and perform pushups. Switch hands, 10 times.

Nutrition Tip:
The color of fruits and vegetables determines the kinds of vitamins and minerals they possess. Eat a variety of colors to get a good mix of these essential health benefits.

Experience Good Thoughts:
"Every time you smile at someone, it is an action of love, a gift to that person, a beautiful thing."

—Mother Teresa

Think Golf:
The leg and hip muscles (quadriceps, hamstrings, and gluteals) are responsible for power production and initiate the golf swing. These muscles generate 80% of a golf swing's power.

Make Me Smile:
A golfer hit his ball into a bunker. His buddies heard — whack, whack, whack — several times until finally he hit the ball out. "How many strokes did it take you to get out of there?" asked his partner. "Three," he answered. "But I heard seven." The golfer replied, "Four of them were echoes."

WEDNESDAY

Name: YOGA/STRETCH: STANDING CHEST OPENER

Goal: Open chest and ribcage for better posture at address and ability to maintain spine angle throughout swing to increase accuracy.

Explanation:

Stand with your feet in address position. Clasp hands behind your back opening up chest cavity. Slowly bend over from waist allowing arms to follow and point up toward sky. Hold belly button in to support spine and keep knees bent. Allow head to hang looking back through knees. Slowly roll back up to standing with head being last to roll. Repeat 3 times.

Nutrition Tip:
It takes a surplus of 3,500 calories to gain 1 pound of fat. Now doesn't it seem easy to lose weight if it takes that many calories to gain just one pound of fat?

Experience Good Thoughts:
"We must teach our children to resolve their conflicts with words, not weapons."
—William J. Clinton, 42nd President

Think Golf:
If the fairways are hard ground from being too dry, be aware of the extra roll that can happen because of it. It can really feel good to hit a long drive but if it rolls too far, it can end up in the rough. Try using a fairway wood or long iron where a ball might run too far and into trouble.

Make Me Smile:
A reporter was sent out to do a "man on the street" interview about women in the 21st century. The first person he came upon was an older gentleman who seemed to be in a hurry. He asked the man his opinion and the old man quickly replied, "Son, I'm 85 years old and haven't thought about women in two years. Now move on, my tee time is in 15 minutes."

THURSDAY

Name: DYNAMIC STRETCH: FRONT KNEE LIFTS

Goal: Increase blood flow and circulation to volatile low back and hip area to prevent injury.

Explanation:

Stand tall with hands on hips and feet hip distance apart. Inhale to prepare. Exhale and lift right knee straight out front. Inhale on lowering and exhale lifting the other leg. Maintain good posture lifting knees as high as possible. Repeat alternating legs 20x.

Nutrition Tip:

Looking for a new fruit to add to your daily diet? Try the papaya. The papaya stands out with a Vitamin A level that exceeds the RDA by 30% plus has enough Vitamin C to meet a full day's allowance three times – all in one piece of delicious fruit.

Experience Good Thoughts:

Take a tip from Thomas Edison, which shows that perseverance and positive thinking are keys to success. In his words, "I have not failed. I have just found 10,000 ways that won't work."

Think Golf:

In 1923, Gene Sarazen won the US Open and the PGA Championship. He played golf until he was 92 years old. When he died in 1999 at 95, he was still financially solvent. Moral of the story: You'll be better off if you play more golf!

Make Me Smile:

The frustrated golfer screamed at his wife, "Shut up or you'll drive me out of my mind." Without skipping a beat his wife responded, "That wouldn't be a drive — that would be a gimme putt."

FRIDAY

Name: BIG BALL: SEATED RIB TILTS

Goal: Increase muscle control of midsection and ribcage with focus on balance.

Explanation:

Sit on ball with feet hip distance apart and directly under knees. Place hands on hips with thumbs facing back to help stabilize and ensure no movement of hips and lower body. Find "neutral spine" and placement of ribs. Inhale to prepare. Exhale and slide ribs side to side controlling direction and range of motion with muscles around ribs and mid spine. Repeat side to side 20x. Enhance control by popping ribs forward and back. Repeat 20x F & B. Use control of breath and muscles to move body, not momentum.

Nutrition Tip:
If you love the taste of garlic but hate garlic breath — just chew on a piece of fresh parsley and presto — no more garlic breath.

Experience Good Thoughts:
People of mediocre ability sometimes achieve outstanding success because they don't know when to quit. Most people succeed because they are determined to succeed. Remember, follow-through is a key ingredient to success.

Think Golf:
"You must always be positive, because your body can only do what your brain sees."
—Chi Chi Rodriguez

Make Me Smile:
A wife asked her husband if he would quit playing golf after she dies. Her husband replies that it will take awhile to get over her death, but eventually he would play golf again. Then she asks if he remarried would he marry a woman who plays golf. He reluctantly replies, "Yes, I probably will." Not giving up, she finally asks him, "Will you give her my clubs?" He answers, "I can't, she's left-handed."

SATURDAY/SUNDAY

GOLFING DAYS ARE GOOD FOR YOUR HEALTH

REFLECTING ON THE PAST WEEK:

What was your basic attitude? Were you a positive thinker or did you need an "attitude adjustment?" Are you having success with eating healthier and doing your exercise program? How do you feel physically? If you went golfing, write down any comments that might be helpful later in improving your game. Remember, that laughter is the best medicine in the face of adversity. Are you seeing the lighter side of life?

The exercise that helped me the most this week was on page:

_____

My nutritional habits this week were:

_____

What made me smile this week?

_____

_____

Looking back at my golf week:
    My Score: _____ What did I do right? _____

_____

_____
    What could I do to improve?

_____

_____

Goals for next week: _____

_____

_____

MONDAY

Name: CARDIO: SIDE SHUFFLING

Goal: Increase cardiovascular endurance and stamina for the 4+ hours of golf; enhance concentration and focus; improve coordination, balance and rhythm.

Explanation:

Side shuffling increases strength in inner and outer thighs. Stand with feet slightly wider than hips. Step right foot toward the left foot then follow with the left foot stepping farther left. Steps will be r-l-r-l-r-l. A slight hop may be added for speed. Be sure to pick up feet vs. drag them. Shuffle 20-30 steps one way then reverse. Take turns doing forward and backward walking.

Nutrition Tip:

Lactose comes in different forms. Although yogurt contains lactose, the yogurt culture provides enzymes that can digest it. Eat yogurt for all of its many benefits especially getting your calcium requirement if you're lactose intolerant.

Experience Good Thoughts:

If not you, then who? If not now, then when?

Think Golf:

Short irons require a three-quarter swing for maximum control. Because the shafts are shorter, move closer to the ball. Of all the full swing clubs, your swing with the short irons is the most compact with the least weight transfer. Try to keep your momentum and swing rhythm steady throughout the entire swing.

Make Me Smile:

The owner of a golf course was confused about paying an invoice, so he decided to ask his secretary for some mathematical help. He called her into his office and said, "Hey, you graduated from college. Could you help me figure this out? If I were to give you $20,000 minus 14%, how much would you take off?" The secretary thought for a minute and then replied, "Everything but my earrings!"

TUESDAY

Name: PILATES: SCISSORS

Goal: Stretch hamstrings of each leg while stabilizing pelvis and compressing abdominals.

Explanation:

Start with upper spine flexed off mat with belly button pulled into spine. Extend one leg toward sky and reach other leg parallel with floor. Hold on to raised leg. Exhale as you switch legs like scissors maintaining a flat back and abdomen tight. Focus on the lengthening of legs and engagement of midsection. Repeat 10 times.

Nutrition Tip:

Do you think pasta is just starch? It really does have substantial nutritional value. Two cups of pasta provide 31% of manganese, 24% of iron, 16% of phosphorus and copper, 12% of magnesium and 9% of zinc that nutritionists recommend. And — pasta retains its minerals during cooking.

Experience Good Thoughts:

"There is one thing stronger than all the armies in the world and that is an idea whose time has come."

—Victor Hugo

Think Golf:

"Forget your opponents; always play against par."

—Sam Snead

Make Me Smile:

An older golfer was told that exercising would be good for his game. He disagreed and quickly responded, "The only reason I would take up exercising is to hear heavy breathing again."

WEDNESDAY

Name: STRENGTH: SUPERMAN ARM/LEG ONLY

Goal: Provide midsection stability and torso strength to assist in rotational action of swing.

Explanation:

Start face down with legs and arms straight out in front and chest resting on the floor. Complete 10 repetitions lifting just arms and upper body while legs form a stable base. Then repeat keeping hands or elbows on floor while legs lift in air initially engaging gluteals to start movement. Focus on balance and exhale on lift.

Nutrition Tip:
Drinking sweet drinks may stimulate your appetite. Too much fructose in the diet could stimulate a person's appetite and encourage you to overeat. Fructose is a form of sugar found in corn syrup, and corn syrup is commonly used to sweeten beverages such as soda, bottled iced tea, and fruit juices.

Experience Good Thoughts:
"Become a possibilitarian. No matter how dark things seem to be or actually are, raise your sights and see possibilities — always see them, for they are always there."
—Dr. Norman Vincent Peale

Think Golf:
Ever wonder about the effect humidity has on the flight of the ball? Does dense air hold your ball back? The fact is that hot, humid air is lighter than cold, dry air. So on a humid day, the air is actually less dense and your ball will fly farther because there is less resistance.

Make Me Smile:
A golfer walks up to a water hazard and notices that he only has two balls left, an old one and a brand new one. So he tees up the old ball. A voice from above booms, "Pick up the old ball and tee up the new ball." A little intimidated, he follows the directions and gets ready to swing. Then he hears the voice again. "First take a practice swing." So he takes a practice swing. The voice from above in a loud and assertive tone says, "Tee up the old ball!"

THURSDAY

Name: BIG BALL: SUPERMAN STANDING

Goal: Increase spatial awareness challenging balance and maintaining proper shoulder stabilization.

Explanation:

Stand with feet together and big ball over head with arms straight. Shift weight to left leg. Slowly allow right leg to extend straight out behind body while arms and ball lean forward. Goal is to form a capital "T" with right leg and body parallel with the floor. Hold for 5 seconds, then return to start. Repeat 5x each leg. Focus on controlled breathing and form.

Nutrition Tip:
Calcium is important for strong teeth and bones and for muscle and nerve function. It is the major mineral in bone. Good sources for calcium include milk and milk products, fish, turnip and mustard greens, almonds, and broccoli.

Experience Good Thoughts:
It's your attitude, not your aptitude, that will determine your altitude!

Think Golf:
If the greens are fast, the ball will break more than on normal greens. So whether it's your approach shot or your putt, plan your shot to stop below the hole. It is always better to putt uphill than to lose control on a downhill putt.

Make Me Smile:
An older couple decided to spend their anniversary at St. Andrews. During the game, the husband confessed that he had an affair many years before. Insisting that it meant nothing, he asked his wife to forgive him. She was hurt but realized they had a wonderful life and quickly forgave him. A few minutes later she said, "Since we're being honest with each other I have something to confess too. 52 years ago I had a sex change operation. I was a man before we met." The husband yelled and screamed and threw his club. "You liar, you shameless cheat! How could you? I trusted you and you've been playing from the ladies' tees all these years!"

FRIDAY

Name: **DYNAMIC STRETCH: LEG KICKOUT SIDE**
Goal: Increase blood flow and circulation to volatile low back and outer hip area to prevent injury and increase flexibility for repetitive weight shifting.

Explanation:

Stand with hands on hips and feet hip distance apart. Inhale to prepare. Exhale and lift right leg out to side maintaining straight posture. Inhale bringing leg back down and exhale lifting other leg to side. Repeat 10x alternating legs.

Nutrition Tip:
Suffering with the embarrassment of excessive flatulence? Here are some culprits that are known to cause it — apples, beans, brussel sprouts, broccoli, cabbage, carbonated beverages, cauliflower, dairy products high in lactose, diet foods sweetened with sorbitol, onions, radishes, and wheat products.

Experience Good Thoughts:
"You can get everything in life you want if you help enough other people get what they want."

—Zig Ziglar

Think Golf:
"You can win tournaments when you're mechanical, but golf is a game of emotion and adjustment. If you're not aware of what's happening to your mind and your body when you're playing, you'll never be able to be the very best you can be."

—Jack Nicklaus

Make Me Smile:
"I have a tip that can take five strokes off anyone's golf game. It's called an eraser.'

—Arnold Palmer

SATURDAY/SUNDAY

GOLFING DAYS ARE GOOD FOR YOUR HEALTH

REFLECTING ON THE PAST WEEK:

What was your basic attitude? Were you a positive thinker or did you need an "attitude adjustment?" Are you having success with eating healthier and doing your exercise program? How do you feel physically? If you went golfing, write down any comments that might be helpful later in improving your game. Remember, that laughter is the best medicine in the face of adversity. Are you seeing the lighter side of life?

The exercise that helped me the most this week was on page:

_____

My nutritional habits this week were:

_____

What made me smile this week?

_____

_____

Looking back at my golf week:
　　My Score: _____ What did I do right? _____

_____

_____

　　　　What could I do to improve?

_____

_____

Goals for next week: _____

_____

_____

MONDAY

Name: YOGA/STRETCH: CAT/COW POSE

Goal: Stretch and strengthen back muscles bringing greater elasticity to the spine reducing risk of injury.

Explanation:

Kneel on all fours with hands directly under shoulders and knees directly under hips. Inhale and draw belly button to spine, pressing spine toward sky rounding back. Gluteals will be tucked under as well as head. Exhale and reverse movement by dropping belly button toward floor while head and hips lift up toward sky. Focus on keeping shoulders away from neck and ears. Repeat 10x.

Nutrition Tip:
No single food can supply all the nutrients in the amounts we need. For example, oranges provide Vitamin C and folate but no Vitamin B12. Cheese provides calcium and Vitamin B12 but no Vitamin C. Be sure to choose from all the food groups to get the nutrients your body needs.

Experience Good Thoughts:
"The quality of a person's life is in direct proportion to their commitment to excellence, regardless of their chosen field of endeavor."

—Vince Lombardi

Think Golf:
"Competitive golf is played mainly on a five-and-a-half inch course: the space between your ears."

—Bobby Jones

Make Me Smile:
Both golfers hit the ball and took a magnificent swing but somehow, something went wrong and a horrible slice resulted. The ball went onto the adjoining fairway and hit a man full force. He dropped. Both players ran up to the man who was on the ground with the ball between his feet. The first guy to arrive yells, "Good heavens, what should I do?" "Don't move him," said his partner, "if we leave him here he becomes an immovable obstruction and you can either play the ball as it lies or take a two club-length drop."

TUESDAY

Name: HEAVY BALL: ROLL UP
Goal: Increase spinal flexion and abdominal strength.

Explanation:

Lie on floor with ball held to chest and toes flexed. Inhale lifting head to look toward feet. As you exhale roll one vertebrae at a time off floor reaching ball forward toward feet. Try not to use momentum. When sitting tall at the top, inhale as you roll back behind tailbone engaging abdominals. Exhale to finish roll down focusing on keeping abdominals tight and being in complete control of the roll down...fighting gravity. Complete 10 repetitions.

Nutrition Tip:
We all need a good supply of iron to build strong bodies. Some food sources that are rich in iron include shellfish, ready-to-eat cereals with added iron, turkey dark meat, sardines, spinach, cooked dry beans, peas, lentils, and whole grain breads.

Experience Good Thoughts:
"Keep away from people who belittle your ambitions. Small people always do that, but the really great make you feel that you, too, can become great."
—Mark Twain

Think Golf:
Strengthening specific muscles related to golf will give a person more distance. These muscle groups include the torso, legs, hips, and shoulders. Ask for advice before you start a fitness program. If you're working out the wrong muscles, it may not help your swing at all AND building up some muscle groups can actually hinder your golf swing.

Make Me Smile:
A wife walked into the bedroom and found her husband in bed with his golf clubs. Seeing the astonished look on her face, he reminded her of the ultimatum she so flippantly gave him, "Well, you said I had to choose, right?"

WEDNESDAY

Name: PRE-ROUND WARMUP: FOOT/ANKLE

Goal: Increase blood flow in ankles to prepare the ankles for unlevel lies while swinging.

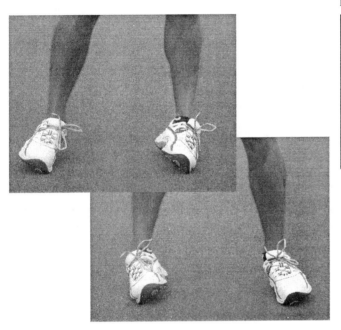

Explanation:

Stand with feet in address position. Hands on hips. Lean, shift weight, and tilt each foot side to side. Keep knees slightly unlocked. Repeat right and left weight shift 20 times. You should feel a stretch on the inside and outside of the ankles.

Nutrition Tip:
Good sources for obtaining Potassium are baked white or sweet potatoes, cooked greens such as spinach, winter squash, bananas, dried fruits such as apricots, prunes, orange juice, and cooked dry beans. Potassium is needed for growth, building muscles, transmission of nerve impulses and heart activity. It is also believed to help lower blood pressure.

Experience Good Thoughts:
"When one door closes, another opens; but we often look so long and so regretfully upon the closed door that we do not see the one which has opened for us."
—Alexander Graham Bell

Think Golf:
Stance is an important aspect of a good set-up. If you're a right-handed golfer, play all your irons a little left of center and all your woods just inside your left heel. This will result in consistent contact at the bottom of your swing arc.

Make Me Smile:
One of the signs that you might be obsessed with golf — It's time to mow your grass and you measure it to 11 on the Stimpmeter.

THURSDAY

Name: CARDIO: INTERVAL SPRINTING

Goal: Increase cardiovascular endurance and stamina for the 4+ hours of golf; develop fast twitch muscles for power; improve coordination, balance and rhythm;

Explanation:

Interval sprinting is the next level up from jogging. Jogging will raise your heart rate and breathing rate quite high. A recommended interval length for a sprint is no longer than 30 seconds. Start by lightly jogging, then sprint (jog fast) to the next quick landmark (mailbox, light post, end of block). Try interval sprinting 3x per week for 10-30 minutes in duration. Focus on deep breaths, light feet, and positive thinking.

Nutrition Tip:
When you reheat sauces, soups, and gravies, make sure they come to a boil. Reheat leftovers thoroughly to at least 165 degrees.

Experience Good Thoughts:
"The human spirit is never finished when it is defeated. It is finished when it surrenders."

—Ben Stein

Think Golf:
Knowing the difference between chipping and pitching can save you many unwanted strokes. When you get close to the green, evaluate your situation. If you're within 10 yards of the green, chip. If you're farther away, pitch.

Make Me Smile:
If you can't wait to get out on the course again but your spouse is not too happy about being a "golf widow" here are some tried and true excuses that seem to carry some weight.
1) I have a meeting at the course, so I'll just play as long as I'm there anyway.
2) I hate Nascar and that's all that's on TV. Do you want Nascar on TV all day?
3) I've been taking golf vitamins. They advertise that I'll be able to hit the ball an extra 10 yards. I have to find out if they're working or not

FRIDAY

Name: TOWEL STRETCH: STANDING INNER THIGH

Goal: Stretch inner thigh musculature helping to prevent imbalances and tightening of low back muscles resulting in injury.

Explanation:

Stand tall on left foot while right foot is placed in middle of towel. Hold both ends of towel in right hand. Balance on left foot while extending right leg straight out parallel to floor in front of body then slowly pull leg out to right side keeping leg straight and upright posture. Hold for 10 seconds, then repeat with other leg. Opposite arm can help balance by extending out to the side or for more support, hold onto wall.

Nutrition Tip:
Some foods have been known to trigger headaches. If you have frequent headaches, check out this list. Beer, coffee, tea, alcohol, red wine, beans (not green beans), cheese, chocolate, cured foods, pork, yogurt, and MSG.

Experience Good Thoughts:
"You cannot do a kindness too soon, for you never know how soon it will be too late."

—Ralph Waldo Emerson

Think Golf:
"All golfers, men and women, professional and amateur, are united by one thing: their desire to improve."   —Judy Rankin

Make Me Smile:
An elderly grandfather had been playing golf for over 75 years. As usual, he went out early and played his 18 holes. Directly after playing golf, he attended the wedding of one of his grandsons. During the reception he was talking with him, offering him advice on how to have a happy marriage. After awhile the young groom said, "Grandpa, what's it like making love at your age?" His grandfather replied, "Well, it's kind of like putting with a rope."

SATURDAY/SUNDAY

GOLFING DAYS ARE GOOD FOR YOUR HEALTH

REFLECTING ON THE PAST WEEK:

What was your basic attitude? Were you a positive thinker or did you need an "attitude adjustment?" Are you having success with eating healthier and doing your exercise program? How do you feel physically? If you went golfing, write down any comments that might be helpful later in improving your game. Remember, that laughter is the best medicine in the face of adversity. Are you seeing the lighter side of life?

The exercise that helped me the most this week was on page:

_____

My nutritional habits this week were:

_____

What made me smile this week?

_____

_____

Looking back at my golf week:
     My Score: _____ What did I do right?

_____

_____

     What could I do to improve?

_____

_____

Goals for next week: _____

_____

_____

MONDAY

Name: DYNAMIC STRETCH: HAMSTRING CURL KICKBACK

Goal: Increase circulation of hamstrings for preparation of correct power and rhythm in swing.

Explanation:

Stand with feet wider than hip distance apart. Place hands on hips with shoulders back. Bend right leg at knee kicking the heel back to the gluteal. Can you touch your buttock? Swith r and l legs 10x while balancing on the opposite leg briefly.

Nutrition Tip:

Vitamin B-6 can be lost in preparation, cooking, or storage. Losses occur when some Vitamin B-6 is dissolved in the cooking liquid. To retain Vitamin B-6, serve fruits raw; or cook foods in a minimal amount of water for the shortest possible time.

Experience Good Thoughts:

"Love and compassion are necessities, not luxuries. Without them humanity cannot survive."

—The Dalai Lama

Think Golf:

"You're never too old to play golf. If you can walk, you can play."

—Louise Suggs

Make Me Smile:

After golf one day, a man stopped in a bar for a beer before heading home. He struck up a conversation with a beautiful young woman. They had a couple drinks, liked each other, and soon she invited him to her apartment. For two hours they made passionate love. On the way home, the man's conscience started bothering him. He loved his wife and didn't want this to ruin their marriage. So he decided to tell her. "Honey, I have a confession to make. After I played golf today, I stopped by the bar for a beer, met a beautiful woman, went to her apartment, and made love to her for two hours. I'm sorry. It won't ever happen again. Please forgive me." His wife glared at him and said, "Don't lie to me, you sorry scum bag! You played 36 holes, didn't you?"

TUESDAY

Name: PILATES: AB PREPS
Goal: Trunk stabilization while flexing the spine, increasing ability for shoulder blades to maintain form during swing for less chance of error.

Explanation:

Lie on back with knees bent and feet flat on floor hip distance apart. Palms down at sides. Inhale and lift head looking between knees. Exhale and flex upperbody off floor sliding ribcage toward hips and reaching arms toward calves. Inhale pausing at top holding belly button in. Exhale as you lengthen back to floor. Repeat 10 times slowly.

Nutrition Tip:
Moderation is the key to good health and a healthy weight. If you crave potato chips or a candy bar, go ahead and enjoy — once in awhile. Don't deny yourself completely. It will lead to binge eating of unhealthy foods.

Experience Good Thoughts:
"Don't aim for success if you want it. Just do what you love and believe in, and it will come naturally."

—David Frost

Think Golf:
Using the "death grip" can prevent a golfer from swinging the club properly. Hold the club in front of you and relax your hands until the club starts slipping through your hands. Your grip pressure should be slightly firmer than the pressure right before the club starts to slip and you will still maintain control.

Make Me Smile:
A sign that you're too old even for the Senior Tour — Every time you swing, the waistband on your pants chafes your nipples!

WEDNESDAY

Name: DB STRENGTH: LATERAL DIAGONAL RAISES

Goal: Increase upper body strength and power; reinforce stabilization of shoulder girdle as well as total back for consistent swing.

Explanation:

Stand with feet hip distance apart holding 3-5-8lb dumbbells in hand with palms facing outer front part of thighs. Inhale to prepare with focus on strong stance and posture. Exhale lifting both arms straight out at a diagonal or "V" angle (to corners of room) to shoulder height. Inhale return hands to thighs. Repeat lifting sequence 10-20x. If weights get too heavy lift one arm at a time. Do not allow body to sway or move during exercise.

Nutrition Tip:

Vitamin A contributes to healthy eyes, healthy skin, and good resistance to infection. Here's a short list of foods rich in Vitamin A. Orange vegetables such as carrots, sweet potatoes, pumpkin, winter squash; Dark green leafy vegetables such as spinach, collards, turnip greens; Orange fruits like mangoes, cantaloupe, apricots; Tomatoes.

Experience Good Thoughts:

"It's not true that nice guys finish last. Nice guys are winners before the game even starts."

—Addison Walker

Think Golf:

One of the most important fundamentals to learn is how to square your body and club to the target. The key is to square both the clubface and the rest of the club — then square your body to the club. If you aim the clubface but not the rest of the club, the body position will be off.

Make Me Smile:

"Give me golf clubs, fresh air, and a beautiful partner and you can keep my golf clubs and the fresh air."

—Jack Benny

THURSDAY

Name: BIG BALL: LYING HIP ROTATION

Goal: Strengthen rotational power of hips while stabilizing upper body and trunk.

Explanation:

Lie on floor with ball between feet straight in the air. Place palms face down on floor at shoulder height. Squeeze inner thighs toward each other. Engage abdominals and obliques and rotate legs over to the right and rest ball on floor. Try to keep upper body still. Inhale to prepare. Then exhale and raise legs back up to middle. Repeat each way 5x. Bend knees if needed to maximize leverage.

Nutrition Tip:
Adolescents and adults over age 50 have an especially high need for calcium. When selecting dairy products to get enough calcium, choose those that are low in fat or fat-free to avoid getting too much saturated fat.

Experience Good Thoughts:
"Live out of your imagination, not your history."
—Steven Covey, Author & Trainer

Think Golf:
Did you know that in 1932 the USGA standardized the golf ball? It had to fall within the parameters of weighing no more than 1.62 ounces and measuring not less than 1.68 inches in diameter. Later modifications were made to regulate the speed of the ball. In 1990, the Royal and Ancient Rules Committee adopted the 1.68-inch ball with an overall distance standard restriction.

Make Me Smile:
When asked where the best place was for spectators to stand during a celebrity golf tournament, Joe Garagiola replied, "The safest place would be in the fairways."

FRIDAY

Name: PILATES: ONE LEG CIRCLE

Goal: Increase stabilization of trunk and hips while increasing range of motion of leg and hip movement during hip shift.

Explanation:

Lie on back with one leg straight on floor and other leg straight in air. Legs form 90 degrees angle. Arms at side palms down. While keeping entire body on floor still, rotate leg in air 10x one way then reverse. Slight pressure of internal muscles will be felt throughout body. Repeat other leg.

Nutrition Tip:

Are you one of the low-carb eaters? When you're looking for a snack, try pork rinds. They have twice as much protein as fat, and more than half of the fat is unsaturated. Seems like they have an undeserved reputation.

Experience Good Thoughts:

"The best and most beautiful things in the world cannot be seen or even touched. They must be felt with the heart."

—Helen Keller, American Blind/Deaf Author

Think Golf:

Putting the word "competition" into proper perspective in your own profession is perfectly addressed in a question posed by Bruce Crampton. "How would you like to meet the top 143 people at what you do each week in order to survive?"

Make Me Smile:

"The income tax has made more liars out of the American people than golf has."

—Will Rogers

SATURDAY/SUNDAY

GOLFING DAYS ARE GOOD FOR YOUR HEALTH

REFLECTING ON THE PAST WEEK:

What was your basic attitude? Were you a positive thinker or did you need an "attitude adjustment?" Are you having success with eating healthier and doing your exercise program? How do you feel physically? If you went golfing, write down any comments that might be helpful later in improving your game. Remember, that laughter is the best medicine in the face of adversity. Are you seeing the lighter side of life?

The exercise that helped me the most this week was on page:

_____

My nutritional habits this week were:

_____

What made me smile this week?

_____

_____

Looking back at my golf week:
     My Score: _____ What did I do right?

_____

_____

     What could I do to improve?

_____

_____

Goals for next week: _____

_____

_____

MONDAY

Name: DYNAMIC STRETCH: CLAP FRONT W/DIAGONAL ARMS

Goal: Open chest and front of shoulders for more range of motion during turn without hindrance.

Explanation:

Stand with feet hip distance apart. Clap straight arms in front of chest and open them on a diagonal line. Repeat clap and open on the opposite diagonal line. Put emphasis on opening vs. the clapping. Repeat 10x each side.

Nutrition Tip:

Need a dip to eat those raw veggies that are so good for you? Mix an envelope of ranch dressing with two cups of plain yogurt for a snack that is low in carbs and calories, satisfies your desire to dip, and tastes great too.

Experience Good Thoughts:

"Your profession is not what brings home your paycheck. Your profession is what you were put on earth to do with such passion and such intensity that it becomes spiritual in calling."

—Vincent Van Gogh, Dutch Painter

Think Golf:

Try this golf game! Bingo-Bango-Bongo: This game allows 2-4 players to be competitive regardless of handicaps. The number of strokes doesn't matter. On every hole players can earn points for different reasons. BINGO means the first ball on the green scores a point. BANGO is awarded to the closest ball to the pin once everyone gets on the green. BONGO is another point for the first one in the hole. The player with the highest point total at the end is the winner.

Make Me Smile:

If you play golf in any areas where palm trees beautify an otherwise mediocre course, here's a head's up —— palm trees eat golf balls! Watch out for the palm trees.

TUESDAY

Name: YOGA/STRETCH: SEATED BUTTERFLY STRETCH
Goal: Open hip joints to allow more mobility during swing, reducing strain on lower back; create coiling affect for increased leveraging and power.

Explanation:

Sit on floor and bring bottoms of feet together. Place elbows on knees while grabbing ankles. Apply gentle pressure with elbows on knees and feel tension and stretch in groin and hips. You may "fly" your knees up and down to increase circulation, but do not ballistically bounce.

Nutrition Tip:
Try sunflower seeds or pumpkin seeds if you're craving a salty snack. You won't eat nearly as many because you have to crack the shells open. They're tasty too.

Experience Good Thoughts:
"At the center of the universe is a loving heart that continues to beat and that wants the best for every person. Anything we can do to help foster the intellect and spirit and emotional growth of our fellow human beings, that is our job."

—Fred Rogers (Mister Rogers of TV)

Think Golf:
"It is a sport in which the whole American family can participate – fathers and mothers, sons and daughters alike. It offers healthy respite from daily toil, refreshment of body and mind."

—Dwight D. Eisenhower, 34th U.S. President

Make Me Smile:
Distance or accuracy? Jim Dent, recognized as one of golf's longest drivers, admits, "I can airmail the golf ball, but sometimes I don't put the right address on it."

WEDNESDAY

Name: BIG BALL: DROP AND CATCH

Goal: Strengthen stabilizing muscles of inner thigh and core for better overall driving power through hips.

Explanation:

Lie on your back with legs straight in the air. Place big ball between ankles and maintain flat spine while keeping legs as straight as possible toward the sky. Drop the ball into hands right above chest while legs separate and stretch inner thighs. Then, throw ball back up between ankles and squeeze ball. Repeat 30-50x. Increase speed.

Nutrition Tip:
Celery is a great snack if you're looking for something refreshing with hardly any calories. One twelve-inch stalk contains fiber and adds about 6 calories to your daily allotment. But be careful if you're one of those who likes to fill the center with peanut butter or cream cheese. Use fillings sparingly and you'll still reap the benefits.

Experience Good Thoughts:
"The most important single ingredient in the formula of success is knowing how to get along with people."
—Theodore Roosevelt, 26th U.S. President

Think Golf:
"Keep your sense of humor. There's enough stress in the rest of your life to let bad shots ruin a game you're supposed to enjoy."
—Amy Strum Alcott, U.S. Golfer

Make Me Smile:
What were you thinking? Jay Knudsen, a very creative entrepreneur, tried marketing the idea of placing cremated remains of golfers into the shafts of their favorite golf clubs! Is that comparable to an urn on the fireplace?

THURSDAY

Name: HEAVY BALL: V-SEAT BOTH KNEES

Goal: Improve lower pelvic and trunk stability and strength.

Explanation:

Sit on floor holding ball in front of chest to prepare. Round back putting weight just back of tail bone or sit bones. Lift legs off floor with knees bent. While maintaining balance and keeping spine flexed with abdominals held tight, take ball clockwise around both legs 10x. Reverse direction 10x.

Nutrition Tip:
Add a little zip to your fruit? Mexicans sprinkle a little chili powder on watermelon, peaches, cantaloupe, and other fresh fruit. It wakes up your taste buds and complements the sweet flavor of the fruit.

Experience Good Thoughts:
"There is overwhelming evidence that the higher the level of self-esteem, the more likely one will be to treat others with respect, kindness, and generosity."
—Nathaniel Branden, Psychologist & Author

Think Golf:
In 1950, the newly formed LPGA kicked off its first tour with the Tampa Open. Polly Riley from Fort Worth, Texas shot a 72-hole score of 295 to win. Looking at the dynamic organization the LPGA is now, it's difficult to imagine that was only 55 years ago.

Make Me Smile:
When asked how to spot the sign of a good golfer, Lee Trevino answered, "It's a tan like mine. It tells you the player is spending a lot of time out on the fairway and the greens — and not in the trees."

FRIDAY

Name: STRENGTH: TAKE AWAY SQUAT I

Goal: Mimic the golf swing from address through top position adding outside resistance to the body to overload the muscles used; promote muscle memory.

Explanation:

In address, hold 3-5-8lb dumbbell in right hand and cross forearm over stomach. Swing weight up and back into top position. Repeat 20-30x focusing on posture and core strength.

Nutrition Tip:
An antioxidant compound found in blueberries appears to lower cholesterol. This same compound also has powerful anti-cancer properties. Sprinkle a few blueberries on your morning cereal for extra cholesterol fighting power.

Experience Good Thoughts:
"Life isn't a matter of milestones, but of moments."

—Rose Kennedy, Kennedy family Matriarch

Think Golf:
Players often lose their tempo in the transition from backswing to downswing. A quick, jerky movement from the top will almost certainly result in your club being out of line as it reaches the ball. If you accelerate gradually on your downswing, you'll be able to control your rhythm.

Make Me Smile:
Gary Nicklaus was asked if it was difficult being Jack's son. Gary answered, "I don't know. I've never been anyone else's son."

SATURDAY/SUNDAY

GOLFING DAYS ARE GOOD FOR YOUR HEALTH

REFLECTING ON THE PAST WEEK:

What was your basic attitude? Were you a positive thinker or did you need an "attitude adjustment?" Are you having success with eating healthier and doing your exercise program? How do you feel physically? If you went golfing, write down any comments that might be helpful later in improving your game. Remember, that laughter is the best medicine in the face of adversity. Are you seeing the lighter side of life?

The exercise that helped me the most this week was on page:

_____

My nutritional habits this week were:

_____

What made me smile this week?

_____

_____

Looking back at my golf week:
    My Score: _____ What did I do right?

_____

_____

    What could I do to improve?

_____

_____

Goals for next week: _____

_____

_____

MONDAY

Name: YOGA/STRETCH: STANDING TWIST
Goal: Enhance golf performance by stretching torso, hips and chest.

Explanation:

Stand sideways to a wall as you lift your knee closest to the wall up 90 degrees. Position the same hip against the wall to stabilize your hips. Inhale and lengthen your spine. Exhale and turn your belly button toward wall. Spread your hands apart on the wall below shoulder height. Hold for 60 seconds then switch sides.

Nutrition Tip:
Take a tip from a famous Chinese restaurant and instead of using bread or tortillas for your stir-fry, sandwich, or burrito -- try using large lettuce leaves. Now you can buy lettuce leaves shaped like a boat and strong enough to hold hot or cold foods.

Experience Good Thoughts:
"Always bear in mind that our own resolution to succeed is more important than any other one thing."

—Abraham Lincoln, 16th President of U.S.

Think Golf:
How high is high enough to tee your ball? The top of the ball should be even with the top of the driver. That should ensure solid contact.

Make Me Smile:
"Golf is like love. One day you think you are too old, and the next day you want to do it again."

—Roberto De Vincenzo

TUESDAY

Name: PRE-ROUND WARMUP: MERRY-GO-ROUND W/ CLUB

Goal: Prepare body for round; decrease risk of injury by loosening up muscles in low back and hips.

Explanation:

Stand with feet hip distance apart holding ends of club in both hands with arms straight in front of chest. Inhale to prepare. Exhale rotating club and upper body to the right as far as possible. Lift up on left toe to allow further rotation. Goal is to rotate club 180 degrees. Inhale return back to start position. Repeat other side. Complete 10 repetitions each side. Focus on tall spine lifting away from hips.

Nutrition Tip:
We know there are many facets to eating a healthy diet. However, eating fruit was the only dietary factor linked to reduced rates of macular degeneration, which is the leading cause of blindness in older adults. So, to protect your vision, eat at least 3 servings of fruit a day such as apples, oranges, bananas, grapes, pears, mangoes, apricots and berries. It's a simple preventative for a debilitating disease.

Experience Good Thoughts:
"You don't have to see the whole staircase, just take the first step."
—Martin Luther King, Jr.

Think Golf:
How important is rhythm in your swing? A good golf swing should go back and forth like the beat of a pendulum. Practice counting "one Mississippi" on your backswing and "two Mississippi" on your forward swing. That will help you to develop a consistent rhythm in your swing.

Make Me Smile:
Just trying to help?? Pro golfer Mary Dwyer hit the prize car that was going to be awarded to the player who shot a hole in one. A spectator who felt the need to explain the rules told her, "I don't think you understand. You have to hit the hole, not the car."

WEDNESDAY

Name: PILATES: ROLL OVER

Goal: Enhance spinal flexibility while strengthening entire core region for better balance, control, power, and focus.

Explanation:

Lie on back with legs extended to sky, toes pointed and hands at sides. Inhale to prepare. Exhale articulating spine off floor slowly from tail bone to upper back.... not neck. Abdominals will tighten throughout movement engaging and pulling the hips against gravity. Allow legs to lower over head and ideally touching mat. Inhale lift legs to parallel. Exhale sequentially rolling spine back down to mat from upper ribcage to tailbone. Complete 10 repetitions focusing on flat abdominals.

Nutrition Tip:

Eating a high protein breakfast and lunch will boost your energy throughout the day. It provides a steady stream of strength without the spikes associated with carbohydrate and sugar intake.

Experience Good Thoughts:

"It's not enough to be busy, so are the ants. The question is, 'What are we busy about?'"
—Henry David Thoreau

Think Golf:

"Remember, your score is only one of many, many ways to measure your success at golf. Other ways include how well you controlled your emotions, how well and how consistently you executed your pre-shot routine, how well you were able to win without bragging, how honorably you took defeat, how much you were able to appreciate the beauty of the golf course and the day, how well you stuck to your game plan, and how much FUN you had."
—Chris Dorris, Performance Psychologist

Make Me Smile:

Groucho Marx said it best — "I don't care to belong to a club that accepts people like me as members."

THURSDAY

Name: STRENGTH: FINISH SQUAT II
Goal: Mimic the golf swing from just before impact through finish adding resistance outside of the body; promote muscle memory.

Explanation:

In wide stance, hold 3-5-8lb dumbbell in left hand. From impact position, follow through with left hand to balance finish position. Keep right shoulder down and flip right heel over. Then bring weight across and bending knees, reach across right foot. Repeat 20-30x with control.

Nutrition Tip:
Eating a light meal with more carbohydrates than protein for dinner will help you to have a better night's sleep. Carbohydrates help produce serotonin, which has a relaxing effect on the body. Getting a good night's sleep will also ensure more energy for the next day's activities.

Experience Good Thoughts:
"A leader takes people where they want to go. A great leader takes people where they don't necessarily want to go but ought to be."

—Rosalynn Carter, Former First Lady

Think Golf:
Setting up for putting is important. Line your forearms with the putter shaft. Position the ball directly under your forward eye (if you're right handed, it's your left eye). Then start practicing your alignment.

Make Me Smile:
A young woman on the golf course was stung by a bee. She quickly went back to the pro shop and told the pro she was just stung. "Do you know anything that will help?" she asked. "Where were you stung?" the pro asked. "Between the first and second hole," she replied. Thinking about it for a minute, the pro says, "Well, first of all, your feet are too far apart."

FRIDAY

Name: TOWEL: SEATED HAMSTRING

Goal: Stretch hamstrings, which helps to prevent imbalances and tightening of low back muscles resulting in injury.

Explanation:

Sit on floor with right leg outstretched in front of body and left leg bent with bottom of foot resting on inside of right knee. Hold onto ends of towel with both hands and place it around bottom of right foot. Gently pull on ends of towel allowing toes to pull toward body stretching entire back of leg. Exaggerate the stretch by leaning chest forward toward knee. Hold 5-10 seconds at a time. Repeat as needed.

Nutrition Tip:
For extra fiber, add green peas to soups, stir-fries, and rice. Put chickpeas in your salads. Throw an extra can of red kidney beans into the chili.

Experience Good Thoughts:
"Always work from a list. Write it out, organize it, and work on your most important task."

—Brian Tracy, Trainer, Speaker & Author

Think Golf:
Your short game is two-thirds of your time on the course. So the experts say to spend two-thirds of your practice time on putting, pitching, and chipping.

Make Me Smile:
The novice golfer was not a very good player, but she was definitely trying very hard. Every stroke missed the ball, scraping the ground either to the right or in front of the ball, and sent chunks of grass and dirt flying in all directions. She looked at her friend and said, "With all this ground moving around, the worms will think we're in the middle of an earthquake." Her partner replied, "I don't think so. The worms around here are pretty smart. I'll bet most of them are hiding right under the ball for protection."

SATURDAY/SUNDAY

GOLFING DAYS ARE GOOD FOR YOUR HEALTH

REFLECTING ON THE PAST WEEK:

What was your basic attitude? Were you a positive thinker or did you need an "attitude adjustment?" Are you having success with eating healthier and doing your exercise program? How do you feel physically? If you went golfing, write down any comments that might be helpful later in improving your game. Remember, that laughter is the best medicine in the face of adversity. Are you seeing the lighter side of life?

The exercise that helped me the most this week was on page:

_____

My nutritional habits this week were:

_____

What made me smile this week?

_____

_____

Looking back at my golf week:
    My Score: _____ What did I do right? _____

_____

    What could I do to improve?

_____

_____

Goals for next week: _____

_____

_____

MONDAY

Name: PRE-ROUND WARMUP: STANDING CALF AND WRIST STRETCH

Goal: Increase warmth of muscles in delicate ankle and wrist joints for preparation of play; decrease injury.

Explanation:

Place both palms against wall with arms out-stretched at shoulder level. Maintain upright posture and step/extend one leg back behind you so the heel can touch the floor. Lean gently forward into hands with body weight while maintaining back heel on ground with stretching feeling in back of lower leg. Repeat other leg holding for 10-20 seconds each.

Nutrition Tip:
Here are some wise words from the Old Farmers Almanac. "You can't lose weight by talking about it. You have to keep your mouth shut."

Experience Good Thoughts:
"When things are bad, we take comfort in the thought that they could always be worse. And when they are, we find hope in the thought that things are so bad they have to get better."

—Malcolm S. Forbes, Financial Expert

Think Golf:
Use targets for practice shots. It's the best way to prepare for playing on the course. Be sure to check your alignment before every swing.

Make Me Smile:
Two friends were golfing and one sliced his shot into a wooded ravine. He picked up his 8-iron and climbed down the hill looking for his ball. After several minutes of hacking at the underbrush, he saw something sparkling in the leaves on the ground. As he came closer, he noticed that it was an 8-iron in hands of a skeleton! He immediately called his friend who was waiting at the top of the hill, "Larry, I've got trouble down here!" "What's the matter?" he asked standing close to the edge. "Bring me my wedge. I don't think I could ever get out of here with an 8-iron."

TUESDAY

Name: HEAVY BALL: PARTNER STANDING TORSO ROTATION
Goal: Promote trunk rotational ability with stabilized lower body.

Explanation:

Begin with feet hip distance apart back to back with a partner. Keeping the feet planted on the ground, rotate torso to the right and left direction focusing on maintaining torso stability. Pass the ball in one direction with partner, then turn to receive it in the opposite direction. The rear foot must pivot and heel will lift on turn. Repeat both ways 10x.

Nutrition Tip:
Try to stay away from stimulants as much as you can. Their effect on your body can be harmful. The most well known stimulants are: refined white sugar, coffee, alcohol, cigarettes, spices, red meat, diet pills, drugs.

Experience Good Thoughts:
"It is a great mistake for men to give up paying compliments, for when they give up saying what is charming, they give up thinking what is charming."

—Oscar Wilde

Think Golf:
If you have problems topping the ball, try to maintain the flex in your right leg during your downswing. If you straighten your leg, your body will rise up, and the outcome will probably be that the club will strike the ball directly in the middle or on the top. Remember, as arms go up, the body must stay down.

Make Me Smile:
"And the wind shall say 'Here were decent godless people; Their only monuments were the asphalt road and a thousand lost golf balls.' "

—T.S. Eliot

WEDNESDAY

Name: DYNAMIC STRETCH: STANDING HIP ABDUCTION
Goal: Promote balance and strengthen muscles around hip joint for easier weight shifting and power production.

Explanation:

Stand tall. Shift weight onto right leg maintaining posture and hip alignment. Try to balance lifting left leg off floor out to the side. If balance can be maintained, continue lifting left leg in and out 10x then switch sides. Repeat 10x each side for 3 sets.

Nutrition Tip:
Eggs are perfect sources of protein. The only downside is that the yolk is high in cholesterol, so limit whole eggs to 3 to 4 per week. Eating the whites of the egg is fine. And the yolk of the egg is not all bad. It contains a number of different vitamins that are very healthy. Just watch how many you eat.

Experience Good Thoughts:
"Recall it as often as you wish, a happy memory never wears out."

—Libbie Fudim

Think Golf:
Visualize your putt for better execution. First select your line of the putt, then visualize the ball rolling on that line and into the cup. Picture the perfect putt. Then execute what you have just visualized. Your mind believes what you tell it.

Make Me Smile:
A foursome of ladies walked into the clubhouse for a drink after playing a round of golf. "How did your game go?" asked the pro. The first answered by saying she did quite well with 20 riders. The second said she did pretty good, too, with 14 riders. The third woman had 10 and the last reported only 2 and admitted that she hadn't played very well. After they left, the pro asked the bartender what they meant by "riders." The bartender smiled and said, "That's when they hit the shot long enough to take a ride on a golf cart!"

THURSDAY

Name: BIG BALL: KNEELING HIP ABDUCTION

Goal: Strengthen muscles around hip joint for easier weight shift and power production during swing.

Explanation:

Kneel on both knees beside big ball. Lean arm over the top of big ball and allow outside leg to extend straight to the side. Try not to slouch over ball and lift outside leg 10-20x feeling "the burn" of the muscles. Switch sides.

Nutrition Tip:

While sugar substitutes have been shown to be safe and helpful for people with certain diseases such as diabetes, do not assume that "sugar-free" means the food product is low in calories. Some "sugar-free" food products provide the same amount of calories as the original version. Look out for xylitol. Xylitol is a sugar substitute used by people with diabetes because it is absorbed into the bloodstream at a slower rate than sugar. BUT — it is not calorie-free. Word of caution: Consuming large amounts of xylitol can cause diarrhea and cramping.

Experience Good Thoughts:

"If you wouldn't write it and sign it, don't say it."   —Earl Wilson

Think Golf:

Work on your balance by holding your follow through position until the ball has landed. This will produce a fundamentally sound swing. If you think that's easy, just try it.

Make Me Smile:

A golfer is a guy who can walk five miles with a heavy bag of clubs on his shoulder, but when he gets home, he expects his dog to get his slippers.

FRIDAY

Name: YOGA/STRETCH: INVERTED TRIANGLE

Goal: Challenge spinal rotation to its fullest while stretching hamstrings; reducing strain to low back area during swing.

Explanation:

Starting from triangle pose with right foot forward and left arm in air, slowly bring left arm down to where right arm is. Rotate body and take right arm in the air with upper body facing opposite direction from first triangle. Focus will be placed on pulling belly button in to help enhance rotation and opening chest. Hold approximately 10 seconds and switch sides.

Nutrition Tip:

A high fiber diet is associated with decreased risk of heart disease, high blood pressure, cancer, and even obesity. Fiber is found ONLY in plant foods, such as fruits, vegetables, and whole grains. Most adults only consume half of the recommended amount each day.

Experience Good Thoughts:

The Buddha says, "All things appear and disappear because of the concurrence of causes and conditions. Nothing ever exists entirely alone; everything is in relation to everything else." Synergy???

Think Golf:

Be in the best possible position to succeed at golf by using suitable equipment. Always have your equipment evaluated. If your clubs are too heavy, too stiff, or not at the proper lie angle, your game will be inhibited by your equipment. Custom club fitting is one way to improve your game.

Make Me Smile:

"A dedicated golfer can be said to be a "divotee."

—Charles McGee Jr.

SATURDAY/SUNDAY

GOLFING DAYS ARE GOOD FOR YOUR HEALTH

REFLECTING ON THE PAST WEEK:

What was your basic attitude? Were you a positive thinker or did you need an "attitude adjustment?" Are you having success with eating healthier and doing your exercise program? How do you feel physically? If you went golfing, write down any comments that might be helpful later in improving your game. Remember, that laughter is the best medicine in the face of adversity. Are you seeing the lighter side of life?

The exercise that helped me the most this week was on page:

_____

My nutritional habits this week were:

_____

What made me smile this week?

_____

_____

Looking back at my golf week:
    My Score: _____ What did I do right? _____

_____

_____

    What could I do to improve?

_____

_____

Goals for next week: _____

_____

_____

MONDAY

Name: STRENGTH: BENCH STEPPING/STEP UPS
Goal: Increase power and endurance strength of lower body as well as balance; prepares golfer for walking 18 holes.

Explanation:

Stand tall behind bench (no higher than 20 inches). Step up with right and allow left leg to follow. Pause on top of bench then return to floor with right leg then left. Focus on posture and placing all weight into heel of leading leg going up and control weight on balls of feet coming down. Repeat each leg 10-15x.

Nutrition Tip:
Major minerals are needed by the body in relatively large amounts. They are: Calcium, Chloride, Magnesium, Phosphorus, Potassium, Sodium, and Sulfur.

Experience Good Thoughts:
"Surround yourself with only people who are going to lift you higher."

—Oprah Winfrey

Think Golf:
Determine the direction of the grain of the grass by locating the brown, sunburned side of the hole, which is due to the exposed roots. That helps you determine which way the grass is growing. Putts down-grain travel faster than putts into the grain.

Make Me Smile:
Golfing vacations are "tee leaves."

TUESDAY

Name: PILATES: BREAST STROKE
Goal: Activate shoulder stabilizers promoting better posture throughout swing.

Explanation:

Lie face down with hands by shoulders and legs squeezing together. Inhale prepare. Exhale reach arms forward and top of head away from body parallel with floor. Inhale and circle arms back toward hips, lengthening and extending upper spine. Repeat 10x. Focus on keeping tension away from upper back and neck. Support spine with abdominals throughout movement.

Nutrition Tip:
Sulfur is needed to make hair, nails and cartilage. It helps in the digestion of fats and controls the metabolism of carbohydrates. It is also essential for the synthesis of Vitamin B1. Good food sources of Sulfur are meat, fish, eggs, legumes.

Experience Good Thoughts:
"Begin to see yourself as a soul with a body rather than a body with a soul."
—Dr. Wayne Dyer, Psychologist

Think Golf:
Posture that keeps the butt end of the club pointed at the midsection of the body will create a more efficient swing.

Make Me Smile:
"Scotland is a peculiar land that is the birthplace of golf and sport salmon fishing — a fact which may explain why it is also the birthplace of whiskey."
—Henry Beard, An *Angler's Dictionary* (1983)

WEDNESDAY

Name: DB STRENGTH: CROSSOVER PUNCHES
Goal: Warm up trunk, hips and shoulders while maintaining proper form with added resistance; reinforce timing and rhythm.

Explanation:

Similar to regular punches, shifting and punching from side to side, but aim arms across body toward corners of ceiling over head. Maintain form and increase weight when needed. Use 3-5-8lb dumbbells. Repeat 20x each side.

Nutrition Tip:
Phosphorus builds and strengthens bones and helps release energy from nutrients. Good food sources of Phosphorus are milk, cheese, meat, fish, poultry, eggs, whole grains, legumes, nuts.

Experience Good Thoughts:
"I have learned silence from the talkative, toleration from the intolerant, and kindness from the unkind; yet, strange, I am ungrateful to these teachers."
—Kahlil Gibran, Poet

Think Golf:
Do you know who was the first player to win the coveted "green jacket"? The great Sam Snead in 1949.

Make Me Smile:
There is a very fine line between "hobby" and "mental illness" — which makes one ask which would describe the average golfer's attitude toward his 6:45 am tee time.

THURSDAY

Name: TOWEL: MERRY GO ROUND
Goal: Increase flexibility of spine for better rotation in backswing and follow-through.

Explanation:

Stand tall with feet slightly wider than hip width and ends of towel in hands with arms extended out chest high. Inhale to prepare. Exhale rotating and pulling towel with right hand to the right. Keep rotating allowing left heel to lift for maximal rotation behind you. Inhale back to center and repeat other side. Alternate focusing on lifting spine higher and higher each time. Repeat 10x.

Nutrition Tip:
Add calcium to your diet by serving sweetened plain yogurt with desserts in place of whipped or sour cream. (300 mg calcium per 3/4 cup). Mix in some sugar-free fruit jam to perk up the taste.

Experience Good Thoughts:
"My advice to you is not to inquire why or whither, but just enjoy your ice cream while it's on your plate — that's my philosophy."
—Thornton Wilder, Novelist & Playwright

Think Golf:
Did you know that the great Ben Hogan kept a notebook with all the swing concepts that worked for him. Keeping a notebook of your favorite exercises and golf tips and periodically looking these over will help you to remember the techniques and nuances that make your game a little better.

Make Me Smile:
The schoolteacher was taking her first golfing lesson. "Is the word that refers to hitting a ball into the hole spelled p-u-t or p-u-t-t?" she asked the instructor.
"P-u-t-t," he replied. "Put means to place something where you want it. Putt means merely a hopeless attempt to do the same thing."

FRIDAY

Name: BIG BALL: SIDE LYING CRUNCH

Goal: Increase strength in obliques and front abdominal area for better reliability and power throughout turn.

Explanation:

Lie on your left side propped up on your midsection and hip on big ball. Place both hands across chest or behind ears for a challenge. Extend legs with left leg crossed behind right for support. Exhale and lift your torso off ball pushing left hip into ball. At the same time, draw your ribcage toward your hip. Pause and return to relaxed position on ball. Complete 10-15 repetitions each side.

Nutrition Tip:
Onions contain substances that prevent blood clots and raise HDL-cholesterol levels. Try to eat them regularly — especially raw. If you're having a high fat meal, try to include onions.

Experience Good Thoughts:
The old adage, 'If at first you don't succeed, try, try again,' has been part of the thinking process for many great people. Henry Ford said, "Failure is only the opportunity to begin again more intelligently." Lucky for us, in golf, we always have the chance to begin again.

Think Golf:
Practice putting for both direction and distance control. Since a good score ends with your final putt, spending time honing your putting skills is well worth the practice time invested. Being able to determine and putt for distance is the one facet that could take several strokes off your score.

Make Me Smile:
"Golf balls are attracted to water as unerringly as the eye of a middle-aged man to a female bosom."

—Michael Green

SATURDAY/SUNDAY

GOLFING DAYS ARE GOOD FOR YOUR HEALTH

REFLECTING ON THE PAST WEEK:

What was your basic attitude? Were you a positive thinker or did you need an "attitude adjustment?" Are you having success with eating healthier and doing your exercise program? How do you feel physically? If you went golfing, write down any comments that might be helpful later in improving your game. Remember, that laughter is the best medicine in the face of adversity. Are you seeing the lighter side of life?

The exercise that helped me the most this week was on page:

_____

My nutritional habits this week were:

_____

What made me smile this week?

_____

_____

Looking back at my golf week:
       My Score: _____ What did I do right? _____

_____

_____

       What could I do to improve?

_____

_____

Goals for next week: _____

_____

_____

MONDAY

Name: CARDIO: JUMP-ROPING
Goal: Increase cardiovascular stamina, focus and coordination of upper and lower body.

Explanation:

To ensure you have the correct length jumprope, stand on the rope with both feet. Handles should come up to shoulder level when pulled at your sides. Practice jumping lightly on both feet. Beginners will focus more on the coordination of the jump. As you progress, increase your time.

Nutrition Tip:
Microwave cooking helps preserve nutrients by cutting cooking time. The cooking liquid from meat and poultry is a rich source of B vitamins. After skimming off the fat, serve it with the meat or use it to make gravy or soup.

Experience Good Thoughts:
If you had to identify, in one word, the reason why the human race has not achieved, and never will achieve, its full potential, that word would be "meetings."

Think Golf:
Exercise your wrists to help your golf swing.
1. Stand with your arm hanging at your side and grab a golf club in one hand towards the end of grip.
2. Raise the club only by cocking your wrist and keeping your arm at side.
3. The club should have the toe pointing up to the sky straight out in front of you.
4. Raise it as high as you can, which will probably be just above parallel to the ground, then lower it and repeat about 10 times.

Make Me Smile:
Did you ever hear a company salesperson say that their golf equipment is so great that it sells itself? If that's the case, why do they spend millions of dollars on marketing?

TUESDAY

Name: PRE-ROUND WARMUP: QUADRICEP STRETCH

Goal: Prevent injury and promote range of motion by warming up before round.

Explanation:

Stand and kick right leg back bending at the knee and grasp ankle with right hand. Gently pull foot back while pushing hip forward to feel stretch in muscle between knee and hip joints in front of leg. Hold 10-15 seconds. Repeat with left leg. Club may be used as prop for balance.

Nutrition Tip:
The outer leaves of vegetables are the most nutritious. Discard as few as possible. Nutrients are often concentrated in or just below the skin. If possible, eat unpeeled fruits and vegetables, or don't peel them too deeply.

Experience Good Thoughts:
"Always look at what you have left. Never look at what you have lost."
—Robert Schuller, Author

Think Golf:
When your ball lands in a hole or is buried in tall grass, use your pitching wedge. Be sure the ball is back in your stance and keep your hands ahead of the ball. Try to hit the ball first on the downswing into your shot. This should create a high shot because of the ball flying off the clubface. Don't forget to follow through. That's what will make it a successful shot.

Make Me Smile:
Do golfers live for abuse? Of course they do. Why else would they play a game that spelled backwards is FLOG??

WEDNESDAY

Name: YOGA/STRETCH: FIGURE 4 STRETCH

Goal: Improve hamstring flexibility.

Explanation:

Sit on the floor with left leg extended and right leg bent so that right foot touches left thigh. Reach left hand forward and grasp left foot, ankle or shin as comfort permits. Hold stretched position for 20-30 seconds. Do not bounce. Switch legs and repeat on right leg.

Nutrition Tip:

Don't wash rice before cooking; cook it in just enough water so that you don't need to drain it off when it is done. This method preserves its healthy benefits. And use long grain white rice or brown rice rather than instant rice to get the most nutrition.

Experience Good Thoughts:

"Optimism is the one quality more associated with success and happiness than any other."

—Brian Tracy

Think Golf:

Many experienced golfers have found that your best game is played both between your ears and in the last 150 yards. If you can master your short game, you can have consistently good scores.

Make Me Smile:

A blonde golfer goes into the pro shop and keeps looking around with frustration. Finally the pro asks her what she wants and she tells him, "I can't seem to find any green golf balls." The pro knows there aren't any in the store but calls manufacturers to determine that are no green golf balls sold. Curiosity gets the best of him and he asks her why she only wants green golf balls. She replied, "Well obviously, because they would be so much easier to find in the sand traps!"

THURSDAY

Name: DYNAMIC STRETCH: OPPOSITE ELBOW/KNEE LIFT

Goal: Increase blood flow and circulation to volatile low back and hip area to help prevent injury.

Explanation:

Stand with feet slightly wider than hip distance apart and arms out to sides with elbows bent upward. Shift weight to right foot. Simultaneously rotate right elbow across body as left knee lifts. Elbow and knee may or may not touch. Do not change posture and take elbow "down" to knee. Shift and repeat other side exhaling on rotation and lift. Repeat 10x alternating.

Nutrition Tip:

Store cereal and grain products in opaque containers to avoid exposure to light, which destroys Riboflavin and Vitamin E.

Experience Good Thoughts:

"It is easy to love the people far away. It is not always easy to love those close to us. It is easier to give a cup of rice to relieve hunger than to relieve the loneliness and pain of someone unloved in our own home. Bring love into your home for this is where our love for each other must start."

—Mother Teresa

Think Golf:

The old cliché, Drive for show and putt for dough, supports the critics who say the professional game amounts to little more than a putting contest.

Make Me Smile:

Your best round of golf will be followed almost immediately by your worst round ever. The probability of the latter increases with the number of people you tell about the former.

FRIDAY

Name: STRENGTH: DUMBBELL LATERAL RAISE
Goal: Endurance and strength of shoulders during swing action.

Explanation:

Stand tall with feet hip distance apart. Hold a 3-5-8lb dumbbell in each hand with elbows at right angles, arms against sides. Raise arms up until parallel to floor. Lower dumbbells to starting position. Repeat 10-15 repetitions for heavier weights; repeat 30-50x for lighter weights.

Nutrition Tip:
Ounce for ounce, avocados have the highest fiber content of any fruit. Try using an avocado when mashing potatoes instead of butter. It tastes great and will add a gram or more of fiber to each serving. Add them to salads for a different flavor.

Experience Good Thoughts:
"Build up your weaknesses until they become your strong points."
—Knute Rockne

Think Golf:
"I know of nothing that can more powerfully affect your ability to realize dreams, enhance health, prevent illness, improve performance — lower golf scores — than controlling your beliefs. When you believe something without doubt, you become free to perform without doubt, you become free to perform without fear or caution. When you are in that state of "full belief," you are uninhibited by notions of what could go wrong. You are instead purely focused upon what is right and what you intend to make happen. You are in flow."
—Chris Dorris, Performance Psychologist

Make Me Smile:
Definition of "local rules" — A set of regulations that are ignored only by players on one specific course rather than by all golfers.

SATURDAY/SUNDAY

GOLFING DAYS ARE GOOD FOR YOUR HEALTH

REFLECTING ON THE PAST WEEK:

What was your basic attitude? Were you a positive thinker or did you need an "attitude adjustment?" Are you having success with eating healthier and doing your exercise program? How do you feel physically? If you went golfing, write down any comments that might be helpful later in improving your game. Remember, that laughter is the best medicine in the face of adversity. Are you seeing the lighter side of life?

The exercise that helped me the most this week was on page:

_____

My nutritional habits this week were:

_____

What made me smile this week?

_____

_____

Looking back at my golf week:
    My Score: _____ What did I do right? _____

_____

_____

    What could I do to improve?

_____

_____

Goals for next week: _____

_____

_____

MONDAY

Name: PILATES: OBLIQUES ROLL BACK

Goal: Aid in muscle memory of stabilizing hips and hip flexors while spine rotates in back swing.

Explanation:

Sit tall with legs bent hip distance apart and feet flat on floor. Arms are extended straight over knees parallel with floor. Inhale to prepare. Exhale rolling torso behind tailbone as far as possible while keeping abdominals flat. Keep upper spine flexed forward with lower spine (c-curve) and rotate torso, sweeping same arm down across floor and back. Inhale maintaining abdominal connection as spine rotates back to center and sit tall in starting position. Complete 3 repetitions each side.

Nutrition Tip:

Eat a low-fat diet consisting of citrus fruits and juices, vegetables, lean meats such as chicken and fish, and low fat dairy products. In addition, eat a lot of fiber. Eating more whole grains, raw fruits and vegetables, and dried beans may lower your levels of cholesterol by 6 to 19 percent. If you do cook your vegetables, don't overcook them. You'll lose most of the nutrients. Cook them al dente to retain the most benefit.

Experience Good Thoughts:

"Everyone who got where he is had to begin where he was."

—Robert Louis Stevenson, Poet

Think Golf:

"As you read the greens, remember: First sight is best sight."

—Charlie Epps, Golf Coach

Make Me Smile:

Brand new golf balls are water magnets. This has not technically been proven, but golfers can attest to the fact that the more a golf ball costs, the greater it is attracted to water.

TUESDAY

Name: **BIG BALL: PLANK PIKES**

Goal: Promote constant shoulder stability for turn while engaging power through midsection to increase club head speed.

Explanation:

Walk out over top ball to a balanced plank pushup position. The farther you walk out toward your toes, the more challenging the move. Once balance has been achieved, pike hips directly in air hinging from the hips. Keep legs as straight as possible. Return to plank and repeat 10x. Maintain posture of upperbody. Walk back to kneeling over ball after the 10 reps.

Nutrition Tip:

Omega-3 fatty acids, found in oily fish such as mackerel, salmon, tuna and herring, help prevent blood clots from forming, reducing the risk of heart disease. You get more benefit from eating the fish itself than from taking fish oil supplements.

Experience Good Thoughts:

"In matters of style, swim with the current; in matters of principle, stand like a rock."
—Thomas Jefferson, 3rd President

Think Golf:

Casual water is a temporary accumulation of water, which is visible before the player takes his stance and is not in the water hazard. Casual water can occur on the green after a hard rain or course irrigation. If there is standing water in your path or water comes up around your shoes when you are on the green, you may drop an equal distance from the hole on dry land with no penalty.

Make Me Smile:

Why is it that electric golf carts always run out of juice when you are the farthest away from the clubhouse?

WEDNESDAY

Name: HEAVY BALL: I LEGGED ROLLUP
Goal: Promote flexibility of spine while engaging abdominals; coordination; hamstring flexibility.

Explanation:

Lie down on back holding ball on chest with legs straight together and toes pointed. Inhale to prepare. As you exhale, roll up reaching ball up toward sky as one leg lifts toward sky as well. Goal is to be able to touch ball to toe of lifted leg. Inhale return to floor and exhale repeat with other side. 20 repetitions total. Focus on rounding spine on the way up and on the way down with control.

Nutrition Tip:
The American Heart Association states that heart disease is the number one killer of American women between the ages of 56 and 76. Although women with diabetes, hypertension, severe obesity, and smoking have greater chances of developing heart disease, any female can fall victim to this disease. Women have one risk factor that men don't, and that is loss of estrogen. Inadequate levels of estrogen in menopausal or pre-menopausal women can lead to heart disease.

Experience Good Thoughts:
"Nothing happens unless first a dream."

—Carl Sandburg, Poet

Think Golf:
Play a courteous game. Leave the green immediately after you complete a hole and wait until you get to the next tee before you record your score.

Make Me Smile:
Do you play regularly at the same course? If so, then you've noticed that — The ball always lands where the pin was yesterday!

THURSDAY

Name: YOGA/STRETCH: TREE POSE

Goal: Challenge balance and focus.

Explanation:

Stand with your feet together. Arms are overhead with palms together. Shift your weight to the left foot and bend your right knee. Place the right heel on the left thigh as you turn the right hip out. Keep your hips facing forward. Raise your arms overhead. Stay in the pose 30 seconds breathing deeply. Repeat on the other side.

Nutrition Tip:
Here are some low-fat treats: fig bars, vanilla wafers, ginger snaps, angel food cake, jelly beans, gum drops, hard candy, puddings made with low-fat (1 percent) skim milk, nonfat frozen yogurt with a fruit topping, or fruit popsicles. Try pretzels or popcorn without butter or oil for an unsweetened treat.

Experience Good Thoughts:
"You cannot teach a man anything; you can only help him find it within himself."
—Galileo, Astronomer & Mathematician

Think Golf:
Never move a loose obstacle from the bunker – not a leaf, not a rock, not a twig, nothing! If you do, it's a rules violation and your partners will probably notice.

Make Me Smile:
The club secretary was apologetic. "I'm sorry but we have no tee times available on the course today." "Now just a minute," the member said. "What if I told you that President Bush and one of his friends wanted to play? Can you find a tee time for them?" "Yes, of course I would," she answered. "Well I happen to know that he's at Camp David at the moment, so we'll take his tee time."

FRIDAY

Name: PILATES: THE MERMAID

Goal: Challenge balance; strengthen shoulders and torso for stabilization during swing.

Explanation:

Begin sitting on your left hip with your legs folded to the right side. Place your left hand on the floor adjacent to your left hip and relax your right arm at your side. Exhale and lengthen up out of your hips straightening your legs and extending your spine. Repeat 5 times each side. Do not allow your base shoulder to sink into your ears.

Nutrition Tip:
Walking is one of the best overall exercises and helps the entire system function better. The metabolism is increased while walking, which burns up fat and promotes weight loss. Blood pressure, blood cholesterol, and sugar levels also tend to fall.

Experience Good Thoughts:
"The secret of success is making your VOCATION your VACATION."

—Mark Twain

Think Golf:
Important to remember: the left elbow and wrist are hinges; they bend. There should be a straight line from the left shoulder to the clubhead. If the left elbow or wrist bend, the clubhead moves away from the ball and target line, which will result in the ball not going where you intended it to go.

Make Me Smile:
One of the laws of golf states that gale force winds that drive your ball back into your face will disappear when it's your opponent's turn.

SATURDAY/SUNDAY

GOLFING DAYS ARE GOOD FOR YOUR HEALTH

REFLECTING ON THE PAST WEEK:

What was your basic attitude? Were you a positive thinker or did you need an "attitude adjustment?" Are you having success with eating healthier and doing your exercise program? How do you feel physically? If you went golfing, write down any comments that might be helpful later in improving your game. Remember, that laughter is the best medicine in the face of adversity. Are you seeing the lighter side of life?

The exercise that helped me the most this week was on page:

_____

My nutritional habits this week were:

_____

What made me smile this week?

_____

_____

Looking back at my golf week:
    My Score: _____ What did I do right? _____

_____

_____

    What could I do to improve?

_____

_____

Goals for next week: _____

_____

_____

MONDAY

Name: TOWEL STRETCH: SIDE BEND

Goal: Increase flexibility of spine laterally; open up ribcage promoting more range of motion throughout turn.

Explanation:

Stand with feet slightly wider than hips. Hold onto ends of hand towel overhead with straight arms. Inhale leaning upper body to the right pushing hips toward the left feeling stretch around left ribcage. Emphasize the stretch by pulling the towel downward with right arm. Exhale return to standing. Repeat alternating sides 10x with control.

Nutrition Tip:
Choose snacks high in antioxidants such as dried fruits, especially apricots and peaches. If you mix dried fruits with nuts and seeds, you'll get even more health benefits. Trail mix combinations are healthful and tasty snacks.

Experience Good Thoughts:
"You can't shake hands with a clenched fist."

—Indira Gandhi

Think Golf:
A good way to practice a full swing at home is to wrap a towel around your chest and hold it under your arms. This will keep your arms close to your body so they react to the body movement instead of trying to hit the ball. Once your body gets the feel for the movement, it will automatically start duplicating it on every swing.

Make Me Smile:
"Shut up, Alice." screamed the golfer at his wife. "Shut up or you'll drive me out of my mind." "That wouldn't be a drive," she said, "it would be a short putt."

TUESDAY

Name: BIG BALL: MERRY GO ROUND
Goal: Increase flexibility and spinal rotation while maintaining balance through backswing and follow-through.

Explanation:

Stand with your feet firmly planted a little wider than hip distance apart extending ball in front of you shoulder height. Rotate 180 degrees facing behind you keeping ball straight out in front of you and maintain weight centered between both feet. Focus on lifting through the spine and be sure to lift your trailing heel for easier rotation. Repeat 5 times each direction.

Nutrition Tip:
Get out of the rut of eating the same old vegetables. Have you ever tried a parsnip? They look like large, light colored carrots and have a sweet but spicy taste. Choose smaller ones that are crisp, plump, and don't have bruises. Serve them boiled or roasted with butter and nutmeg or you can use them in stews, soups, or boiled dinners. Parsnips are in season all winter so buy them and freeze a few while in their prime. Blanche, cool and dry before freezing.

Experience Good Thoughts:
"Don't spend your precious time asking 'Why isn't the world a better place?' It will only be time wasted. The question to ask is 'How can I make it better?' To that there is an answer."

—Leo F. Buscaglia

Think Golf:
Driving accuracy is crucial. Hit your best tee shot possible. It is extremely difficult to advance the ball with power toward the target from the rough.

Make Me Smile:
A golfer has one advantage over a fisherman. He doesn't have to produce anything to prove his story.

WEDNESDAY

Name: DYNAMIC STRETCH: ARM CIRCLES FORWARD/BACK

Goal: Increase blood flow and circulation around shoulder joint to enable more range of motion throughout turn without hindrance.

Explanation:

Stand tall with feet hip distance apart. Circle right arm forward and up above your head trying to get elbow as close to ear as possible and reach toward back wall. Continue alternating between right and left arms. Reverse circles 10x each.

Nutrition Tip:
Garlic helps to reduce high blood pressure, cholesterol, and dangerous blood clotting. It fights potent carcinogens and helps to strengthen the immune system.

Experience Good Thoughts:
"It is literally true that you can succeed best and quickest by helping others to succeed."

—Napoleon Hill

Think Golf:
Visualize yourself with a good swing and hitting your target area. Attitude has as much to do with improving your swing as your physical ability does. So try not to get upset with yourself. When you lose control of your emotions, you lose control of your swing.

Make Me Smile:
When paying your greens fee, do the math. Golfers who regularly shoot par are paying nearly a quarter for every shot they take. A player with a high handicap is paying only eight or nine cents a stroke. Moral of story — a mediocre player gets more for his money which makes his favorite sport a thrifty sport!

THURSDAY

Name: CARDIO: BURPIES (SQUAT THRUSTS)

Goal: Increase range of motion throughout body with focus on power around shoulders and knees.

Explanation:

Stand tall. 1) Squat down in ball with hands on floor. 2) Jump feet back to pushup plank position 3) Hop legs back into squat ball position. 4) Jump back up to standing position. Focus on breathing and rhythm. Repeat 10x.

Nutrition Tip:
Eggplants have antioxidant properties and boost immunity by stimulating activity of protective enzymes. They are part of the nightshade family — but try to avoid eating them if you have problems with arthritis.

Experience Good Thoughts:
"It's not what happens to you; it's what you do about it that makes the difference.'
—W. Mitchell, Businessman & Speaker

Think Golf:
Never place your bag on the green or on the fringe. The weight of the bag along with the legs of the stand can damage the green. Lay it down away from the putting surface and on the side of the green that is toward the next tee. This will also speed up play.

Make Me Smile:
Two ants sat on the grass watching a golfer create huge divots on every stroke. One ant said to the other, "Let's get on top of the ball before he kills us!"

FRIDAY

Name: YOGA/STRETCH: SEATED TWIST
Goal: Loosen and promote range of motion in low back.

Explanation:

Sit on floor with your legs outstretched and knees slightly bent. Lift your left calf and cross it over your right thigh, placing the left foot flat on the floor next to the right leg. Sit up tall and rotate your shoulders and head as far left as is comfortable, keeping your shoulders relaxed. Hold for 10-30 seconds each side. You may reach opposite arm across body and press slightly on outside of knee for increased stretch.

Nutrition Tip:
Tomatoes contain carotenoids such as lycopene. Studies have shown their protective effects on many forms of cancer, heart and circulatory diseases. Tomatoes can be used in so many ways, raw and cooked. They add flavor and healthy benefits to dishes from salads to soups to sauces.

Experience Good Thoughts:
"Only those who will risk going too far can possibly find out how far one can go."
—T.S. Eliot, Poet

Think Golf:
An important rule of etiquette is to always shake hands with your partners and thank them after playing a round. It promotes good sportsmanship and keeps the game friendly. After all, we play golf to have a good time, right?

Make Me Smile:
"What's your golf score?" the pro asked the prospective member. "Not so good," said the golfer. "It's 69." "Hey, that's not a bad score. Actually, it's a pretty good score." "Glad you think so. I'm hoping to do even better on the next hole."

SATURDAY/SUNDAY

GOLFING DAYS ARE GOOD FOR YOUR HEALTH

REFLECTING ON THE PAST WEEK:

What was your basic attitude? Were you a positive thinker or did you need an "attitude adjustment?" Are you having success with eating healthier and doing your exercise program? How do you feel physically? If you went golfing, write down any comments that might be helpful later in improving your game. Remember, that laughter is the best medicine in the face of adversity. Are you seeing the lighter side of life?

The exercise that helped me the most this week was on page:

My nutritional habits this week were:

What made me smile this week?

Looking back at my golf week:
     My Score: _____ What did I do right? _____

     What could I do to improve?

Goals for next week: _____

MONDAY

Name: BIG BALL: ELBOW PLANK & PUSHUP

Goal: Strengthen shoulder girdle to keep constant stabilization during swing; promote balance and core stability.

Explanation:

Lie face down on ball with hands in fists and elbows tucked under chest. With control and maintaining straight spine, lift upper body off ball by pushing forearms into ball and engaging entire shoulder girdle and abdominals. Exhale on the lift. Lift and lower 10x.

Nutrition Tip:
Pumpkin seeds are high in zinc. This festive vegetable is also high in fiber, beta-carotene, and potassium; acts as a diuretic and laxative; and is antagonistic to intestinal worms. Bet you didn't know just how beneficial they were! Grab a bag next time you're at a grocery store.

Experience Good Thoughts:
"When we do the best that we can, we never know what miracle is wrought in our life, or in the life of another."

—Helen Keller

Think Golf:
According to *Golf for Women* magazine, it is proper to tip a locker-room attendant $1.00 for a towel and $2.00 if she cleans your shoes.

Make Me Smile:
Doesn't it seem like a golfer hitting into your group is always bigger than anyone in your group? And doesn't it always happen that a group you accidentally hit into will have the scariest players ever — like a professional boxer, a convicted murderer or a weightlifting champion?

TUESDAY

Name: STRENGTH: WIDE SQUAT

Goal: Promote lower body stability and strength for base of support throughout swing; emphasize inner thighs so knees don't collapse.

Explanation:

Stand with feet wider than hips and toes aiming diagonally outward. Inhale and sit back with your hips as you bend your knees into a squat. Make sure knees stay over heels not outside toes. Exhale return back to standing keeping abdominals tight and gluteals squeezed. Repeat 10-20x.

Nutrition Tip:

Peppers inhibit production of cancer-causing nitrosamines during digestion; they are high in Vitamin C, bioflavonoids, and Vitamin A. They also contain folic acid, potassium, and niacin.

Experience Good Thoughts:

There are no great people in this world— only great challenges, which ordinary people rise to meet.

Think Golf:

The ancient Dutch word for club was "kolf". The Dutch played a game similar to today's golf and taught it to their trading friends in Scotland. The Scottish pronunciation "golf" seemed to stick internationally. Since that time, Scotland has become known as the game's home.

Make Me Smile:

Here's a great reason to go golfing — that is if you need a reason — Golf teaches patience, and everyone could use a lesson in patience. How could your spouse disagree with that?

WEDNESDAY

Name: PILATES: BREAST STROKE PREPS
Goal: Activate shoulder stabilizers, which promotes better posture throughout swing.

Explanation:

Lie face down on floor with arms by sides and palms touching outer thighs. Inhale to prepare. As you exhale slide hands down legs and shoulder blades down back to bring upper body to slight extension. Hold throughout exhale. Legs should squeeze together, toes pointed and buttocks tight with belly button supporting low back. Inhale returning back to rest position on floor. Important: keep tops of feet on floor.

Nutrition Tip:
Have a sweet tooth? Grab a piece of dark chocolate. Recent research suggests it may help relax blood vessels and improve blood flow. It's rich in flavonoids, a type of antioxidant believed to fight aging and disease. Watch your portion, though, because chocolate is high in fat and calories.

Experience Good Thoughts:
"What we see depends mainly on what we look for."
—John Lubbock, British Statesman

Think Golf:
Has anyone ever told you "you're shanking?" That means your ball goes far to the right. It can happen if you stand too close to the ball or if you reach forward through impact. Hitting the ball with the center of the clubface will help your ball to fly straight.

Make Me Smile:
Here's a silly joke. Why should golf be in the Special Olympics rather than the Olympics? Because everyone who plays has a handicap.

THURSDAY

Name: PRE-ROUND WARMUP: OPPOSITE KNEE/ELBOW

Goal: Increase blood flow to hips and back to prepare for constant movement during entire round and help to prevent trauma to areas.

Explanation:

Stand tall feet wider than hip distance apart. Hold club parallel to ground in front of body with hands on grip and hozzle. Inhale to prepare. As you exhale, lift right knee up and rotate upper body to the left trying to connect right knee and left elbow. Return foot to place and repeat on left leg. Controlled movement 20x.

Nutrition Tip:

Cabbage can help trigger the production of enzymes that protect the cell's DNA from being damaged by carcinogens. It increases healthy metabolism of estrogen too.

Experience Good Thoughts:

"One can have no smaller or greater mastery than the mastery of oneself."

—Leonardo da Vinci

Think Golf:

If you find your ball buried in the sand, close your clubface and stance, swing firmly downward and aim one inch behind the ball.

Make Me Smile:

A golfer out to enjoy a round alone is addressing the ball when a man runs up to him yelling, "Wait. Before you tee off, I have something really amazing to show you." Although he was annoyed, he asked the man what it was. "It's a special golf ball," says the man who identifies himself as a salesman, "you can never lose it." "I don't believe that," says the golfer. "What if you hit it into the water?" "It floats," answers the salesman, "and you can see it right away." "What if you hit it into the woods?" the golfer asked. "Then it emits a beeping sound and you can hear where it landed. And it glows in the dark so you can play at night too." "I'm telling you, sir, you just can't lose this ball." The golfer, really interested in this amazing ball, finally asks the salesman, "Where did you get it?" To which the salesman replied, "I found it!"

FRIDAY

Name: HEAVY BALL: I LEGGED WITH TWIST
Goal: Promote flexibility of spine while engaging abdominals and obliques much needed for power in turn; coordination.

Explanation:

Lie down on back holding ball on chest with legs straight together and toes pointed. Inhale to prepare. Exhale as you roll up halfway turning upper body toward the left as left leg bends and lifts toward chest. Goal is to touch right elbow to left knee. Inhale returning body to flat and exhale repeat on other side. 20 repetitions total. Focus on rounding spine on the way up and on the way down with control.

Nutrition Tip:
Make your own ice cream sandwiches. Spread fat-free ice cream on chocolate or vanilla wafer cookies and cover with plastic wrap. Place in freezer until ready to eat.

Experience Good Thoughts:
The Bible offers practical advice that has proven valuable over the centuries. "Do not use harmful words, but only helpful words, the kind that build up and provide what is needed, so that what you say will do good to those who hear you."
— Paul's letter to the Ephesians 4:29

Think Golf:
If you have a sidehill lie – be sure the ball is higher than your feet, use one club longer, shorten your backswing and stay low to the ball, keep your weight on your heels, widen your stance, center your ball in your stance, and allow for fade.

Make Me Smile:
"I'm sorry to have to say this," said the doctor to his patient, "but there's nothing we can do, and you have very little time left." "Oh, no!" cried the patient. "What do you mean, little time? How long do I have? Can I play a few more rounds of golf?" "10", said the doctor. "10 what -- Months? Weeks? Years?" asked the golfer. "10 hours," said the doctor sadly. "Whew," said the golfer relieved. "Then I can play at least 36 more holes."

SATURDAY/SUNDAY

GOLFING DAYS ARE GOOD FOR YOUR HEALTH

REFLECTING ON THE PAST WEEK:

What was your basic attitude? Were you a positive thinker or did you need an "attitude adjustment?" Are you having success with eating healthier and doing your exercise program? How do you feel physically? If you went golfing, write down any comments that might be helpful later in improving your game. Remember, that laughter is the best medicine in the face of adversity. Are you seeing the lighter side of life?

The exercise that helped me the most this week was on page:

_____

My nutritional habits this week were:

_____

What made me smile this week?

_____

_____

Looking back at my golf week:
    My Score: _____ What did I do right? _____

_____

_____

    What could I do to improve?

_____

_____

Goals for next week: _____

_____

_____

MONDAY

Name: BIG BALL: HAND TO TOE TOUCH

Goal: Enhance flexibility of hamstrings and low back with focus on posture and trunk stability.

Explanation:

Stand tall with feet together and arms overhead with ball. Lengthen ball forward as right leg lifts to touch toe to ball. Exhale during reach forward and try not to hunch over. Maintain posture and keep abdominals tight. Return with ball overhead and repeat with left leg.
Switch legs 10x.

Nutrition Tip:

Protein boosts the metabolism! Proteins are made up of 23 amino acids linked together in complicated configurations. For movement to take place, protein molecules must be broken down and then reassembled to build cells. That is a lot of work! A 20% to 25% metabolic boost is the result of protein ingestion. Eat protein!

Experience Good Thoughts:

Ability is what you're capable of doing. Motivation determines what you do. Attitude determines how well you do it.

Think Golf:

"Identify those beliefs that keep you from excelling well beyond your typical round: "I've never broken 80, so it probably won't happen today," "I've never beaten this guy before," "I haven't practiced much lately, so I probably won't play that well." Catch yourself speaking and thinking this nonsense, and replace it with something much more powerful, something you WANT to have happen. Fool yourself into believing the best-case scenarios."

—Chris Dorris, Performance Psychologist

Make Me Smile:

The person you would most hate to lose to will always be the one who beats you.

TUESDAY

Name: **YOGA/STRETCH: BOUND ANGLE**
Goal: Open and release tension in low back, hip, and groin area to help increase ability for club head speed and weight shifting on downswing.

Explanation:

Sit tall with bottoms of feet together. Press elbows down lightly on inner thighs to promote stretch. Pull belly button to spine and lean chest forward toward feet for greater stretch. Do not bounce without control. Stretch and focus on breathing for 30 seconds.

Nutrition Tip:
Eating one cup of cooked spinach will give us 840 mg of potassium, one of the best sources for this mineral.

Experience Good Thoughts:
Contentment is not the fulfillment of what you want but the realization of how much you know you already have. Use today to think about the riches you already have and find the contentment that is inside your spirit.

Think Golf:
Your USGA Handicap Index compares your scoring ability to that of an expert amateur on a course of standard difficulty. It indicates your skill and changes as your game improves. It disregards high scores and promotes continuity by adding scores from one season or year to the next. To have an accurate handicap, each player is expected to score the best possible on each hole in every round played. That's what makes the USGA Handicap Index System work!

Make Me Smile:
People who say a shank is close to a perfect shot have never had four in a row!

WEDNESDAY

Name: PILATES: THE SEAL

Goal: Relax shoulder area; repetitive motion that relaxes and massages spine in flexed position.

Explanation:

Sit and put the bottoms of both feet together. Place hands under and on outside of feet while leaning back and balancing. Flex your spine, bringing your chin toward your chest. Using your abdominals to assist in balancing behind your sit bones, inhale and roll backwards. Exhale and return to the starting position. Repeat 10 times.

Nutrition Tip:

Some food combinations make up a complete protein. Here are a few: Baked potato with yogurt, potato and egg salad, rice pudding, cereal with milk, corn and lima beans, macaroni and cheese, pasta and tomato sauce.

Experience Good Thoughts:

"Individual commitment to a group effort is what makes a team work, a company work, a society work, a civilization work."

—Vince Lombardi

Think Golf:

According to the USGA, men and women playing from the same set of tees will have different USGA Course Ratings. Women receive additional strokes since the women's Course Rating is usually higher.

Make Me Smile:

The oldest man ever to shoot his age in a round of golf was 103 year-old Arthur Thompson. On his birthday in 1973, Thompson shot a 103 over the 6,215 yard Uplands course in Ontario, Canada. Now that's an interesting piece of trivia. Care to top that record?

THURSDAY

Name: DYNAMIC STRETCH: SIDE BENDS

Goal: Lengthen muscles on both sides of spine as well as obliques to aid in maximum coil and recoil.

Explanation:

Stand tall with feet a little wider than hip distance apart. Clasp arms over head reaching tall. Slowly bend to the right without shifting weight in hips or feet first. Then slowly shift weight in hips and feet to the left slightly for maximum stretch. Continue pulling arms away from body. Repeat each side 5x.

Nutrition Tip:

Drink Green Tea! Green tea contains significant amounts of zinc, manganese, potassium, niacin, folic acid and vitamin C. It is a powerful antioxidant helping rid the body of environmental toxins, lowering cholesterol, decreasing chance of heart disease, and aiding in weight management. Studies show that the only side effect from drinking the recommended 4-5 cups daily may be insomnia from the caffeine.

Experience Good Thoughts:

"Is there anyone so wise as to learn by the experience of others?"

—Voltaire

Think Golf:

Etiquette to remember: ALWAYS replace your divots on the fairways and some-times even the rough. Take advantage of the sand/seed mixture on some carts if divot is not available.

Make Me Smile:

The frustrated golfer sadly said to his friend, "I've played so awful today. I think I'm going to drown myself in that lake." Noticing how he had been playing all day, his friend replied, "I don't think you could keep your head down that long."

FRIDAY

Name: STRENGTH: SQUATS ON TOES
Goal: Promote balance and stability in stabilizing muscles of ankles, knees,and hips; increase endurance strength of legs.

Explanation:

Stand tall with feet a little wider than hip distance apart. Clasp arms over head reaching tall. Slowly bend to the right without shifting weight in hips or feet first. Then slowly shift weight in hips and feet to the left slightly for maximum stretch. Continue pulling arms away from body. Repeat each side 5x.

Nutrition Tip:
Sift through your pantry and remove as many high-calorie, high-fat foods as possible. If you have snacks for your children, move them out of your view so that the temptation is less. You will find that if those foods and snacks are not around the kitchen, you won't go out to get them. You'll just do without. In doing that, you'll cut down your calorie intake considerably.

Experience Good Thoughts:
"Forget injuries, never forget kindnesses."

—Confucius

Think Golf:
The Jack Nicklaus co-designed, New St. Andrews course in Tochigi, Japan boasts futuristic technology. Golfers are transported by monorail around the course and their golf bags are carried by an electronic system.

Make Me Smile:
Q: What is the hardest thing about playing golf with your boss?
A: Having to say, "Great shot!" 100 times.

SATURDAY/SUNDAY

GOLFING DAYS ARE GOOD FOR YOUR HEALTH

REFLECTING ON THE PAST WEEK:

What was your basic attitude? Were you a positive thinker or did you need an "attitude adjustment?" Are you having success with eating healthier and doing your exercise program? How do you feel physically? If you went golfing, write down any comments that might be helpful later in improving your game. Remember, that laughter is the best medicine in the face of adversity. Are you seeing the lighter side of life?

The exercise that helped me the most this week was on page:

_____

My nutritional habits this week were:

_____

What made me smile this week?

_____

_____

Looking back at my golf week:
  My Score: _____ What did I do right? _____

_____

_____

  What could I do to improve?

_____

_____

Goals for next week: _____

_____

_____

MONDAY

Name: CARDIO: JUMPING JACKS

Goal: Increase cardiovascular endurance as well as coordination and rhythm.

Explanation:

Stand tall with feet together and hands at sides. Jump feet out wide as arms swing overhead. Jump feet back in to starting position as hands come back down to sides of legs.

Nutrition Tip:

Bananas are a good source of potassium no matter how ripe they are. Potassium helps to avoid high blood pressure and if you have it, it will assist in regulating it. Very ripe bananas are high in sugars that are readily assimilated and can improve stamina. Less ripe bananas counter constipation. Bananas are also an excellent natural choice to treat anemia.

Experience Good Thoughts:

"Health and cheerfulness mutually beget one another."

—Joseph Addison

Think Golf:

Don't just "hit and hope" when you go to the driving range. Most golfers practice inefficiently. Jack Nicklaus suggests that you "Never practice without a firm plan. And for every practice session, always focus on one particular goal. Do not address every problem every time."

Make Me Smile:

Is it true that swimming will help you to stay fit and trim? I don't think so. If swimming is so great, then explain whales to me!

TUESDAY

Name: YOGA/STRETCH: BOAT
Goal: Strengthen core muscles supporting healthy back and good posture and reinforce straight spine at address.

Explanation:

Sit back behind sit bones (tailbone area). Pull belly button into spine for support and lift legs off floor. Body and legs should be in "V" position. Arms and legs are straight with arms reaching toward toes. Hold for 10 seconds. Repeat 3x. Maintain good posture keeping chin lifted and eyes forward.

Nutrition Tip:
Everyone knows that oranges are loaded with Vitamin C but do you know all the health benefits they provide? Oranges help the body's defenses to resist infection; they have anti-cancer properties, especially in the stomach; the pectin in them helps lower cholesterol; they can improve the strength of small blood vessels; and they are excellent for treating over-acid body conditions or a sluggish intestinal tract.

Experience Good Thoughts:
Ways to reduce stress...........laugh and smile, look on the bright side, don't take yourself too seriously, and count all your blessings.

Think Golf:
Butch Harmon, golf coach, suggests "the only way to effectively improve your golf swing is to understand precisely what it is you are doing wrong in a swing." Of course that means you need to be able to see your swing. The best way to observe yourself is to see a video of what you are doing. It's most helpful if you have a pro analyze it as you watch.

Make Me Smile:
What do you call a compulsive golfer? Answer: A crackputt.

WEDNESDAY

Name: BIG BALL: PLANK AND PUSHUPS

Goal: Strengthen entire shoulder girdle to help prevent collapsing in swing, promoting width; increase strength in small muscles for club control.

Explanation:

Place hands directly on top of ball shoulder width apart with fingertips aiming downward and thumbs forward. As you gain balance and control, start to put more weight on ball as you walk your feet away from you. Once a plank is achieved, as a challenge, lower your entire body down to the ball in push up fashion, and push back up to straight arms.

Nutrition Tip:
If you're not a fish lover, get essential fatty acids through flaxseed. Essential fatty acids play a vital role in keeping your skin, hair, heart and brain healthy. Put ground flaxseed in shakes, yogurt, over cereal, or when baking whole grain breads. They have a pleasant nutty flavor so sprinkle them over a stir-fry or add them to soups, stews, or other dinner casseroles. You CAN get your fatty acids even if you don't eat fish.

Experience Good Thoughts:
Jesus said, "Happy are those who are merciful to others; God will be merciful to them."
—Matthew 5:7, Sermon on the Mount

Think Golf:
"You miss 100% of the shots you don't take." —Wayne Gretsky

Make Me Smile:
A grandfather was teaching his granddaughter to play golf and reminiscing about when he played as a youngster. On a very difficult dog-legged par 4, the grandfather said, "When I was your age, I'd aim right over those trees and hit the green every time." His granddaughter thought about it and thought if he could do it so could she. She hit a perfect drive, but it landed right in the middle of the woods covered with 50 ft trees. She looked sadly at her grandfather who said, "Of course when I was your age, those trees were only 6 feet tall!"

THURSDAY

Name: **HEAVY BALL: WOODCHOP**

Goal: Warm up entire body; increase circulation and flexibility for large muscles involved in golf swing.

Explanation:

Stand with feet slightly wider than hips distance apart holding ball straight over head. Swing ball in large arc from top to bottom through legs and back up again. Bending must start from hips and knees then allow spine to flex forward while being supported with abdominals. Repeat 20x exhaling down and inhaling up.

Nutrition Tip:
The basis for interest in Vitamins E and C are for their antioxidant effect. Although oxygen is essential for life, normal cell processes produce certain highly reactive oxygen molecules that can damage cell structures. This damage may play a role in aging as well as in alzheimer's and cancer. Antioxidants like E and C protect cells from the damaging effects of these highly reactive oxygen-containing molecules.

Experience Good Thoughts:
Words of advice: When you are in it up to your ears, keep your mouth shut!

Think Golf:
"Golf tournaments are won or lost with your wedges and your putter," advises Sam Snead. When practicing, Tiger Woods claims that you should putt, chip, pitch, then lob in that order to achieve a higher rate of success. Practice your short game!

Make Me Smile:
"All you ever do is think about your old golf game. I bet you don't even remember the day we were married," said the neglected newlywed. "Sure I do, honey, it was the day I sank that thirty-foot putt."

FRIDAY

Name: PILATES: THE SAW

Goal: Increase flexibility of torso and rotational muscles; improve posture and alignment.

Explanation:

Sit tall with legs extended slightly wider than hip width apart. Extend you arms open and out to sides. Keeping the spine lifted, exhale and drop the right arm down over the left leg as if to saw off the left pinky toe with the right pinky finger. Using your abdominals, roll up and return to starting position. Repeat 4-5 times on each side.

Nutrition Tip:
Eat breakfast! People who don't perform well mentally or physically are usually ones who skip breakfast. This is related to a rise in blood sugar levels that are low after an all night fast, but return to normal after a nutritious breakfast. Eating breakfast everyday increases metabolic or calorie-burning rate and skipping breakfast has the opposite effect on metabolism, which makes weight loss even more difficult.

Experience Good Thoughts:
"The sovereign invigorator of the body is exercise, and of all the exercises, walking is best."
—Thomas Jefferson

Think Golf:
"Reverse every natural instinct and do the opposite of what you are inclined to do, and you will probably come very close to having a perfect golf swing."
—Ben Hogan

Make Me Smile:
A beginner golfer was playing golf. His game was turning out to be a pathetic round and it was getting to be difficult for his caddie to watch. At one point the ball was about 180 yards from the green and as the duffer sized up his situation, he asked his caddie, "Do you think I can get there with a 5-iron?" To which his caddie replied, "Eventually."

SATURDAY/SUNDAY

GOLFING DAYS ARE GOOD FOR YOUR HEALTH

REFLECTING ON THE PAST WEEK:

What was your basic attitude? Were you a positive thinker or did you need an "attitude adjustment?" Are you having success with eating healthier and doing your exercise program? How do you feel physically? If you went golfing, write down any comments that might be helpful later in improving your game. Remember, that laughter is the best medicine in the face of adversity. Are you seeing the lighter side of life?

The exercise that helped me the most this week was on page:

_____

My nutritional habits this week were:

_____

What made me smile this week?

_____

_____

Looking back at my golf week:
    My Score: _____ What did I do right? _____

_____

_____

    What could I do to improve?

_____

_____

Goals for next week: _____

_____

_____

MONDAY

Name: DYNAMIC STRETCH: CROSS & CLAP

Goal: Open chest muscles and front of shoulders to ensure appropriate turn during swing without hindrance.

Explanation:

Stand with feet hip distance apart. Cross straight arms in front of body then try to clap them behind your back. Repeat 10x alternating hand on top during cross in front.

Nutrition Tip:
Safety in your kitchen counts! Never throw water on a grease fire. Use salt or baking soda. If it's a small outbreak in a pan, just cover the fire with a metal lid.

Experience Good Thoughts:
"He that will not apply new remedies must expect new evils."

—Francis Bacon
(How's your golf game?)

Think Golf:
Did you know? At age three, in 1979, Tiger Woods shot a 48 over nine holes at the U.S. Naval Golf Course in Cypress, California. Although, he wasn't exactly conforming to USGA rules…Woods used a tee for shots made from the fairway.

Make Me Smile:
"So the doctor told me that he would have me on my feet and golfing in three weeks," said the patient to her friend. "That's good!" replied the friend. "Did he do as he promised?" "You bet. I had to sell my car to pay the bill and now I walk to the course."

TUESDAY

Name: PRE-ROUND WARMUP: HIP OPENING

Goal: Open ball and socket joint of the hip providing more space for weight shifting and prevent muscle imbalance around low back and gluteals.

Explanation:

Hold on to fixed pole of golf cart. Cross R ankle over L knee and proceed to lower hips back and down as if to sit down. You will feel the stretch around your right hip and down the outer thigh while pulling on the cart to help stretch the mid back. Repeat on other leg and frequently during your round to prevent tightening.

Nutrition Tip:
This Chinese proverb offers indisputable advice: "He that takes medicine and neglects diet wastes the skills of the physician."

Experience Good Thoughts:
In the words of Walt Whitman, "If anything is sacred, the human body is sacred." Treat it thoughtfully. Nurture it physically, mentally, and spiritually to stay healthy.

Think Golf:
John Daly was asked to hit tee shots off an airport runway in Denver to determine how much further a ball might travel in the thin mile-high air. With the roll, one of Daly's smashes traveled over 850 yards.

Make Me Smile:
The doctor called his golfer patient with test results right before he was to begin a tournament with a purse of $100,000. "I'm afraid I have good news and bad news," he said. "What's the good news?" replied the patient. "I'd rather hear that first." "You have 24 hours to live." "That's the good news?" said the golfer. "And the bad news?" "I wasn't able to reach you yesterday."

WEDNESDAY

Name: BIG BALL: HIP CIRCLES

Goal: Increase range of motion and circulation to low back and hip area; help separate trunk from hips to aid in turn during swing.

Explanation:

> Sit on top of ball with feet hip distance apart and directly under knees. Keep upper torso and head still. Rotate hips on ball in clockwise motion 10x then repeat counterclockwise 10x. Sit tall and elongate spine throughout movement.

Nutrition Tip:

The Journal of Agricultural and Food Chemistry released their list of the top foods with the most antioxidants. These foods fight damage from free radicals, which are linked to heart disease, cancer, aging, and other diseases. Here they are — small red beans, blueberries, red kidney beans, pinto beans, cranberries, artichokes, blackberries, prunes, raspberries, strawberries, apples, pecans, cherries, and plums.

Experience Good Thoughts:

"Perseverance is the secret of all triumphs."

—Victor Hugo

Think Golf:

The term "birdie" first came into use in the fall of 1903. At the time, a "bird" was a description of excellence. One day at the Atlantic City Country Club in New Jersey, a man named Abe Smith yelled out to a friend after one of his shots, "That's a bird of a shot!" It originally meant a great shot, but it soon became identified with a stroke that produced one under par.

Make Me Smile:

The advantage of exercising everyday is that you die a healthier person.

THURSDAY

Name: STRENGTH: FRONT SQUAT-MEDIUM
Goal: Strengthen lower body for good base of support for swing.

Explanation:

Stand with feet facing forward and hip distance apart. Squat sitting hips back in imaginary chair as arms go out in front parallel to floor to counterbalance sitting back. Place weight mostly in heels. Exhale pushing through heels and squeezing buttocks to stand. Repeat 10-20x.

Nutrition Tip:
To help keep blood sugar even, instead of just eating whole strawberries, try sliced strawberries with their juice on top of a whole wheat bagel or piece of toast with cream cheese to balance out the meal. Always think carb-protein-fat!

Experience Good Thoughts:
"The way you think, the way you behave, the way you eat, can influence your life by 30 to 50 years."

—Deepak Chopra

Think Golf:
Did you know? Tiger Woods became the fastest golfer in history to reach $1 million in earnings just after his first nine PGA Tour events. Ernie Els was the previous record holder after 28 tournaments.

Make Me Smile:
A woman goes to the doctor because she keeps seeing spots. She tells him that it's really affecting her golf game. "Very interesting," the doctor says. "Did the glasses I prescribed for you help at all?" "Not with my golf game," she answered, "but now I see much clearer spots."

FRIDAY

Name: PILATES: JACKKNIFE
Goal: Target control of entire abdominal column and ability to articulate one vertebrae at a time.

Explanation:

Lie on back with legs directly up toward sky and arms down at sides. Inhale flexing hips and hinging legs toward torso. Then sequentially articulate spine off mat from tailbone to mid back reaching legs overhead parallel to mat. Exhale extend hips and reach legs toward sky. Inhale staying in place reaching toes toward sky. Exhale maintain extension in hips as much as possible and sequentially articulate spine back down to mat. Repeat entire sequence 5x.

Nutrition Tip:
Nuts can spoil so storing them correctly is imperative. Shelled nuts should be stored in a tightly covered container in a cool, dry place or in the freezer. Nuts with shells on will keep for a minimum of two months in the refrigerator and may last for a year.

Experience Good Thoughts:
"You win the victory when you yield to friends."   —Sophocles

Think Golf:
Al Geiberger is known as "Mr. 59" since he shot the first-ever PGA tournament below 60 in 1977. He accomplished this on Colonial Country Club's challenging 7,249 yard course with a 29 on the back nine.

Make Me Smile:
A 78 year old man was saddened by the fact that he couldn't see well enough to play golf anymore. Trying to be supportive, his wife suggests he ask his brother who is 83 to go with him. "He still has good sight and he can watch your ball for you," she said. So he decided to try it. The next day he and his brother are out on the course. He steps up to the tee and hits a great drive, which disappears down the middle of the fairway. Excitedly he asks his brother, "Did you see where the ball went?" "Sure did," answered his brother. "Well, where did it go?" he said as they began to walk down the fairway. "I saw it just fine, but I forgot where it landed!"

SATURDAY/SUNDAY

GOLFING DAYS ARE GOOD FOR YOUR HEALTH

REFLECTING ON THE PAST WEEK:

What was your basic attitude? Were you a positive thinker or did you need an "attitude adjustment?" Are you having success with eating healthier and doing your exercise program? How do you feel physically? If you went golfing, write down any comments that might be helpful later in improving your game. Remember, that laughter is the best medicine in the face of adversity. Are you seeing the lighter side of life?

The exercise that helped me the most this week was on page:

_____

My nutritional habits this week were:

_____

What made me smile this week?

_____

_____

Looking back at my golf week:
    My Score: _____ What did I do right? _____

_____

_____

    What could I do to improve?

_____

_____

Goals for next week: _____

_____

MONDAY

Name: YOGA/STRETCH: KNEE TO CHEST
Goal: Reduce risk of injury to low back by stretching hip flexors and hamstrings.

Explanation:

Lie on your back. Bring one knee into the chest and hold for approximately 5 seconds. Release slightly and repeat 3x total. Switch legs. At the end, bring both legs into chest. Knees can be slightly apart as to not put too much stress on abdominal wall. Breathe slowly and allow body to "give in" to the stretch. Relax the head and neck.

Nutrition Tip:
To help stabilize blood sugar, instead of just eating a banana, try putting banana slices in low or no-fat yogurt or spread peanut butter on top of a banana! Always think carb-protein-fat!

Experience Good Thoughts:
Truly successful people persistently pursue their biggest dreams and do not give up because of obstacles along the way. They know that realizing big dreams naturally means big challenges. These people often write down daily, weekly, monthly, yearly, 5, 10, even 20 year goals. Once goals are set, they break them down into steps toward achieving them. What are your goals? Write them down.

Think Golf:
Did you know? The term "caddie" has been linked back to Mary, Queen of Scots who was an avid golfer in the mid 1550's. While studying in France she recruited "cadets" (pronounced "ka-day" by the French) to carry her clubs on her golfing retreats. The word became associated with golf ever since.

Make Me Smile:
"If you're going to throw a club, it is important to throw it ahead of you, down the fairway, so you don't waste energy going back to pick it up."

—Tommy Bolt

TUESDAY

Name: DYNAMIC STRETCH: DIAGONAL KNEE LIFTS
Goal: Increase blood flow and circulation to volatile low back and hip area to prevent injury.

Explanation:

Stand tall with hands on hips and feet hip distance apart. Inhale to prepare. Exhale and lift right knee to right corner. Inhale on lowering and exhale lifting the other leg. Maintain good posture. Repeat alternating legs 20x.

Nutrition Tip:
When eating salad, make sure you get enough healthy monounsaturated fat! Try mixing a tablespoon of your favorite NONFAT salad dressing with a teaspoon of olive oil. It will help satisfy your craving for more!

Experience Good Thoughts:
How we see ourselves – positively or negatively – colors the way we view others and our relationships with them. Recognizing the feelings we have about ourselves is often the first step toward developing healthy relationships with others.

Think Golf:
Did you know? Bent grass is faster grass than Bermuda but does not take the heat as well. Consequently, you will find more bent-grass greens in the north and the heat-enduring Bermuda grass more apparent in the South. USGA specifications call for greens to be cut at 1/32nd of an inch.

Make Me Smile:
What would be a good lunch at a golf course? How about a club sandwich with sliced tomatoes and french-fried puttatoes!

WEDNESDAY

Name: TOWEL: STANDING QUADRICEP

Goal: Open up and stretch hip flexors and front of thigh to help prevent imbalanced muscularity caused by the golf swing.

Explanation:

Stand with ends of towel in hands behind body. Balance on left leg and lift right foot behind to rest in towel. Top of foot (shoelaces) should be in the middle of towel. Place both ends of the towel in right hand only. Slightly pull towel up toward sky while leg lifts back to administer more of a stretch. Hold and balance for about 10 seconds then switch legs. For more support, hold onto a wall.

Nutrition Tip:
Eat summer squash and zucchini! They both have substantial amounts of Vitamin C especially when eaten raw, and provide fiber, potassium, and magnesium. Keep the skin on. Add just a little olive oil as you grill or saute them.

Experience Good Thoughts:
The difference between CAN and CANNOT are only three letters — three letters that determine your life's direction. Be a positive thinker.

Think Golf:
The first person to hole out is responsible for replacing the flagstick. It is courteous and well-known etiquette among avid golfers.

Make Me Smile:
A couple went to Ireland for a golf vacation. They drive into a gas station out in the country with their classy BMW rental. An Irish station attendant came out to greet them. "Top of the mornin' to ya, sir," says the attendant. The American says "hello" and bends over to reach the gas nozzle. A couple of tees fall out of his shirt pocket onto the ground. "What are those?" asked the attendant. "They're called tees," answers the golfer. "What on earth are they for?" asks the Irishman. "They're for resting balls on when you're driving." "Holy cow," says the Irishman, who obviously knew nothing about golf, "BMW thinks of everything!"

THURSDAY

Name: PRE-ROUND WARMUP: STANDING TWIST W/ CLUB
Goal: Promote muscle memory; increase blood flow and circulation to spinal rotation.

Explanation:

Stand in address position with same hip tilt and spine angle. Rest club parallel with ground across back of shoulders holding on to ends. Inhale prepare. Exhale rotate upper body as if in backswing trying to turn shoulders and club 90 degrees. Pause. Inhale repeat to start. Repeat backswing 10x. Then proceed to follow through on opposite side. Focus on controlled movements.

Nutrition Tip:
Eat your crusts! Baking changes the amino acid lysine, contained in flour, into a compound called pronyl-lysine that not only helps darken and sweeten a bread's crust, but also activates enzymes that zap cancer-causing free radicals. There is more than eight times as much of this antioxidant in the crusts than in the inside of the bread loaves! Best crusts? Pumpernickel and whole wheat.

Experience Good Thoughts:
"Optimism is the faith that leads to achievement. Nothing can be done without hope or confidence."
—Helen Keller

Think Golf:
Pick the putter that is right for you! If you are a player who moves the club straight back and straight through the stroke, you need a putter that's face balanced. This will keep the ball on a straight line to the hole. If you use a more inside to inside stroke, you'll fare better with a toe-balanced putter designed specifically for that motion.

Make Me Smile:
"You know the old rule — He who has the fastest cart never has to play a bad lie."
—Mickey Mantle in Esquire (1971)

FRIDAY

Name: STRENGTH: TRICEP DIPS

Goal: Increase clubhead speed with stronger arm musculature; better execution of short game shots for accuracy.

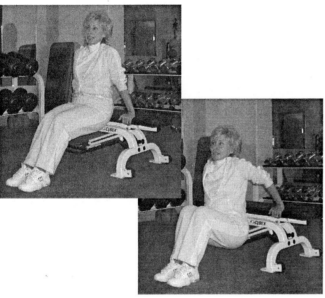

Explanation:

Using a flat bench or chair, go from a straight-arm position to having your arms bent at the elbow at a 90-degree angle, then push back up. Keep shoulders, and hips in alignment. To increase intensity, move feet farther from bench, but do not move hips away from bench. Repeat 3 sets of 15 dips.

Nutrition Tip:

Best cereal on the market? Kashi Go-Lean cereal has the highest combination of protein and fiber of any cereal. One serving contains 13 grams of protein and 10 grams of fiber, which can be a great breakfast or dinner!

Experience Good Thoughts:

When your life seems difficult and you feel down, take time to visualize. Think good thoughts — imagine what you would like your life to be — and always expect the best.

Think Golf:

Do you have a face-balanced putter or a toe-balanced putter? Here is how you find out: Balance the shaft on your left index finger while holding the grip lightly with your right hand. If the face of the putter stays parallel to the ground, it's face-balanced. If the toe of the putter points down toward the ground, your putter is toe-balanced.

Make Me Smile:

"Your financial cost of playing golf can best be figured out when you realize if you were to devote the same time and energy to business instead of golf, you'd be a millionaire in approximately six weeks."

—Buddy Hackett

SATURDAY/SUNDAY

GOLFING DAYS ARE GOOD FOR YOUR HEALTH

REFLECTING ON THE PAST WEEK:

What was your basic attitude? Were you a positive thinker or did you need an "attitude adjustment?" Are you having success with eating healthier and doing your exercise program? How do you feel physically? If you went golfing, write down any comments that might be helpful later in improving your game. Remember, that laughter is the best medicine in the face of adversity. Are you seeing the lighter side of life?

The exercise that helped me the most this week was on page:

_____

My nutritional habits this week were:

_____

What made me smile this week?

_____

_____

Looking back at my golf week:
    My Score: _____ What did I do right? _____

_____

_____

    What could I do to improve?

_____

_____

Goals for next week: _____

_____

_____

MONDAY

Name: YOGA/STRETCH: LYING QUADRICEP STRETCH
Goal: Relieve tension and promote range of motion/flexibility in hip joint through upper leg musculature to knee joint.

Explanation:

Lying face down, bend one knee bringing foot up towards the hip. Reach back with the arm on the same side and grasp the ankle or lower leg and pull the foot towards the hip until a gentle stretch is felt along the front of the hip and thigh. Keep abdominals pulled in and both hip bones on the ground. Hold each side 10 to 15 seconds.

Nutrition Tip:
If you're over 20 years old, you should have your cholesterol level checked regularly. High cholesterol can increase your chance of getting coronary heart disease. HDL or "good" cholesterol actually helps to clean arteries and keep them unblocked. LDL or "bad" cholesterol clogs artery walls and can cause heart attacks. If it is high, it is time to make some lifestyle changes including better diet and more exercise. Cut back on high fat foods and eat more fruits and vegetables.

Experience Good Thoughts:
Diane Sawyer, TV Newscaster, said it best when she described the importance of listening. "I think the one lesson I have learned is that there is no substitute for paying attention."

Think Golf:
When in doubt — PUTT! Your putter is your best friend, even when the ball is off the green. If you're a 100+ shooter, your chipping touch is probably erratic, which could be costing you valuable strokes. Whenever the grass is short enough to be called fairway or fringe, take a putter instead of a wedge. You'll have better control and probably better results.

Make Me Smile:
My butcher and my golf game have one thing in common. They both have a slice that's cost me a fortune.

TUESDAY

Name: DB STRENGTH: OVERHEAD CROSSOVER PUNCH

Goal: Increase upper body strength and power; reinforce stabilization of shoulder girdle for consistent swing.

Explanation:

Stand with feet hip distance apart. Hold 3-5-8 lb. dumbbells in hands at shoulders with palms facing each other. Inhale to prepare. Exhale pushing right arm over head and diagonally to left corner. Inhale pulling it back to start and repeat with left arm reaching to the right corner. The same heel of the reaching arm may and should lift off the floor slightly. Repeat 20x alternating punches.

Nutrition Tip:
To find out how much water you need, divide your body weight in half; the resulting number is said to be the number of ounces you should drink daily. Drink more when sweating and exercising. During meals, 4-6 ounces should be enough to aid in digestion. Most of your daily intake of fluids should be consumed one half hour before meals and between meals.

Experience Good Thoughts:
Never underestimate the importance of success in small matters. It proves that with persistence, bigger success is possible too. Small successes build confidence.

Think Golf:
Distance control is critical on long putts, so you need to develop a stroke that you can trust to putt the ball the same distance every time. Using a pendulum motion is by far the most reliable way to accomplish this. Imagine that your shoulders and hands form a triangle at address, and try to maintain that triangle as you move the club back and through the stroke. Don't allow your wrists to break through impact. It's difficult to control distance with a wristy putting stroke.

Make Me Smile:
Words from Billy Graham, Evangelist: "God listens to me everywhere — except on the golf course."

WEDNESDAY

Name: BIG BALL: PIKES W/ROTATION

Goal: Promote constant shoulder stability for turn while engaging power through midsection to increase club head speed.

Explanation:

This is advanced exercise once plank pike has been successful. Once in plank position overtop ball, pike hips in air with slight rotation of hips to incorporate oblique muscles. Return to plank and repeat each rotation 10x.

Nutrition Tip:

Don't skip meals! Skipping meals actually slows down the body's metabolic rate (the rate in which the body burns calories). A person who consumes a 2,100-calorie meal all at once for a day will often gain more weight than someone who eats three 700 calorie meals, or even better, six 350 calories meals.

Experience Good Thoughts:

"Would you like me to give you a formula for success? It's quite simple, really. Double your rate of failure. You're thinking of failure as the enemy of success. But it isn't at all. You can be discouraged by failure, or you can learn from it. So, go ahead and make mistakes. Make all you can. Because, remember, that's where you'll find success – on the far side of failure."

—Thomas J. Watson, founder of IBM

Think Golf:

When putting, take a high line. It's always better to overestimate the break of a putt. The ball will never go in if you start it on a line that's lower than the correct line. However, if you start the putt higher, you can still hole it with the right speed.

Make Me Smile:

Golf and eating have at least one thing in common. Both are a lot more satisfying to do than they are to watch.

THURSDAY

Name: PRE-ROUND WARMUP: FIGURE 8 BEHIND BACK W/CLUB

Goal: Increase range-of-motion around shoulders to aid in shoulder turn; loosen muscles for more rhythmic, fluid swing.

Explanation:

Stand feet hip distance apart with ends of club in both hands, arms extended straight overhead. Bend both elbows bringing club directly behind head in line with ears. Lower elbows as much as possible and try to straighten arms still holding club behind low back against buttocks. Reverse, bending arms at elbows bringing club back overhead. Do not force stretch. Repeat 5x.

Nutrition Tip:
Protein travels to repair and rebuild muscle tissues by way of water. Healthy muscles are made up of 72% water. If you are dehydrated, the process does not work efficiently.

Experience Good Thoughts:
Never be afraid to try something new. Give your ideas a fair shake and have confidence in your abilities. Remember that a lone amateur built the Ark. And a large group of professionals built the Titanic.

Think Golf:
"It is as easy to lower your handicap as it is to reduce your hat size."
—Henry Beard, Mulligan's Law (1994)

Make Me Smile:
A couple met on vacation and decided to keep seeing each other when they returned home. The guy, being an honest and forthright gentleman, says, "It's only fair to tell you that I'm a golf nut. I live, eat, sleep, and breathe golf." "I guess I should be honest with you then too," his new love says. "I'm a hooker." Thinking quietly for a moment he finally replies, "Well, it's probably because you're not keeping your wrists straight when you hit the ball."

FRIDAY

Name: PILATES: TEASER PREP

Goal: Increase complete core stabilization, trunk control and balance so crucial for generating clubhead speed while maintaining balance.

Explanation:

Lie on back with arms overhead. Knees bent and feet flat on floor approximately 12-18 inches away from hips and hip width apart. Inhale reaching arms to ceiling and keeping spine and back of ribcage flat on floor. Exhale rolling up one vertebrae at a time to balance just back of tailbone. Arms reach forward on a diagonal. Inhale reach arms by ears without changing spine shape. Exhale roll down with control. Complete 8-10 repetitions.

Nutrition Tip:

Studies show that many adults worldwide cannot digest the sugar lactose that is in cows' milk. After consuming milk products, symptoms of lactose intolerance show up such as indigestion, bloating, diarrhea, and stomach cramps. Some people with lactose intolerance can eat cheeses and yogurts, because the bacteria used to process these foods predigest lactose.

Experience Good Thoughts:

"A professional is a person who can do his best at a time when he doesn't particularly feel like it."

—Alistair Cooke, Journalist

Think Golf:

Simple rule of golf – Hit the ball hard and straight and not too often.

Make Me Smile:

"The hardest shot is the chip at 90 yards from the green, where the ball has to be played against an oak tree, bounces back into a sandtrap, hits a stone, bounces onto the green, and then rolls into the cup. That shot is so difficult, I have only made it once!"

—Zeppo Marx

SATURDAY/SUNDAY

GOLFING DAYS ARE GOOD FOR YOUR HEALTH

REFLECTING ON THE PAST WEEK:

What was your basic attitude? Were you a positive thinker or did you need an "attitude adjustment?" Are you having success with eating healthier and doing your exercise program? How do you feel physically? If you went golfing, write down any comments that might be helpful later in improving your game. Remember, that laughter is the best medicine in the face of adversity. Are you seeing the lighter side of life?

The exercise that helped me the most this week was on page:

_____

My nutritional habits this week were:

_____

What made me smile this week?

_____

_____

Looking back at my golf week:
    My Score: _____ What did I do right? _____

_____

    What could I do to improve?

_____

_____

Goals for next week: _____

_____

_____

MONDAY

Name: CARDIO: BACKWARDS WALKING

Goal: Increase cardiovascular endurance and stamina for the 4+ hours of golf; enhance concentration and focus; improve coordination, balance and rhythm.

Explanation:

Walking backwards works all the same muscles as walking forward, but in a different order. It opens up the hip flexors, which tighten during a swing. When walking backwards, stand erect and reach back with your toe hitting the ground first. Squeeze each buttock as the same leg reaches back. Try walking backwards on a treadmill approximately 2.0 mph. With the help of a buddy, try walking backward on a wide path or street. Use the arms as you would when walking forward. Try walking backward for 2-3 minutes at a time switching it with forward walking.

Nutrition Tip:
Although they are advertised as fat-free, packaged fat-free foods are often loaded with sugar. Watch your sugar intake. Read the labels.

Experience Good Thoughts:
A person who is nice to you but rude to the waiter, is NOT a nice person!

Think Golf:
Want to hit longer drives? It all hinges on pure, solid contact with the ball. If you can learn to rotate your shoulders on a consistent plane, without lifting your body up, from set-up through ball contact, then you'll be on your way to longer drives every time you tee up.

Make Me Smile:
"I have a furniture problem. My chest has fallen into my drawers."

—Billy Casper

TUESDAY

Name: YOGA/STRETCH: WIDE SPLIT
Goal: Test inner thigh, hamstring, and low back flexibility; baseline assessment for golf "readiness".

Explanation:

Sit tall with legs extended straight and wide apart. Goal is to maximize and widen the "V" position. Place hands on floor between legs to start. Inhale to prepare. Exhale hinging from hips forward leading with chest to floor. Pause. Return to start position and repeat 5x slowly. Do not bounce in this position! Hold abdominals tight throughout exercise.

Nutrition Tip:
Consuming too much table salt can cause the body to retain water. This water retention can lead to dizziness, swelling, weight gain, and can even cause the body to lose important nutrients. Consuming too much salt increases one's risk of developing high blood pressure. When people with high blood pressure lower their salt intake, their blood pressure usually drops.

Experience Good Thoughts:
"You have within you right now, everything you need to deal with whatever the world can throw at you."

—Brian Tracy, Trainer, Speaker & Author

Think Golf:
Having a happy social life may be as important to your health as not smoking. By making good physical decisions (like playing golf for its fitness value) and having a network of friends, you could live a completely healthy life. So the next time you're asked why you play golf so much, the answer is simple — Because it's good for your health.

Make Me Smile:
When you're too old to chase the opposite sex, you can always chase golf balls.

WEDNESDAY

Name: TOWEL: GOLF SWING

Goal: Increase flexibility of spine in backswing and follow through while maintaining correct spine angle.

Explanation:

Stand in address position holding ends of towel in both hands parallel to body as if holding it on top of ball path. Inhale to prepare. Head should remain still and stable as if eyes stay on ball. Exhale and pull with right hand and bring arms back as if in backswing. Inhale back to center and repeat other side as if in follow through. Swing with core control keeping head still 10-20 repetitions.

Nutrition Tip:

Need to become more stress-free? Let your diet help! A diet that is high in water and low in saturated fats, starches, salt, protein, and caffeine may help. Also, eat 6 small meals spread throughout the day to give the body a steady energy supply. Ideally, meals should consist of mostly whole grains, beans, vegetables, and fruits and nuts. Lean fish, eggs, and poultry may be tolerated as well.

Experience Good Thoughts:

Motivational and inspirational words are like vitamins for your soul. Take your daily vitamin.

Think Golf:

Ever notice how the pros squat down to read the green before putting? The closer you are to the surface of the green, the better you'll see its contours. So, follow the pros, and don't be afraid to squat! Get behind your ball far enough away to get a good view, squat down and take in the slopes of the green.

Make Me Smile:

What must a golfer shoot to assure tournament victory? — The rest of the players.

THURSDAY

Name: DB STRENGTH: FRONT RAISES
Goal: Increase upper body strength and power; reinforce stabilization of shoulder girdle as well as total back for consistent swing.

Explanation:

Stand with feet hip distance apart holding three 5 to 8lb dumbbells in hands with palms facing front of thighs. Inhale to prepare with focus on strong stance and posture. Exhale lifting both arms straight forward to shoulder height and width. Inhale return hands to thighs. Repeat lifting sequence 10-20x. If weights get too heavy, lift one arm at a time. Do not allow body to sway or move during exercise.

Nutrition Tip:
Eating fish may help your health and you don't even have to eat it regularly. Researchers discovered that including a small amount of fish in your diet can give you the benefit of reducing your risk of having a stroke. According to those analyzing information from several studies, eating fish as seldom as 1 to 3 times per month was enough to have a beneficial effect on the risk of ischemic stroke, the most common kind of stroke.

Experience Good Thoughts:
Is your glass half full or half empty? Walter Winchell's definition of an Optimist is "A man who gets treed by a lion but enjoys the scenery."

Think Golf:
Pay attention to your partners' putts or chips toward the hole. As Yogi Berra once said, "You can observe a lot just by watching." It is especially important if one of your partners has a putt that is on a line similar to yours.

Make Me Smile:
The infamous Lorena Bobbitt was lucky enough to have a golf shot named after her — every man should remember her — they call it the "nasty slice".

FRIDAY

Name: BIG BALL: KNEELING STRETCH

Goal: Open muscles in front of body which, when tight, can hinder range of motion throughout turn and extra torque of low spine.

Explanation:

Kneel with hands stretched out in front of you on top of ball. Slowly sit back into heels while walking ball as far as you can away from you. Lower head down underneath elbows and feel stretch throughout arms, chest, and back. Focus on breathing. Hold for 10 seconds and repeat 3x.

Nutrition Tip:

So you say you don't eat much sugar? Think again. Watch for hidden sugar in foods you eat. Sugar is often listed as corn syrup, maltodextrin, honey, maple syrup, sucrose and other "ose" ingredients. Read your labels!

Experience Good Thoughts:

Cheerfulness is contagious. If you choose cheerful people for your friends, you'll become cheerful too.

Think Golf:

It is important that the pace of the swing be consistent. It is no good swinging slowly through one shot and quickly through the next. You'll get very inconsistent results. Try to imagine a pendulum and the way it moves backward and forward at the same pace. Try to feel this in all of your pitch shots.

Make Me Smile:

"Doctor," said the patient, "I'm concerned about this procedure. Will I be able to golf after I've recovered? "Absolutely," replied the doctor. "Great! I've never been able to golf before!"

SATURDAY/SUNDAY

GOLFING DAYS ARE GOOD FOR YOUR HEALTH

REFLECTING ON THE PAST WEEK:

What was your basic attitude? Were you a positive thinker or did you need an "attitude adjustment?" Are you having success with eating healthier and doing your exercise program? How do you feel physically? If you went golfing, write down any comments that might be helpful later in improving your game. Remember, that laughter is the best medicine in the face of adversity. Are you seeing the lighter side of life?

The exercise that helped me the most this week was on page:

_____

My nutritional habits this week were:

_____

What made me smile this week?

_____

_____

Looking back at my golf week:
　　　My Score: _____ What did I do right? _____

_____

_____

　　　What could I do to improve?

_____

_____

Goals for next week: _____

_____

_____

MONDAY

Name: STRENGTH: PRONE SPINAL EXTENSION WITH ROTATION

Goal: Increase low back strength and endurance during constant rotation of swing while maintaining shoulder stability and open chest.

Explanation:

Lie face down on floor with fingertips behind ears to keep shoulders and elbows back. While keeping legs and toes on floor, slowly extend the spine (lift chest off floor) and rotate one elbow high in air while other elbow touches ground. Pause at the top of each movement before returning to center. Repeat both side 10x each.

Nutrition Tip:

The acid in fizzy drinks, even diet drinks, may contribute to enamel erosion that can weaken your teeth. Rinse your mouth or chew sugar-free gum after you drink soda to neutralize acid and minimize the damage to your teeth.

Experience Good Thoughts:

"If you smile when no one else is around, you really mean it."
—Andy Rooney, TV News Personality

Think Golf:

The golden rule in chipping is: Fly the ball as little as possible and roll the ball as much as possible.

Make Me Smile:

The nice thing about these golf books is that they usually cancel each other out. One book tells you to keep your eye on the ball; the next says not to bother. Personally, in the crowd I play golf with, a better idea is to keep your eye on your partner.

—Jim Murray

TUESDAY

Name: DYNAMIC STRETCH: NECK FLEX/EXTEND STRETCH
Goal: Increase range of motion of neck reducing risk of neck injury; aid golfer in keeping head still on backswing.

Explanation:

Stand or sit keeping chin slightly elevated and think about a long neck. Inhale to prepare. On exhale, drop chin toward chest allowing back of neck to lengthen. Inhale back to center. Exhale and allow head to drop back lengthening front of neck. Open mouth to release neck flexors. Repeat slow and controlled 10x.

Nutrition Tip:
Hard cheeses that were derived from the milk of grass-fed Swiss cows contained higher levels of omega-3 fatty acids. Their diet of high-altitude grass seemed to be the reason for the difference. So eat hard alpine cheeses as a healthier choice.

Experience Good Thoughts:
You must learn day by day, year by year, to broaden your horizon. The more things you love, the more you are interested in, the more you enjoy, the more you are indignant about — the more you have left when anything happens.

—Ethel Barrymore, Actress

Think Golf:
The wrists play an important role in your golf swing: Why? Because they control the club throughout the golf swing and they provide power through impact or the "hitting zone".

Make Me Smile:
What's the definition of a golf course manager? He's the keeper of lawn order.

WEDNESDAY

Name: HEAVY BALL: PUSHUP ONE HAND BODY ROTATION

Goal: Promote total body stability with focus on shoulder girdle strength for optimal turn and consistency of swing.

Explanation:

Assume plank position with ball under right hand and feet placed slightly wider than hips. Perform one pushup. As you straighten back up, push left hand off floor and rotate body toward the left reaching right hand to sky. Try balancing body weight on both feet and right hand on ball. This is an advanced move, which takes much strength and power. Work up to it slowly just slightly lifting hand off floor at a time. Try 5 repetitions then switch sides.

Nutrition Tip:
According to a large Harvard study, men with the highest omega-3 blood levels (omega-3 fish oils are found in salmon and other fatty fish) were the least apt to suffer fatal heart attacks.

Experience Good Thoughts:
"The foolish man seeks happiness in the distance; the wise grows it under his feet."
—James Oppenheim

Think Golf:
The key to consistent pitch shots is acceleration, and the key to acceleration is follow through. Golfers often take the club back too far and then slow down as the club reaches the ball. Follow through should be longer than the backswing. The easiest way to picture this is to imagine that you are standing next to a clock. If you take the club back to the 9 o'clock position you should follow through to the 2 o'clock position.

Make Me Smile:
Why is it that the same spouse who can't add when it comes to the family budget at home turns into a mathematician on the golf course?

THURSDAY

Name: PRE-ROUND WARMUP: VERTICAL SWING WITH CLUB
Goal: Loosen and relax muscles for more smooth and fluid swing; increase circulation and range of motion around spine and shoulders.

Explanation:

Assume address position and/or golf ready stance with strong spine angle. Hold club parallel with ground with one hand on grip and other hand on hozzle. Keep head still and inhale rotating as if in backswing then exhale swinging the opposite way. Each direction may stay symmetrical keeping head still or mimic the asymmetric backswing and follow through. Repeat swings 10x each way.

Nutrition Tip:
Consuming soybean products is said to reduce cancer and heart disease risks in men and women. It may also lessen PMS symptoms in women. As little as 10 ounces of soy milk per day may help.

Experience Good Thoughts:
"My great concern is not whether you have failed, but whether you are content with your failure."

—Abraham Lincoln

Think Golf:
Learning the art of "weight transfer" is crucial to a good swing. If you slide your hips instead of rotating them, your swing will be unbalanced and your shot will result in a slice or a hook. Keeping your left side firm through impact eliminates the slide movement and reinforces body rotation.

Make Me Smile:
Golf helps people to stay in shape. As Ellen DeGeneres said, "my grandmother started walking five miles a day when she was 60. She's 97 today and we don't know where the hell she is."

FRIDAY

Name: BIG BALL: ROLL SIDE TO SIDE
Goal: Reinforce rhythm, balance, and core control; promote consistent timing of movement during swing.

Explanation:

Lie face down on ball resting on crossed arms under chest. Legs remain straight and slightly wider than hips. As one unit, turn entire body to the right, which places left side on ball. Keep rotating to back side and switch left leg under right leg to maintain balance. Reverse rotation back to chest down and repeat process to the left. Repeat 5 times each side.

Nutrition Tip:
Research has shown that walnuts, which are high in antioxidants, can improve vascular health for people who have high cholesterol. So, eat a small handful of walnuts as a snack instead of something sweet and you'll be giving your heart the extra-added protection it needs to keep you healthy.

Experience Good Thoughts:
"It takes less time to do things right than to explain why you did it wrong."
—Henry Wadsworth Longfellow

Think Golf:
According to Henry Beard Golfing (1985), "A golf cart is a two-wheeled bag carrier that decreases the exercise value of playing 18 holes of golf from about the level of two sets of doubles tennis to the equivalent of an hour and a half of shopping." Message here: Walking the course is part of the golf experience and good for your health. Only use a motorized cart when you absolutely must.

Make Me Smile:
The one good round of golf you so proudly boast in a month will be the one to drop your handicap and place you into a flight you can't hope to compete in.

SATURDAY/SUNDAY

GOLFING DAYS ARE GOOD FOR YOUR HEALTH

REFLECTING ON THE PAST WEEK:

What was your basic attitude? Were you a positive thinker or did you need an "attitude adjustment?" Are you having success with eating healthier and doing your exercise program? How do you feel physically? If you went golfing, write down any comments that might be helpful later in improving your game. Remember, that laughter is the best medicine in the face of adversity. Are you seeing the lighter side of life?

The exercise that helped me the most this week was on page:

_____

My nutritional habits this week were:

_____

What made me smile this week?

_____

_____

Looking back at my golf week:
    My Score: _____ What did I do right? _____

_____

    What could I do to improve?

_____

_____

Goals for next week: _____

_____

_____

MONDAY

Name: PILATES: SIDE KICK

Goal: Reinforce stability of abdominals, spinal extensors, and pelvis; stretch hip flexors and extensors, which open up and aid in range of motion during swing.

Explanation:

Lie on side with body hinged at hips approximately 10 degrees forward. All joints are stacked and feet are flexed. Top leg is slightly lifted up toward sky approximately 2 inches. Bottom arm is extended under ear and top arm is in front of chest with palm on floor for support. Inhale reaching top leg forward as far as possible with two pulses. Exhale kick same leg back with no pulse. Use momentum allowing the leg to stretch. Focus is on maintaining upper body and hips still and stable. Complete 8-10 kicks each side.

Nutrition Tip:
Did you know we have about 10,000 working taste buds as young adults? But as we age, our taste buds disappear to about half. That explains why many people in their later years tend to eat foods that have more intense flavors and use more spices.

Experience Good Thoughts:
Don't underestimate the power of love. In I Corinthians 13, it is written, "These three remain: faith, hope and love; and the greatest of these is love."

Think Golf:
Practice makes perfect. Get your grip, posture, ball position and alignment right when swinging from a practice tee. Perfect your pre-swing every time you prepare to swing.

Make Me Smile:
"I'd move heaven and earth to be able to break 100 on this course," sighed the golfer. "Try heaven," said his caddie. "You've already moved most of the earth."

TUESDAY

Name: PRE-ROUND WARMUP: CHEST OPENER W/CART
Goal: Open up front of shoulders and chest before round for better rotation in swing and reduction of risk of injury.

Explanation:

Stand facing cart. Outstretch right arm and place open palm against cart support pole (or wall). Lift chest slightly and rotate 180 degrees to the left facing upper body and hips away from cart. Push palm into cart pole to promote stretch in front of shoulder and chest. Pause during exhale. Inhale release and stretch again. Repeat 3x each arm.

Nutrition Tip:
Instead of staying away from bitter vegetables and salad greens, which are so good for your health, temper the bitterness with a dab of sweet butter or a little creamy salad dressing.

Experience Good Thoughts:
We only have one life and one chance to do all the things we want to do. So — dream your loftiest dreams. Go where you want to go — travel stimulates our minds and provides the R&R we need for every day life. Be where you want to be — don't be caught in a place that is unfulfilling.

Think Golf:
Course etiquette tells us to take only one practice swing before making your shot. The exception is if you are waiting to play. Then you can use that time to perfect your swing.

Make Me Smile:
"I have never played this bad before," said the golfer to the caddie. "I didn't realize you EVER played before," said the caddie.

WEDNESDAY

Name: YOGA/STRETCH: STAFF (SEATED TOE TOUCH)

Goal: Test flexibility of hamstrings, calves, hips and low back; baseline assessment for golf "readiness".

Explanation:

Sit tall with spine straight and legs out straight with feet flexed. Place hands by hips. Remain seated on sit bones, not behind. Goal is to keep body at 90 degree angle. Inhale sitting taller drawing chest up and belly button to spine. Exhale hinging from the hips (not rounding the back) and reach straight arms toward toes. Pause. Return back to starting position with hands at sides to stretch spine. Complete 5x. Great exercise to test starting flexibility before workout or round and after.

Nutrition Tip:

Many of us choose not to eat foods prepared with monosodium glutamate because of certain side effects associated with it. But the reason chefs use monosodium glutamate is because it's a flavor enhancer. So instead of using a chemical to make foods taste better, try using parmesan cheese, mushrooms, tomatoes, or other foods that naturally contain small amounts of monosodium glutamate. You'll be surprised how these additions can enhance the natural flavor of foods.

Experience Good Thoughts:

You can only attain a bright future if you can forget your past. Although you can learn from past mistakes, you can't go forward in life until you let go of your past failures and heartaches. Start looking ahead today.

Think Golf:

The pitching shot should be a shorter version of the golf swing, which includes the arms and the legs. So don't try to guide the ball to the target with the arms only. You need your legs to make a consistent stroke.

Make Me Smile:

It seems like the only downwind holes are par threes.

THURSDAY

Name: DB STRENGTH: OVERHEAD "V" PUNCHES

Goal: Increase upper body strength and rotational power; reinforce stabilization of shoulder girdle and total back for consistent swing.

Explanation:

Stand with feet hip distance apart holding 3-5-8lb dumbbells directly in front of shoulders with palms facing inward toward each other. Inhale to prepare. Exhale alternating punches (lifts) with arms crossing over midline of body to opposite corners of room overhead. Palms slightly face downward. Complete 20 (10x each side). Focus on breathing and strong back posture throughout exercise. The heel of the punching arm may lift off floor slightly for control and power.

Nutrition Tip:
We develop a taste for foods that are given to us on a regular basis. However, sometimes these foods are not good for us. TEACH your taste buds to LIKE healthy foods. It's just a matter of doing it!

Experience Good Thoughts:
When choosing a mate or a friend, go for someone who makes you smile. It only takes a smile to make a dark day seem bright. So find the one who makes your heart smile. That's what makes a relationship last.

Think Golf:
Some people believe that the secret to a good swing is in the "feel" of it. We can learn all the mechanics of the perfect swing, but once we know the "feel" of it we can duplicate that feeling over and over.

Make Me Smile:
Golfer: "Please stop checking your watch all the time. It's very distracting to me."
Caddie: "This isn't a watch, sir. It's a compass!"

FRIDAY

Name: TOWEL: DIAGONAL WOOD CHOP

Goal: Enhance total body flexibility in all planes of motion; increase rhythm and coordination in timed movement.

Explanation:

Stand tall with feet slightly wider than hip distance apart. Hold towel from ends in each hand directly in front of chest on a diagonal line. Inhale and reach towel to top left corner over shoulder slightly raising up on right toe. Exhale pulling towel with right hand down toward right ankle. Legs will bend into a slight lunge lifting left heel off floor. Focus on good form and rhythm. Repeat 10x on one side, Then switch to other side.

Nutrition Tip:

When you're craving something sweet, eat fresh berries, cherries or sweet fruits such as peaches instead of cookies or other desserts. They will satisfy your sweet tooth and add a lot of extra vitamins to your diet.

Experience Good Thoughts:

When you were born, you were crying and everyone else was smiling. Live life so that at the end – you're the one who is smiling and everyone around you is crying.

Think Golf:

Setting up is extremely important to the result of the shot. When you use your driver, play off the front heel. Long irons should be played just forward of center and mid irons should be played in the center.

Make Me Smile:

Zig-zag, downhill, left-to-right putts are usually followed by zig-zag, uphill, right-to-left putts.

SATURDAY/SUNDAY

GOLFING DAYS ARE GOOD FOR YOUR HEALTH

REFLECTING ON THE PAST WEEK:

What was your basic attitude? Were you a positive thinker or did you need an "attitude adjustment?" Are you having success with eating healthier and doing your exercise program? How do you feel physically? If you went golfing, write down any comments that might be helpful later in improving your game. Remember, that laughter is the best medicine in the face of adversity. Are you seeing the lighter side of life?

The exercise that helped me the most this week was on page:

_____

My nutritional habits this week were:

_____

What made me smile this week?

_____

_____

Looking back at my golf week:
      My Score: _____ What did I do right? _____

_____

      What could I do to improve?

_____

_____

Goals for next week: _____

_____

_____

MONDAY

Name: BIG BALL: RIB CIRCLES

Goal: Increase range of motion of mid back and shoulder girdle area promoting the ability to coil and generate more club head speed in swing.

Explanation:

Similar to rib tilts, sitting tall on top of big ball with hands on hips to help prevent any movement of lower body. Rotate ribcage in clockwise motion 10x, then repeat counterclockwise 10x. Practice increasing size of circle of rib rotation. Sit tall and maintain long spine to avoid compressing and shearing.

Nutrition Tip:
Research has shown that for about a quarter of the people in the U.S. genes are responsible for making sugar taste sweeter. So you can genuinely blame your ancestors for having that uncontrollable sweet tooth!

Experience Good Thoughts:
Don't count the candles on your birthday cake — count the memories!

Think Golf:
The leading hand is important in hitting short putts. The back of the left hand should extend straight at the hole if you are right-handed. Just putt the ball with the back of the hand facing the hole throughout the stroke.

Make Me Smile:
A foursome that included the fire chief was playing when one of the players hit a ball into the rough. As the golfer went toward the brush to find his ball, the fire chief yelled to be careful because of rattlesnakes. He said people had been calling all week for them to remove the snakes. The golfer was surprised and said, "People actually call the fire department for that. What do you say to them?" The chief responded quickly. "The first thing I ask is, 'Is it on fire?'"

TUESDAY

Name: DYNAMIC STRETCH: OVERHEAD REACH

Goal: Lengthen body and aid in stretching and decompressing vertebrae; increase circulation.

Explanation:

Stand with feet together. Reach and clasp hands together overhead. Stand as tall as possible squeezing and engaging all muscles of the body. Lengthen fingertips to sky, pull elbows close to the ears, squeeze inner thighs together all at one time. Hold for 5 seconds, then release. Repeat 3x.

Nutrition Tip:
Pork tenderloin is nearly as low in fat as skinless chicken breast. It is extremely tender and has a delicious flavor. It is best suited to frying, broiling, grilling, or sautéing. The best ones are small — about 8 to 12 ounces each. So eat pork, the other white meat!

Experience Good Thoughts:
A Scottish Proverb states, "What may be done at any time will be done at no time." If there's no deadline or commitment, you'll have no reason to get started. So prioritize and set goals. Finishing a project can generate such tremendous satisfaction.

Think Golf:
Properly fitted clubs make all the difference in your game. The price of the clubs is not the important part — even less expensive clubs should be fit to the golfer. If you find that you have to alter your stance and swing to suit the club, then you should consider getting custom fitted clubs. The clubs should conform to your physical specifications.

Make Me Smile:
One of the unofficial Laws of Golf reads — Golf balls from the same sleeve tend to follow one another, particularly out of bounds or into the water!

WEDNESDAY

Name: PRE-ROUND WARMUP: HANDS ON WALL ROTATIONS

Goal: Aid in turn during backswing; increase spinal rotation through repetitive stretching.

Explanation:

Stand facing away from a wall with feet hip distance apart and about 12 inches from the wall. Rotate clockwise and place hands parallel with floor on wall behind you. Rotate the other way and do the same. Focus on lifting spine upward. Repeat 20x. Then practice rotating without lifting up bottoms of feet off floor.

Nutrition Tip:

Grapes contain antioxidant compounds that may effectively lower cholesterol and triglycerides. Grapes also contain Vitamin C, lutein, and zeaxanthin — compounds that may reduce the risk of cardiovascular disease by inhibiting atherosclerosis.

Experience Good Thoughts:

"It's a funny thing about life: if you refuse to accept anything but the very best, you will very often get it."

—W. Somerset Maugham, Playwright

Think Golf:

"The legs are the foundation of the backswing. They will give us balance and control and keep us from overswinging."

—Roger Ide, Golf Professional

Make Me Smile:

An older couple are playing in the annual Husband and Wife Club Championship. They're playing in a play-ff hole and it is down to a six inch putt that the wife has to make. She takes her stance and her husband can see her trembling. She putts and misses. They lose the match. On the way home in the car her husband is fuming. "I can't believe you missed that putt. That putt was no longer than my 'willie.' The wife just looked over at her husband and smiled, "Yes, dear, but it was much harder!"

THURSDAY

Name: **PILATES: HUNDRED**

Goal: Stabilization of spine and hips while in a flexed position challenging abdominals with resistance.

Explanation:

Lie on back with legs straight in the air over hips squeezing inner thighs together. Arms at sides with palms down. Inhale to prepare. As you exhale, flex upper spine off floor while reaching arms slightly off ground. Extend straight legs away from body while maintaining a flat back to floor. Keep body still as arms pulse up/down an inch off floor counting to 100. Inhale on 5 breaths, exhale on 5 breaths.

Nutrition Tip:
The FDA reported that producers of olive oil could say on their labels that there was "limited and not conclusive" evidence that people could reduce the risk of coronary disease by replacing saturated fats with olive oil. It is only the 3rd time that the agency has approved such a claim for a food label. The other two foods were walnuts and omega-3 fatty acids.

Experience Good Thoughts:
"Do not go where the path may lead. Go instead where there is no path and leave a trail."

—Ralph Waldo Emerson

Think Golf:
Do you know where the first course in the United States was built? In Yonkers, New York in 1888. It was named St. Andrews.

Make Me Smile:
Definition of a Target Line — An imaginary line from a player's lie to the target, which the ball would follow if an imaginary golfer hit it.

FRIDAY

Name: **YOGA/STRETCH: KNEELING PIGEON**
Goal: Open and increase range of motion in low back, hips and groin allowing for maximal power in swing and less risk of injury.

Explanation:

Begin kneeling on all fours. Bring right knee forward between hands and turn right foot inward toward the outside of the left hand. Slowly slide the left leg back moving it away from the left hand. There should not be any pain in right knee. As flexibility allows, fold forward onto elbows and relax head and neck toward floor. Hold for 10 seconds letting your body relax fully with every exhale.

Nutrition Tip:
A recent study at the University of Arizona and the University of Arkansas showed higher levels of bone mineral density in postmenopausal women who ate at least 18 mg. of iron a day. Raisins are a good source of iron. Pound for pound, raisins have as much iron as most red meat. As with all plant products high in iron, eat with a food high in Vitamin C (raisins have virtually no Vitamin C) to realize maximum absorption.

Experience Good Thoughts:
"Life is ten percent what happens to you and ninety percent how you respond to it."
—Lou Holtz, Football Coach

Think Golf:
On October 4, 1895, the first U.S. Open golf tournament was held at the Newport Country Club in Rhode Island.

Make Me Smile:
The term "woods" has two definitions in golf. It can mean the types of clubs used to drive the ball a long distance or it can mean the place where the ball lands after you try to drive it a long distance.

SATURDAY/SUNDAY

GOLFING DAYS ARE GOOD FOR YOUR HEALTH

REFLECTING ON THE PAST WEEK:

What was your basic attitude? Were you a positive thinker or did you need an "attitude adjustment?" Are you having success with eating healthier and doing your exercise program? How do you feel physically? If you went golfing, write down any comments that might be helpful later in improving your game. Remember, that laughter is the best medicine in the face of adversity. Are you seeing the lighter side of life?

The exercise that helped me the most this week was on page:

_____

My nutritional habits this week were:

_____

What made me smile this week?

_____

_____

Looking back at my golf week:
        My Score: _____ What did I do right? _____

_____

_____

        What could I do to improve?

_____

_____

Goals for next week: _____

_____

_____

MONDAY

Name: HEAVY BALL: V-SEAT FIGURE 8
Goal: Improve lower pelvic and trunk stability and strength; coordination.

Explanation:

Sit on floor holding ball in front of chest to prepare. Round back putting weight just back of tailbone or sit bones. Lift legs off floor with knees bent. While maintaining balance and keeping spine flexed with abdominals held tight, take ball around legs in a figure 8 pattern 10x. Reverse direction 10x.

Nutrition Tip:
Looking for physical activity to help burn calories and get rid of unwanted fat? Did you know that one hour of reading burns 100 calories and one hour of brisk walking burns 310 calories? Go out, walk the golf course, and burn some calories!

Experience Good Thoughts:
"Repeat anything often enough and it will start to become you."
　　　　　　　　　　　　　　　—Tom Hopkins, Speaker & Author

(Are you thinking more positive thoughts, nurturing your sense of humor, becoming a healthier person?)

Think Golf:
Wearing a golf glove helps you maintain a secure grip. But have you noticed one hand with a rich tan and the other fairly pale? One suggestion is to buy a glove with the back of the hand exposed to let the sunshine in. Another suggestion is to buy a newly introduced glove that allows the sun to come through the special fabric. Costly but effective.

Make Me Smile:
A Hole-in-One is when a ball is hit from the tee directly into the hole on a single shot by a golfer playing all ALONE!

TUESDAY

Name: STRENGTH: JUMP LUNGES

Goal: Increase explosive strength of lower body with focus on fast twitch muscles for power.

Explanation:

Stand in static lunge position with good posture and weight evenly distributed between front foot heel and back foot toes. Use arms to help lift body upward with momentum and jump switching legs and landing with feet in opposite positions. Land lightly. Switch 20x maintaining good form with abdominals held in tightly.

Nutrition Tip:
Researchers say we can slow down the brain's aging process. Whenever we learn something new, we form new brain connections. Keeping our brains active by lifelong learning can help to keep us thinking clearly. It can also be said that although eating habits form over long periods of time, we CAN change those habits to eating healthier and choosing more fruits and vegetables in our diets. No excuses.

Experience Good Thoughts:
"Stay committed to your decisions, but stay flexible in your approach."
—Tony Robbins, Motivational Speaker

Think Golf:
Golf associations throughout the nation are licensed to offer players an official Handicap Index. Beware of fast-growing internet companies that offer Handicap Indexes. Be certain they are recognized by the USGA before doing business with non golf-related companies. Peer review is one of the necessities for reporting scores and keeping Handicap Indexes honest and fair.

Make Me Smile:
It is a known fact in the golf world that your spouse either hates golf or is a better player than you are.

WEDNESDAY

Name: DYNAMIC STRETCH: SHOULDER SHRUGS

Goal: Release tension and increase circulation around shoulder joints for better and unhindered movement during swing.

Explanation:

Stand with feet hip distance apart, palms facing toward outer thighs. Inhale and lift shoulders up toward ears. Exhale and return shoulders back down reaching fingertips to floor. Try to increase intensity of movement and distance. Repeat 30x controlled.

Nutrition Tip:

Portion control is the hardest part of eating a healthy meal. A healthy serving of protein should be about 3 to 4 ounces and a serving of pasta or mashed potatoes is considered about 1/2 cup. If we could keep to these portions, it would be easy to maintain a healthy weight. More is definitely not better!

Experience Good Thoughts:

"The best thing about the future is that it comes only one day at a time."
—Abraham Lincoln, 16th President

Think Golf:

Always pick a target when you are setting up a shot. When you are 150 yards out or closer to the green, the flag does NOT have to be your target. Aim at something midway between you and the flag to help your direction. That will compensate for poor judgment in aiming and will aid in getting your ball where you want it to go.

Make Me Smile:

Why is it harder to hit a ball over water and sand? Because the water beckons you, the sand mocks you, and your partners tease you. And golf is supposed to be a friendly, quiet game.

THURSDAY

Name: BIG BALL: GOLF SWING

Goal: Increase circulation and range of motion around spine; promote width in swing.

Explanation:

Stand with feet slightly wider than hip distance apart. Arrange body in address position with big ball in hands. Maintain correct spine angle. Swing ball back and forth in backswing and follow through utilizing core. Swing ball R and L 10 times.

Nutrition Tip:
People eat a great deal of food additives each year — many of which are thought to be linked to cancer, allergies, asthma, and other illnesses. Eating less processed or fast foods, buying organic foods, and washing produce and meats thoroughly to remove pesticides will help.

Experience Good Thoughts:
"When you judge another, you do not define THEM, you define YOURSELF."
—Dr. Wayne Dyer, Psychotherapist & Author

Think Golf:
How high should you tee the ball on your tee shot? Tee it up to where the top of the ball is even with the top of the driver as it hits the ball.

Make Me Smile:
Has anyone noticed that par three holes are obsessed with the desire to humiliate golfers? It seems that the shorter the yardage, the greater its desire.

FRIDAY

Name: CARDIO: JOGGING

Goal: Increase cardiovascular endurance and stamina for the 4+ hours of golf; enhance concentration and focus; improve coordination, balance and rhythm.

Explanation:

Jogging is the next level up from power walking. Make sure you feel comfortable walking at a fast pace before you start jogging. Start by lightly jogging to short landmarks, then to the next one (mailbox, lightpost, end of block). Gradually, as you feel comfortable without pain, don't speed up, but continue jogging for longer durations. Try jogging a 15-minute mile (4mph). Jog 3x per week for 30 minutes each time. Focus on light feet, calm breathing, and positive thinking.

Nutrition Tip:

Research has shown that eating oats with Vitamin C helps to curb the formation of arterial plaque. By combining Vitamin C rich fruits such as strawberries or melon with oatmeal or drinking orange juice with an oatmeal breakfast, you can help your body to keep your arteries clear.

Experience Good Thoughts:

"Failures are like skinned knees — painful but superficial."
—H. Ross Perot, Businessman

Think Golf:

Don't try to scoop the ball into the air. It will only lead to hitting the top of the ball. A striking motion is the way to achieve a better shot.

Make Me Smile:

When hitting over a water hazard, golfers have two choices — either hit one more club OR hit two more balls.

SATURDAY/SUNDAY

GOLFING DAYS ARE GOOD FOR YOUR HEALTH

REFLECTING ON THE PAST WEEK:

What was your basic attitude? Were you a positive thinker or did you need an "attitude adjustment?" Are you having success with eating healthier and doing your exercise program? How do you feel physically? If you went golfing, write down any comments that might be helpful later in improving your game. Remember, that laughter is the best medicine in the face of adversity. Are you seeing the lighter side of life?

The exercise that helped me the most this week was on page:

_____

My nutritional habits this week were:

_____

What made me smile this week?

_____

_____

Looking back at my golf week:
     My Score: _____ What did I do right? _____

_____

_____

     What could I do to improve?

_____

_____

Goals for next week: _____

_____

_____

MONDAY

Name: PILATES: SWAN DIVE

Goal: Enhance strength and endurance of spine extensors helping to prevent lifting of head and shoulders during swing.

Explanation:

Lie face down with hands by shoulders and legs slightly apart and toes pointed. Inhale prepare. Exhale curl head, neck, and ribcage off floor using hands for added assistance. Feel stretch in front of body while activating gluteals and lengthening through spine. Inhale returning back to floor. Repeat 10x focusing on opening up through ribcage.

Nutrition Tip:

In order to preserve antioxidants when microwaving vegetables, use only a couple tablespoons of water to fresh vegetables and no water to frozen vegetables. Water siphons out nutrients when cooking vegetables.

Experience Good Thoughts:

"Time never stops to rest, never hesitates, never looks forward or backward. Life's raw material spends itself now, this moment — which is why how you spend your time is far more important than all the material possessions you may own or positions you may attain."

—Dennis Waitley, Author, Speaker

Think Golf:

Who is the only player to lose The Masters in a play-off twice? Answer: Ben Hogan.

Make Me Smile:

We all try to be good examples. However, if you can't be a good example, then be content in knowing that you can be a terrible warning. Now get in shape, think positive, and practice your short game.

TUESDAY

Name: BIG BALL: LEG LIFTS

Goal: Promote body awareness for balance and posture.

Explanation:

Sit on ball feet hip distance apart and knees over feet. With arms to the side and spine erect, lift right foot off floor 10x. Repeat with left leg. For challenge, lift leg and extend straight then bend and return back to floor. Focus on posture and head position.

Nutrition Tip:

Summer snacks good for dipping are celery, cucumbers, green peppers and cauliflower florets. Of all these, cucumbers have the most calories, with a whole one tipping the caloric scale at a modest 45 calories.

Experience Good Thoughts:

You can make more friends in two months by becoming interested in other people than you can in two years by trying to get other people interested in you.

—Dale Carnegie, Author & Trainer

Think Golf:

Golfing Feat: Australian meteorologist, Nils Lied, working at Mawson Base in Antarctica in 1962, drove a ball 2,640 yards across the ice.

Make Me Smile:

Yes, walking the golf course does contribute to better health but where does that get you in the end? Health fanatics will feel pretty stupid someday when they're lying in a hospital bed dying of nothing!

WEDNESDAY

Name: YOGA/STRETCH: ONE LEGGED DOWNWARD DOG
Goal: Stabilize shoulder girdle while challenging flexibility of back, hamstrings, and calves.

Explanation:

Start in downward facing dog pose, hands down with hips in air, maintaining straight spine and straight legs. Reach right foot off ground and up to the sky keeping leg straight and rotating hips slightly for further stretch. Challenge movement: Kick/lift leg 5 times tapping toe to floor each time and trying to stretch toe farther to sky. Switch legs and repeat.

Nutrition Tip:
Drink a minimum of 64oz. of water daily. This will ensure you're replacing fluids lost during exercise. You need not wait until you are thirsty. By then, you are in a depleted state. Drink glasses throughout the day, not all at once!

Experience Good Thoughts:
"My religion is very simple. My religion is kindness."   —The Dalai Lama

Think Golf:
A player may only have 14 clubs in the bag during any round. Penalty strokes are assessed if more clubs are found in the bag. Be careful not to pick up another player's club from the ground and place it in your bag. Count your clubs and be sure all you have in your bag are your own clubs.

Make Me Smile:
A guy was on the phone with one of his buddies who asked him if he wanted to go golfing. He offered that he had already checked it out with his wife and it was OK. Wanting to sound macho, he said, "Well, I'm the king of this castle and I can play golf anytime I want to."   "But hold on a minute, let me just check to see if I really want to."

THURSDAY

Name: STRENGTH: JUMP SQUATS

Goal: Increase explosive strength focusing on lower body muscular power.

Explanation:

Stand tall with feet slightly wider than hips. Lower down to a squat with weight remaining mostly in heels. Spring upward as high as you can reaching arms to the sky. When returning to the ground, decelerate body and use joints as shock absorbers by landing first on toes, then balls of feet, then heels. Repeat 10x for 3 sets.

Nutrition Tip:
Evidence suggests that nutritious foods work best when combined with other nutritious foods. Include a variety of healthful foods at each meal. Vitamin-rich vegetables and fruits, fiber-rich whole grains, fish or poultry, and heart-healthy fats are choices to include in most meals.

Experience Good Thoughts:
"Nobody can make you feel inferior without your permission."
—Eleanor Roosevelt, Former First Lady

Think Golf:
"Tee your ball high . . . air offers less resistance than dirt."
—Jack Nicklaus

Make Me Smile:
You can tell when a golfer is really old. The other day I was talking about a good grip and an old duffer heard me and thought I was talking about dentures.

FRIDAY

Name: DYNAMIC STRETCH: ROUNDED FORWARD REACH

Goal: Release tension in mid back and shoulder blades; increase circulation and range of motion to help promote backswing rotation.

Explanation:

Stand with feet a little wider than hips. Arms over head with hands clasped together. Inhale to prepare. Exhale as arms reach forward pulling shoulders forward and rounding back. Tuck hips under to emphasize full flexion of spine. Breathe throughout and hold for 10 seconds. Repeat 2x.

Nutrition Tip:
Eating a cup of vegetable soup for lunch can help you eat your required amount of vegetables needed in a day. If you buy it canned, read the label for salt content. Adding a small salad to the meal will boost the number of vegetables significantly.

Experience Good Thoughts:
"What this power is, I cannot say. All I know is that it exists . . . and it becomes available only when you are in that state of mind in which you know exactly what you want – and are fully determined not to quit until you get it."
—Alexander Graham Bell

Think Golf:
A player is entitled to remove any loose impediment, which is described as natural objects that are not fixed or growing, not solidly embedded and do not adhere to the ball. It does not matter how large (it could be a boulder) or how much it weighs.

Make Me Smile:
Golf is a game where the ball may not lie well, but the players sure do.

SATURDAY/SUNDAY

GOLFING DAYS ARE GOOD FOR YOUR HEALTH

REFLECTING ON THE PAST WEEK:

What was your basic attitude? Were you a positive thinker or did you need an "attitude adjustment?" Are you having success with eating healthier and doing your exercise program? How do you feel physically? If you went golfing, write down any comments that might be helpful later in improving your game. Remember, that laughter is the best medicine in the face of adversity. Are you seeing the lighter side of life?

The exercise that helped me the most this week was on page:

_____

My nutritional habits this week were:

_____

What made me smile this week?

_____

_____

Looking back at my golf week:
     My Score: _____ What did I do right? _____

_____

     What could I do to improve?

_____

_____

Goals for next week: _____

_____

_____

MONDAY

Name: HEAVY BALL: UP THROWS

Goal: Increase explosive power as well as endurance for chest, shoulders, and arms; improves accuracy.

Explanation:

Stand in slightly staggered stance (one foot more forward than the other) holding ball into chest. Look up throwing ball as far and as straight as possible overhead. Ball should return back to hands. Absorb shock of ball lowering it back to chest and explode ball back into sky again. Repeat up throws 20-30 repetitions. As accuracy improves, so will height.

Nutrition Tip:

Researchers speculate that fruit can help you control your weight because fruit fiber is filling and helps to control your appetite. Fruit is low in calories and is high in water content.

Experience Good Thoughts:

"There are two ways to live your life. One is as though nothing is a miracle. The other is as though everything is a miracle."   —Albert Einstein

Think Golf:

Try this golf game! In a SKINS game, the player with the lowest score on a hole wins a skin. But if two or more players shoot the same for that hole, then no one wins the skin. Most skins games are played with carryovers. That means if no skins are won on a hole, then that skin is added as a carryover to the next hole. For example, there's a tie on three consecutive holes, then the next hole would be worth four skins. Groups usually assign the point value or dollar value to a skin before the round begins. Using players' handicaps usually makes everyone hunker down and concentrate more, knowing they have a shot at winning the hole's skin.

Make Me Smile:

I'm hitting my woods just great — but I'm having a terrible time getting out of them!

TUESDAY

Name: BIG BALL: SUPERMAN OPPOSITE ARM/LEG

Goal: Provide midsection stability and torso strength to assist in rotational action of swing; challenges balance and mental focus.

Explanation:

Start in regular superman position face down over ball with tips of toes on floor behind you and fingertips on floor under shoulders. Slowly lift opposite arm and leg up and away from body. Hold for 10 seconds trying to maintain balance. Return to center and repeat other side. Repeat each side 5 times keeping abdominals engaged.

Nutrition Tip:
If your Energy intake (which is the number of calories you eat) is greater than your Energy expenditure (which is the number of calories you use), your body weight will increase (because you have an energy surplus).

Experience Good Thoughts:
"There's no scarcity of opportunity to make a living at what you love. There is only a scarcity of resolve to make it happen."

—Dr. Wayne Dyer, American Psychotherapist

Think Golf:
Etiquette to remember: ALWAYS repair your ball marks on the green. Be aware at all times where your ball landed on the green and make sure there is no mark visible. If you don't have a ball mark repair tool, use your tee.

Make Me Smile:
The poor widow went to the funeral home to make arrangements after her husband died. The funeral director asked, "How would you like the obituary to read?" "Peter Duncan died," she said. Surprised by the lack of information she provided to make the obituary more personal, he asked if she was sure that was all she wanted him to submit. Finally she said, "OK, add 'Golf Clubs for Sale.'"

WEDNESDAY

Name: **DYNAMIC STRETCH: ROLLUP/ROLL DOWN**
Goal: Increase range of motion and lengthens entire back of body from neck through spine; increase flexibility in low back and hamstrings.

Explanation:

Stand tall with feet together and hands down at sides facing outer thighs. Inhale to prepare and lengthen back of neck, dropping chin toward chest. As you exhale, roll down as if rolling back off a wall behind you, one vertebrae at a time. Allow head to hang and engage abdominals pulling belly button to spine. Bend down allowing hands and arms to drop weightlessly toward feet. Inhale at the bottom pausing for a moment, then exhale and reverse the process standing back up.

Nutrition Tip:

Most nutritionists agree that only about 15% of your daily calories should come from protein. Eating less meat can help you eat less fat and fewer calories. Meat contains more fat and calories than vegetables and fruits do.

Experience Good Thoughts:

"A good friend who points out mistakes and imperfections and rebukes evil is to be respected as if he reveals a secret of hidden treasure."

—The Buddha

Think Golf:

You may protect yourself from the rain by holding an umbrella and making your shot. But you cannot have another person hold the umbrella for you while making a stroke.

Make Me Smile:

The union and company were deep in negotiations. The union completely denied that workers were abusing their sick leave benefits. One day at the bargaining table, the company's representative held up a newspaper and yelled, "This man called in sick yesterday!" On the front page of the sports section was a photo of the supposedly ill employee who won a golf tournament with an outstanding score. There was complete silence in the room. Then the union rep said, "Wow, just think of the score he could have had if he wasn't feeling sick!"

THURSDAY

Name: PILATES: SIDE DOUBLE LEG LIFT
Goal: Strengthen side muscles to prevent lateral bending during swing.

Explanation:

Lie on one side, supporting your head with the lower arm. Your upper arm is in front of your body to help with balance and alignment. Extend both legs along same line as body. Inhale to prepare. Exhale and lift both legs off floor to hip height using muscles on side of hip and waist. Return to floor. Repeat 10x each side.

Nutrition Tip:
Complex carbohydrates such as those found in whole grain breads take longer to digest, causing glucose to enter the bloodstream slower. They are also fiber-filled, which helps you feel full.

Experience Good Thoughts:
"Every time you are tempted to react in the same old way, ask if you want to be a prisoner of the past or a pioneer of the future."
—Deepak Chopra, M.D. & Author

Think Golf:
The midsection or core muscles (erector spinae, abdominals, and obliques) transfer force from the legs to the torso to accelerate even more.

Make Me Smile:
What is the definition of Lie as it relates to golf?
First meaning – where the ball comes to rest after being hit by a golfer.
Second meaning — the number of strokes it took to get it there according to that golfer.

FRIDAY

Name: YOGA/STRETCH: STOP STRETCH
Goal: Help to keep forearms loose for more clubhead speed at impact.

Explanation:

Extend left arm, hand flexed, palm facing away. With the right hand, pull left fingers toward chest while pushing the heel of the left hand out. Repeat three times and switch sides.

Nutrition Tip:
Antioxidant compounds in grapes may help to reduce cholesterol. Chemicals found in grape skins appear to have cancer-fighting and anti-inflammatory properties too. They are easy to eat as snacks throughout the day with health benefits hard to beat.

Experience Good Thoughts:
"Even if you are on the right track, you will get run over if you just sit there."
—Will Rogers

Think Golf:
Simple rule of golf – Hit the ball hard, straight and not too often. Sounds easy enough, doesn't it?

Make Me Smile:
There are two things you can learn by stopping your backswing at the top and checking the position of your hands: first — how many hands you have, and second — which one is wearing the glove.

SATURDAY/SUNDAY

GOLFING DAYS ARE GOOD FOR YOUR HEALTH

REFLECTING ON THE PAST WEEK:

What was your basic attitude? Were you a positive thinker or did you need an "attitude adjustment?" Are you having success with eating healthier and doing your exercise program? How do you feel physically? If you went golfing, write down any comments that might be helpful later in improving your game. Remember, that laughter is the best medicine in the face of adversity. Are you seeing the lighter side of life?

The exercise that helped me the most this week was on page:

_____

My nutritional habits this week were:

_____

What made me smile this week?

_____

_____

Looking back at my golf week:
       My Score: _____ What did I do right? _____

_____

_____

       What could I do to improve?

_____

_____

Goals for next week: _____

_____

_____

MONDAY

Name: DB STRENGTH: PUNCHES

Goal: Warm up trunk, hips, and shoulders while maintaining proper form with added resistance; reinforce timing and rhythm.

Explanation:

Stand with feet hip width apart with elbows bent at your sides and 3-5-8lb dumbbells in hand. Punch with your right hand across the left side at same direction as left foot. Shift weight to left foot and lift right heel (pivot). Do not hyperextend or bounce elbow. Pull arm back in and repeat other side.

Nutrition Tip:

When choosing cabbage, fresh cabbage and pickled RED cabbage seem to be the highest in flavonoids, which fight cancer and aging. Use red cabbage as a replacement for lettuce in sandwiches and salads.

Experience Good Thoughts:

"The most damaging phrase in the language is: 'It's always been done that way.' "
—Admiral Grace Hopper, Navy Officer

Think Golf:

Did you know that a player can leave the course during play and go to the clubhouse or restroom as long as he does not unduly delay play.

Make Me Smile:

Your best round of golf will most likely be followed by your worst round ever. The probability of this phenomenon increases with the number of people you tell about your best round.

TUESDAY

Name: HEAVY BALL: SIDE BEND W/REACH AWAY

Goal: Increase lateral flexibility of spine to help prevent injury during sidebending; strengthen small muscles of arms for club control.

Explanation:

Stand with feet hip distance apart holding ball straight overhead in both hands. Inhale bending to the right side and shifting hips to the left. When you've reached maximum side bend, balance ball in right hand. Continue lowering ball down toward right leg and lengthen left hand toward sky for extra stretch. Exhale pushing right arm and ball back up to meet left hand returning to standing position. Repeat alternating sides 10x.

Nutrition Tip:
When thinking about losing weight, eat fruits high in water content. Some of them in this category are: watermelon, cantaloupe, grapes, apples, and strawberries.

Experience Good Thoughts:
Take this French Proverb to heart and sleep well every night. "There is no pillow so soft as a clear conscience."

Think Golf:
Here's a new way to enjoy golf and add a little fun to the game. WOLF is a game for 3 or 4 players. On a rotating basis one player is designated as the wolf on each tee. The wolf hits first, then chooses a partner from the other players after seeing the results of all the tee shots. The partners then team up and play out the hole in a best-ball format.

Make Me Smile:
When you look up and cause a terrible shot, you will always look down again at exactly the moment when you ought to start watching the ball if you ever want to see it again.

WEDNESDAY

Name: DYNAMIC STRETCH: TOE RAISES
Goal: Strengthen shin muscles while stretching calves for better mobility of ankle joint.

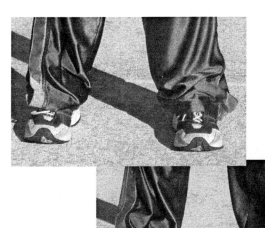

Explanation:

Stand with feet hip distance apart. Place hands on hips and maintain good posture in upright position with knees slightly unlocked and abdominals engaged. Balance on heels and lift toes up and down as if toe-tapping the sky. Complete a set of 30 reps.

Nutrition Tip:
Vegetarians need to guard against a lack of Vitamin B-12, which is found primarily in meat, dairy products, and eggs. Vitamin B-12 is necessary for the proper function of nerves and the production of red blood cells.

Experience Good Thoughts:
"Take your life in your own hands and what happens? A terrible thing — no one else is to blame."

—Erica Jong, Author

Think Golf:
Because golf is played without supervision or a referee, it relies on the integrity of the players. Keep up the reputation of the game and the individuals who play it by following the Rules of Golf. Although you may have a strong competitive spirit, playing by the Rules is mandatory and all players should conduct themselves in a polite and courteous manner.

Make Me Smile:
The best way to play a particular hole will become obvious as soon as you have finished playing that particular hole.

THURSDAY

Name: BIG BALL: ELBOW PLANK TO STANDING

Goal: Strengthen shoulder girdle to keep constant stabilization during swing; promote balance and core stability.

Explanation:

Prop forearms on ball in plank position with feet hip distance apart balancing on toes. Pike hips backward while rolling ball back toward knees to standing. Reverse and roll out over ball back to plank. Repeat 10 times keeping abdominals tight.

Nutrition Tip:
Cooking vegetables is a matter of preference when it comes to doneness. A rule of thumb is when you start to smell the fragrance of the vegetables, they are at the point of being fully cooked. Some vegetables like cabbage, onions, and rutabagas get sweeter when cooked until soft.

Experience Good Thoughts:
"The nearest way to glory is to strive to be what you wish to be thought to be."
—Socrates

Think Golf:
A ball that is embedded in its own pitch-mark in the ground in any closely mown area through the green may be lifted, cleaned and dropped, without penalty, as near as possible to the spot where it lay but not nearer the hole. The ball when dropped must first strike a part of the course through the green. "Closely mown area" means any area of the course, including paths through the rough, cut to fairway height or less. USGA Rule #25-2

Make Me Smile:
When you're looking for your ball and there is a ball in the fringe and a ball in the bunker, guess which one is yours? Right again — the one in the bunker.

FRIDAY

Name: YOGA/STRETCH: ELEVATED TOE TOUCH
Goal: Stretch calves, hamstrings, gluteals, and low back — all muscles in the golf swing most susceptible to tightening due to swing.

Explanation:

Sit tall with straight back and legs extended together in front of body. Lift right foot and rest right heel on top of left toes. Inhale lifting spine as arms extend in front of chest. Exhale hinging from hips reaching hands to toes. Inhale back to start and repeat movement 5x. Switch legs.

Nutrition Tip:
Worrying about keeping your mind sharp as you get older? Thought-provoking activities such as reading or doing crossword puzzles along with eating omega-3-fatty-acid-rich fish, nuts, and olive oil will help to stimulate your mind and keep you alert.

Experience Good Thoughts:
"None will improve your lot in life if you yourself do not."
—Bertolt Brecht, German Poet

Think Golf:
William Wordsworth, a British poet, described golf as "a day spent in strenuous idleness." But to 26 million Americans and millions of others around the world who play the game, golf is much more than an idle pastime. To those who accept the challenge of both physical and mental growth it inspires, golf is a true passion.

Make Me Smile:
Here's one your kids will love. Why do golfers carry an extra pair of pants in their bags? Answer: In case they get a hole in one.

SATURDAY/SUNDAY

GOLFING DAYS ARE GOOD FOR YOUR HEALTH

REFLECTING ON THE PAST WEEK:

What was your basic attitude? Were you a positive thinker or did you need an "attitude adjustment?" Are you having success with eating healthier and doing your exercise program? How do you feel physically? If you went golfing, write down any comments that might be helpful later in improving your game. Remember, that laughter is the best medicine in the face of adversity. Are you seeing the lighter side of life?

The exercise that helped me the most this week was on page:

_____

My nutritional habits this week were:

_____

What made me smile this week?

_____

_____

Looking back at my golf week:
    My Score: _____ What did I do right? _____

_____

_____

    What could I do to improve?

_____

_____

Goals for next week: _____

_____

_____

MONDAY

Name: PRE-ROUND WARMUP: HAMSTRING STRETCH
Goal: Lengthen back of legs as well as low back for preparation of round.

Explanation:

Swing leg up onto cart of platform that is high enough to challenge you, but low enough that you are able to keep base leg straight and tall. Lean over from hips focusing on good posture. Reach toward lifted foot and feel stretch from ankle to buttocks. Do not bounce! Hold for approx. 10 seconds then switch legs.

Nutrition Tip:
Antioxidant-rich foods come in all shapes and sizes. Smother your pasta in tomato sauce and add onions, garlic and red peppers for added nutrients. For dessert make pumpkin pudding using canned pumpkin and condensed milk. Great for you and tastes good too.

Experience Good Thoughts:
"Personally, I'm always ready to learn, although I do not always like being taught."
—Winston Churchill, British Prime Minister

Think Golf:
I know we all love to give advice. But according to USGA Rule #8-2b, When a player's ball is on the putting green, the player, his partner or either of their caddies may, before but not during the stroke, point out a line for putting, but in so doing the putting green must not be touched. A mark must not be placed anywhere to indicate a line for putting.

Make Me Smile:
If you aim right for the center of the bunker, you'll never hit it. Now that's a novel strategy!

TUESDAY

Name: STRENGTH: BACKWARD LUNGES
Goal: Promote balance and all over lower body strength for good base of support.

Explanation:

Stand tall with hands on hips. Lean slightly forward from hips as you reach back with right leg and dip right knee toward floor. Keep feet in alignment and put only right toes on floor…never heel. Shift weight slightly more toward back foot and bring upperbody back to upright position. Return back to start position by pushing through left heel…not toe…and buttocks muscles. Slow and controlled movements. Repeat other side.

Nutrition Tip:
Fruits and vegetables are most nutritious served raw. The best cooking methods for vegetables are quick and use little or no water; these include steaming, blanching, stir-frying, pressure-cooking, and microwaving. If you boil vegetables, leave them whole (with skins on, if possible) or cut them into big pieces.

Experience Good Thoughts:
Ways to reduce stress: Play and do something fun. Breathe deep, long breaths. Enjoy soothing music. And, if you are in a committed relationship, make love often!

Think Golf:
For shots around the green, solid contact is essential. Without it, direction and distance cannot be achieved. Keep the handle of the golf club in front of the clubface as you strike the ball, never behind it. A lead wrist that is bent and a shaft that leans away from the target is a universal error for players. After you are consistently making solid contact, work on swing length, which controls the distance of your shot. Short shots should be equidistant meaning the backswing length and forward swing length are the same.

Make Me Smile:
One of Bob Hope's famous golf jokes — How long have I been playing golf, you ask? I've been playing so-o-o-o long that my handicap is in Roman numerals.

WEDNESDAY

Name: TOWEL: BENT OVER CHEST OPENER
Goal: Increase circulation and blood flow around shoulders, back, and hips; help facilitate more fluid range of motion throughout swing.

Explanation:
Stand with feet hip distance apart. Hold towel at ends with both hands behind back. Arms should be straight. Slightly bend at knees then at waist leaning entire body forward. Hang from the waist with head looking between knees. Arms will follow over the back and head weighted by gravity. Allow arms to hang as far as comfortable. Do not force stretch. Slowly return to standing rolling up one vertebrae at a time. Return to start. Repeat 2-3x.

Nutrition Tip:
Remember that germs grow quickly at room temperature. Keep hot foods hot and cold foods cold. Wash your hands, cooking utensils, and cutting boards frequently. Refrigerate leftovers as soon as they are cool. Better safe than sorry.

Experience Good Thoughts:
"The great pleasure in life is doing what people say you cannot do."
—Walter Bagehot, British Economist

Think Golf:
Did you know that the USGA reserves the right to change the Rules relating to artificial devices and unusual equipment and make or change the interpretations relating to these Rules? A player who is not sure if they are using an item that is acceptable for use by the USGA should consult them about Rule 14-3.

Make Me Smile:
Special golf rules for rednecks: You can move the ball if it's under a car on blocks, but you can't putt until the goat finishes "mowing" the green.

THURSDAY

Name: BIG BALL: WALL SQUATS
Goal: Increase strength and endurance of total lower body.

Explanation:

Stand with feet hip distance apart. Place big ball in center of back between you and wall. Bend knees and squat down to a 90 degree bend of legs. Make sure knees are directly over heels, not toes. Continue to squat 20-30x with control. Variation: Hold squat at bottom with goal being ability to hold 60 seconds.

Nutrition Tip:
When you're craving something sweet, don't try to fight it. Just be careful in choosing the right snack. Eating a handful of dried blueberries or cherries instead of cookies will keep your energy level up and be a healthy snack.

Experience Good Thoughts:
"To insure good health: Eat lightly, breathe deeply, live moderately, cultivate cheerfulness, and maintain an interest in life."

—William Londen

Think Golf:
USGA Rule #17-3 states that the player's ball must not strike a) the flagstick when it is being attended, removed or held up; b) the person attending or holding up the flagstick; or c) the flagstick in the hole, unattended, when the stroke has been made on the putting green. The penalty for breach of this rule is loss of hole in match play and two strokes and the ball must be played as it lies in stroke play.

Make Me Smile:
If your golf swing feels natural, you're probably doing it wrong.

FRIDAY

Name: PILATES: OPEN LEG ROCKER

Goal: Reinforce spinal stability in flexed position while strengthening and compressing abdominals toward pelvis for more connection of muscles of hip region for power.

Explanation:

Balance in seated position with weight behind tailbone and back slightly rounded engaging abdominals tight toward spine. Legs extend in air in a V position with hands placed behind knees. Inhale by deepening the C curve of the spine allowing entire spine to flex and roll backward without touching head to floor. Maintaining shape, exhale rolling forward and return to starting position. Focus will be placed on consistent abdominal engagement throughout entire movement. Do 10 X.

Nutrition Tip:
Here's a great afternoon pick-me-up. Combine applesauce and cinnamon into a cup of low-fat vanilla yogurt. Tastes great and it's a healthy snack. You'll get calcium and a serving of fruit in an easy and delicious combination.

Experience Good Thoughts:
"A good man's words are wise, and he is always fair. He keeps the law of his God in his heart and never departs from it."

—Psalm 37: 30-31

Think Golf:
According to Rule 5-3, a ball is unfit for play if it is visibly cut, cracked or out of shape. A ball is not unfit for play solely because mud or other materials adhere to it, its surface is scratched or its paint is damaged or discolored.

Make Me Smile:
We've all heard that the most important inches in golf are those between the ears; through years of observation, I have noted that the most important inches in golf are actually the ones between your ball and the hole, especially on the fourth putt!

SATURDAY/SUNDAY

GOLFING DAYS ARE GOOD FOR YOUR HEALTH

REFLECTING ON THE PAST WEEK:

What was your basic attitude? Were you a positive thinker or did you need an "attitude adjustment?" Are you having success with eating healthier and doing your exercise program? How do you feel physically? If you went golfing, write down any comments that might be helpful later in improving your game. Remember, that laughter is the best medicine in the face of adversity. Are you seeing the lighter side of life?

The exercise that helped me the most this week was on page:

_____

My nutritional habits this week were:

_____

What made me smile this week?

_____

_____

Looking back at my golf week:
    My Score: _____ What did I do right? _____

_____

_____

    What could I do to improve?

_____

_____

Goals for next week: _____

_____

_____

MONDAY

Name: HEAVY BALL: BACKSWING IN THIRDS

Goal: Promote muscle memory in torso for backswing; overload midsection muscles to increase strength and power during downswing.

Explanation:

Stand in address position holding heavy ball where club would be for golf swing. Inhale to prepare. Exhale and move ball back to 1/3 of golf swing. Inhale returning to address. Exhale moving ball 2/3 of golf swing. Inhale return to address. Exhale moving ball entire golf swing with slight pause at the top. Inhale return to address. Repeat sequence 5 times focusing on keeping head still and mimicking backswing as correct as possible. You will feel the extra weight of ball throughout stabilizing muscles of body. Keep good form.

Nutrition Tip:
Romaine lettuce is an excellent source of the B vitamin folate, a high source of Vitamin A, and a source of zinc and Vitamins C and E.

Experience Good Thoughts:
"In politics, if you want anything said, ask a man. If you want anything done, ask a woman."

—Margaret Thatcher, British Prime Minister

Think Golf:
Do you know when the USGA was formed? The year was 1894 and it was formed by representatives of five U.S. clubs: St. Andrews (Yonkers), Shinnecock Hills, Newport, Chicago, and The Country Club of Brookline (Massachusetts).

Make Me Smile:
It always happens that the people in front of you are playing too slow and the people behind you are playing too fast.

TUESDAY

Name: STRENGTH: PUSHUP WIDE

Goal: Increase base strength of chest and shoulders with focus on shoulder stability; aid in less breakdown at top of swing.

Explanation:

Start in basic pushup position. Whether knees remain down or up, keep a straight line between head, shoulders, spine, hips, and knees. Place hands one hand width wider than shoulders and sternum between thumbs. Keeping spine and abdominals tight, lower body straight down to the floor by bending at elbows and return to straight arms. Repeat 10x for 3 sets. Inhale as you lower down, exhale on the return push back up.

Nutrition Tip:

According to the University of California Wellness Letter, the average American gains about two pounds a year. 3,500 calories equals one pound so two pounds would mean cutting back on 7,000 calories a year. Shouldn't be hard. Small changes in daily intake could easily compensate for those extra calories. Use mayo sparingly; use skim milk instead of whole milk; eat less whole grain cereal in the morning; buy tuna packed in water; cut out soft drinks and drink more water.

Experience Good Thoughts:

"Happiness is a perfume you cannot pour on others without getting a few drops on yourself."

—Ralph Waldo Emerson, Poet

Think Golf:

No funny business allowed. USGA Rule # 14-1 states that the ball must be fairly struck at with the head of the club and must not be pushed, scraped or spooned.

Make Me Smile:

Definition of a "whiff" is a stroke that completely misses the ball. For those of us who have had the unfortunate timing to have experienced this shot, it has been sensitively named a "warm-up swing."

WEDNESDAY

Name: YOGA/STRETCH: REVOLVING SIDE ANGLE

Goal: Improve shoulder turn in backswing and support better posture at address and throughout swing.

Explanation:

Start in lunge position with right foot out in front and left heel off the floor in back. Gravity is centered in middle and right heel. Hands are in prayer position in front of chest. Lean forward and rotate upper body so that left elbow is on outside of right knee. Maximize stretch by pushing left elbow against right knee, belly button pulled into spine, hold for 10 seconds, then switch sides.

Nutrition Tip:

Potassium helps muscles contract, maintains fluid balance, sends nerve impulses, and releases energy from protein, fat and carbohydrates. Great sources of potassium are fruits, vegetables, beans, and fish.

Experience Good Thoughts:

"I do not know what path in life you will take, but I do know this: If, on that path, you do not find a way to serve, you will never be happy."

—Albert Schweitzer, Theologian

Think Golf:

Did you know that a normal player rarely plays a game at his handicap level? It's usually several strokes more than what is shown on a USGA Handicap Index. That's why players often complain, "I wish I could just play what is supposed to be my normal game."

Make Me Smile:

You know it's too cold to play golf when you get dressed to leave the house and you choose your wool visor with furry ear flaps.

THURSDAY

Name: PRE-ROUND WARMUP: SLINKY ARMS

Goal: Loosen up tight joints and small muscles of shoulders, elbows, wrists, hands and fingers before round; prevent injury.

Explanation:

Stand with fingers interlaced together and palms open in front of chest. Flap arms like a wave keeping fingers interlocked. Keep rhythm going 5x one direction then reverse. Elbows will be out wider than shoulders. Perform loosely and without too much control.

Nutrition Tip:

You are not the victim of your metabolism. You are the creator of it! Depriving your body of nutrients can only lead to a metabolic slowdown. Be sure to eat! Think of your body as a furnace. Keep the fire going and growing by providing kindling a little at a time and consistently. Your body will become a food-burning machine!

Experience Good Thoughts:

"Experience is a revelation in the light of which we renounce our errors of youth for those of age." —Ambrose Bierce, Author

Think Golf:

In Stroke Play, Rule 3-2 tells us that every player must hole out. If a competitor fails to hole out at any hole and does not correct his mistake before he makes a stroke on the next teeing ground or, in the case of the last hole of the round, before he leaves the putting green, he is disqualified. So finish up.

Make Me Smile:

An American golfer went to Scotland to play golf at the birthplace of the game. Meeting a Scottish golfer in the clubhouse, he asked if he would like to play a round of golf with him. After a bad tee shot, the American played a "mulligan" which turned out to be an outstanding shot. So trying to find out more about playing in Scotland, he asks him, "What do you call a mulligan here in Scotland?" The Scot replied, "We call it three!"

FRIDAY

Name: PILATES: ROLL UP/ROLL DOWN
Goal: Target core by compressing abdominals while lengthening spine. Help stabilize pelvis through swing.

Explanation:

Lying down, flex feet and feel the lengthening of your legs away from you. Reach arms to sky, but focus on trying to flatten belly button to spine and spine to floor. Lift head and inhale. As you exhale, reach arms toward feet and roll up keeping spine flexed (rounded) and ribs tucked in toward hips. Reach toward feet, then roll back down slowly with control never allowing a stretch between ribcage.

Nutrition Tip:
Stay away from eating trans fats. Trans fats are artery clogging ingredients in foods that must be listed on food labels next year. The FDA notes that trans fat, like saturated fat, raises the risk of heart disease.

Experience Good Thoughts:
"Light is the task where many share the toil."   —Homer

Think Golf:
What is the accepted definition of a "stroke" by the USGA? A stroke is the forward movement of the club made with the intention of striking at and moving the ball, but if a player checks his downswing voluntarily before the clubhead reaches the ball, he has NOT made a stroke.

Make Me Smile:
We hear lots of jokes about people shooting their age, but you know you're a pretty bad player when you shoot your cholesterol level!

SATURDAY/SUNDAY

GOLFING DAYS ARE GOOD FOR YOUR HEALTH

REFLECTING ON THE PAST WEEK:

What was your basic attitude? Were you a positive thinker or did you need an "attitude adjustment?" Are you having success with eating healthier and doing your exercise program? How do you feel physically? If you went golfing, write down any comments that might be helpful later in improving your game. Remember, that laughter is the best medicine in the face of adversity. Are you seeing the lighter side of life?

The exercise that helped me the most this week was on page:

_____

My nutritional habits this week were:

_____

What made me smile this week?

_____

_____

Looking back at my golf week:
  My Score: _____ What did I do right? _____

_____

  What could I do to improve?

_____

_____

Goals for next week: _____

_____

_____

MONDAY

Name: **TOWEL: STANDING HAMSTRING**

Goal: Stretch hamstrings which help to prevent imbalances and tightening of low back muscles resulting in injury; enhance balance.

Explanation:

Stand tall holding ends of towel in both hands. Balance on left foot while lifting right foot and placing it in middle of towel. Stand tall lifting right knee up toward chest. Maintain balance. Slowly extend right leg out straight to parallel with floor while retaining upright posture. Hold for 10 seconds, then repeat with other leg. For more support if needed, lean against wall.

Nutrition Tip:
The Institute of Medicine says that you should not consume more than 1,500 milligrams of sodium per day. The average person eats more than 4,000 mg per day. Watch your salt intake. Too much can contribute to many health problems.

Experience Good Thoughts:
"The successful warrior is the average man, with laser-like focus."

—Bruce Lee, Martial Artist

Think Golf:
A player is said to have "addressed the ball" when he has taken his stance and has placed his club on the ground. (The exception is that when a player in a hazard has taken his stance, it is considered addressing the ball.) If a player has not placed his club on the ground, he has not technically addressed the ball and cannot be penalized under Rule 18-2b.

Make Me Smile:
You know you're deep in the rough when your partner asks if your cart is equipped with 4-wheel drive.

TUESDAY

Name: YOGA/STRETCH: LYING LEG CROSSOVER

Goal: Improves flexibility across back and gluteals for a pain free swing... reducing strain during repeated swings.

Explanation:

Lie on your back with legs straight out in front of you. Raise one leg and bend at the knee to 90 degrees in knee and hip. Cross that leg over extended leg, while opposite shoulder stays on the ground. Feel a slight pull in the back and buttock. Hold and repeat on the other side. Repeat 2x.

Nutrition Tip:
Finding it hard to eat enough fruit in a day? Try carrots dipped in peanut butter, a three-bean salad with low-fat dressing or a sweet potato cut into bite size pieces. Or buy a bag of dried fruit such as apricots, which are soft, sweet and are good for your health.

Experience Good Thoughts:
"Talent is cheaper than table salt. What separates the talented individual from the successful one is a lot of hard work."

—Stephen King, American Writer

Think Golf:
If you hit the ball into a position that makes par almost impossible, don't get upset and lose control. Think about what you need to do to make a bogey. Hit your next shot so that you're back on the fairway, the next onto the green, and with smart planning you have managed to get out of that bad position and end up with a bogey.

Make Me Smile:
"The uglier a man's legs are, the better he plays golf."

—H.G. Wells

WEDNESDAY

Name: STRENGTH: SUPERMAN OPPOSITE ARM/LEG

Goal: Increase strength and endurance of low back musculature and gluteals to help prevent injury.

Explanation:

Similar to regular superman...Lie face down on floor with arms and legs straight out. Inhale. As you exhale lift right arm and left leg as high and as far away from your body as possible. Inhale, release and repeat with other side. Repeat each side 10x.

Nutrition Tip:

Drinks with fruit can help get your five servings of fruit a day. Make a fruit smoothie with non-fat milk, mix unsweetened juice concentrate with gelatin and chill for a healthy jellied snack, or put some unsweetened fruit juice in ice cube trays and add frozen cubes to a glass of water.

Experience Good Thoughts:

"Great things are not done by impulse, but by a series of small things brought together."

—Vincent Van Gogh, Dutch Painter

Think Golf:

Cleanliness is next to Godliness – even in golf! Keep your irons clean. The grooves in the iron create the spin that allows the ball to fly for the proper distance. If the grooves are dirty, you have less of a chance to hit a solid shot that will make it all the way to the green.

Make Me Smile:

Correcting the faults you have developed in your swing can NEVER be treated in just ONE lesson from a professional.

THURSDAY

Name: HEAVY BALL: PUSHUPS W/BOTH HANDS ON BALL
Goal: Promote total body stability and balance while strengthening chest and shoulder girdle for power control with extra focus on triceps.

Explanation:

Place both hands on ball: thumbs facing forward and fingertips aiming downward. Lift into plank position with legs straight and feet together. Chest remains directly over ball. Inhale and bend arms lowering chest toward ball. Exhale and push back up to straight arms keeping body straight and abdominals tight. Goal: 10 repetitions.

Nutrition Tip:
Healthier choices just take a little imagination. Toss your salad with fresh avocado slices and balsamic vinegar or eat some tortilla chips dipped in guacamole instead of potato chips and dip.

Experience Good Thoughts:
"Thousands of candles can be lighted from a single candle, and the life of the candle will not be shortened. Happiness never decreases by being shared."
—The Buddha

Think Golf:
Do your putts often end up short? Try a shorter backstroke and accelerate through impact to a finish where your putter is in the air and facing the hole. Hit through the impact instead of jabbing the ball.

Make Me Smile:
For all wives who play golf with their husbands, just think if your husband was Jack Nicklaus. Barbara Nicklaus was playing the 9-hole Tour Wives Championship with Jack as her caddie. Yes, we know part of a caddie's role is to give advice, but really, 165 tips in 9 holes. She didn't win but he won the award for "Most Advice" given by a husband.

FRIDAY

Name: BIG BALL: STRAIGHT LEG HIP LIFTS
Goal: Engage muscles in back of body – low back, gluteals, hamstrings, calves…used in power production and stability.

Explanation:

Lie on floor with legs straight out and toes pointed just barely on the ball. Abdominals engaged at all times. Squeeze glutes while pushing toes into ball pulsing hips off the floor. Complete 20-25 repetitions maintaining neutral spine.

Nutrition Tip:
Watch your portions when going out to eat. One sure way to eat less is to divide your meal in half as soon as you receive it from the server. Ask for a container and place half of your dinner in the container to take home for the following day. This ensures that you won't overeat when dining out.

Experience Good Thoughts:
"The quality of a leader is reflected in the standards they set for themselves."
—Ray Kroc

Think Golf:
The USGA offers players many benefits but its main purpose is to write and interpret the Rules of Golf. It also provides a National Handicap System, funds turf grass and environmental research, provides financial grants, and maintains equipment standards. It keeps all golfers on the same page.

Make Me Smile:
Everyone warns us about going out on a limb. But if you give it just a little thought you'll find out that's where the fruit is! Try a new shot, a new club, a different course, a different exercise. Who knows what you'll find when you do.

SATURDAY/SUNDAY

GOLFING DAYS ARE GOOD FOR YOUR HEALTH

REFLECTING ON THE PAST WEEK:

What was your basic attitude? Were you a positive thinker or did you need an "attitude adjustment?" Are you having success with eating healthier and doing your exercise program? How do you feel physically? If you went golfing, write down any comments that might be helpful later in improving your game. Remember, that laughter is the best medicine in the face of adversity. Are you seeing the lighter side of life?

The exercise that helped me the most this week was on page:

_____

My nutritional habits this week were:

_____

What made me smile this week?

_____

_____

Looking back at my golf week:
    My Score: _____ What did I do right? _____

_____

_____

    What could I do to improve?

_____

_____

Goals for next week: _____

_____

_____

MONDAY

Name: CARDIO: ROLLERBLADING

Goal: Increase cardiovascular endurance and stamina for the 4+ hours of golf; enhance concentration and focus; improve coordination, balance and rhythm.

Explanation:

Rollerblading is a cardiovascular activity using the whole body. Be careful! Wear a helmet, shin, wrist, and elbow guards always. It is a great way to enhance coordination and strengthen stabilizing muscles of the legs. Try to blade 3x a week for a 30 minute duration. Don't focus on speed. Focus on technique and breath.

Nutrition Tip:
If you drink bottled water, it is recommended to take supplements. Distilled water and bottled water lack necessary minerals. Buying a filter for your faucet is a good alternative. It will remove harmful chemicals and microorganisms but will allow healthful minerals to pass.

Experience Good Thoughts:
"Good health and good sense are two of life's greatest blessings."

—Publius Syrus

Think Golf:
How long can a player search for his ball? The player can look for his ball for five minutes before having to go back to play another ball. But don't take all that time if at all possible. Remember to be a courteous player.

Make Me Smile:
"Did you know that I'm a scratch golfer?" said the player to her new friend. "How do you do that?" her friend asked. "I mark down my good scores, and I scratch off the bad ones."

TUESDAY

Name: PRE-ROUND WARMUP: LUNGE W/CART

Goal: Prepare body for round; stretch and open up hip flexors, hamstrings, inner thighs, and pelvis for unhindered swing.

Explanation:

Stand approximately 3 feet away from cart. Swing right foot up on cart so that right knee is higher than hip. Gently lean body forward placing more weight on right foot. Lift up on back toe to enhance stretch. Keep chest lifted pushing left hip forward to open hip flexors. Pause then return to start. Repeat 5x each leg.

Nutrition Tip:

Trying to lose weight? Do not go below 1,200 calories a day or try to lose more than 1-2 pounds a week. Try cutting 250 calories a day from your diet and burn off 250 more with exercise. Exercising 30 minutes a day is needed to maintain good health.

Experience Good Thoughts:

"Our greatest battles are that with our own minds."

—Jameson Frank

Think Golf:

The upper torso (pectorals, latissimus dorsi, and deltoids) produces the actual swing action and plays a critical role in club head speed.

Make Me Smile:

Did you hear about the golfer who told his psychiatrist he thought he was a dog? The doctor asked him to sit down and tell him more about it. The golfer answered that he couldn't – he wasn't allowed on the furniture. "I think this is why I chase a ball around outside so much too," he added.

WEDNESDAY

Name: YOGA/STRETCH: DANCER QUAD STRETCH
Goal: Promote balance while stretching hip flexors and quadriceps, which are constantly flexed throughout swing.

Explanation:

Stand and kick left foot back into left hand. You may use your golf club for support in right hand. Press the knee back and hip forward of left leg to promote greater stretch and pull left heel to left buttock. Pull belly button in throughout stretch. Hold 10 seconds. Repeat other leg.

Nutrition Tip:
Beverages add more calories than you think, especially non-diet sodas and alcoholic drinks. By watching what you drink and how often, you can lessen your calorie intake substantially.

Experience Good Thoughts:
"All comes by the body. Only health puts one in rapport with the universe."
—Walt Whitman

Think Golf:
A helpful hint about keeping the clubhead in front of your hands during your backswing — pull the club with your right hand. That will force the club to move correctly during the backswing.

Make Me Smile:
It seems that I always hit the ball really good. It just lands in places that are really bad.

THURSDAY

Name: PILATES: TEASER II
Goal: Increase complete core stabilization, trunk control and balance so crucial for generating clubhead speed while maintaining balance.

Explanation:

Lie on back with spine imprinted into floor and legs straight to ceiling pointed and arms long overhead. Inhale slide shoulder blades down back and reach arms toward ceiling then sequentially roll spine off mat one vertebrae at a time to balance just behind sit bones. Arms stay by ears. As you exhale, maintain torso in place while lowering straight legs down to floor. Inhale return legs to "V" position. Exhale and roll spine down to mat through imprint and arms stay by ears. Repeat 5x.

Nutrition Tip:
Grapes are considered one of the most medicinal fruits. No wonder they were known as the fruit of the kings. They have an impressive record with tumor reduction, they purify the blood, invigorate the immune system, and promote the action of the bowel. They also clean the liver and aid in kidney function. They have a high content of iron so they are good for your blood too. Grapes anyone?

Experience Good Thoughts:
"Persistent people begin their success where others end in failure."
—Edward Eggleston, Writer & Historian

Think Golf:
Simple but important safety Rules to follow: Always be sure the players in front are out of range before hitting. That is far better than having to yell "fore" because you put another player in danger.

Make Me Smile:
My husband has a hard time breaking par when he plays golf. But he has managed to break his putter and a window in the clubhouse.

FRIDAY

Name: **STRENGTH: PUSHUP NARROW**

Goal: Increase base strength of chest and shoulders with focus on shoulder stability aid in less breakdown at top of swing.

Explanation:

Start in basic pushup position. Whether knees remain down or up, there should be a straight line between head, shoulders, spine, hips, and knees. Place hands directly under chest with index fingers and thumbs touching in the shape of a diamond. Keeping spine and abdominals tight, lower body straight down to the floor by bending at elbows and return to straight arms. Repeat 10x for 3 sets. Inhale as you lower down, exhale on the return push back up.

Nutrition Tip:

Here's rule-of-thumb formulas for the amount of calories you need in a day. This calculation takes into account age, activity level and gender.

Males: Sedentary — Body weight X 13; Moderate activity — Body weight X 15;
Active lifestyle — Body weight X 17.

Females: Sedentary — Body weight X 12; Moderate activity — Body weight X 14;
Active lifestyle — Body weight X 16.

Experience Good Thoughts:

"All results no matter how magnificent are infinitesimal when compared to future possibility."
—James A. Ray

Think Golf:

The National Golf Foundation reports that only 22 percent of all golfers regularly score better than 90 for 18 holes on a regulation length course. For women golfers, it is just 7 percent and for men it is 25 percent.

Make Me Smile:

Sometimes men complain that women ask too many questions when they go golfing with them — like "Why did you hit that ball into the sand? I thought you were aiming for the green." Seems like a valid question to me!

SATURDAY/SUNDAY

GOLFING DAYS ARE GOOD FOR YOUR HEALTH

REFLECTING ON THE PAST WEEK:

What was your basic attitude? Were you a positive thinker or did you need an "attitude adjustment?" Are you having success with eating healthier and doing your exercise program? How do you feel physically? If you went golfing, write down any comments that might be helpful later in improving your game. Remember, that laughter is the best medicine in the face of adversity. Are you seeing the lighter side of life?

The exercise that helped me the most this week was on page:

My nutritional habits this week were:

What made me smile this week?

Looking back at my golf week:
    My Score: _____ What did I do right? _____

    What could I do to improve?

Goals for next week: _____

MONDAY

Name: HEAVY BALL: DIAGONAL WOODCHOP

Goal: Help to improve timing, rhythm, and form utilizing all muscles of body working together in synchronicity.

Explanation:

Stand with feet slightly wider than hips with ball in hands reaching up toward the right. Lower the ball diagonally across the front of body and touch ball to floor on the outside of the left foot. Bending should occur in ankles, knees, and hips vs. just back. Return back up to reaching over right shoulder. Repeat 10x same side then switch sides. Keep good form. Action imitates picking object off floor on one side and putting up onto shelf on opposite side.

Nutrition Tip:

Eat at a slower pace. It takes several minutes for your brain to realize that your stomach is full so take a break, chat a little, and be sure you give your brain enough time to catch up with your eating.

Experience Good Thoughts:

"Hatred paralyzes life; love releases it. Hatred confuses life; love harmonizes it. Hatred darkens life; love illuminates it."

—Martin Luther King, Jr.

Think Golf:

Etiquette to remember: ALWAYS mark your ball when on the green. Even when your ball is not physically in the way of another player's line, it may be visually in the way. Mark it before they have to ask.

Make Me Smile:

Do you ever get the feeling that your caddie might not be on your side? If you hear a remark like 'Well I just lost 20 bucks' after you sink a 30 foot birdie putt, you know.

TUESDAY

Name: DYNAMIC STRETCH: STATIC LUNGE
Goal: Promote balance and strengthen lower body musculature for good solid base throughout swing.

Explanation:

Stand with both feet together. Reach right foot back about 3-4 feet so legs are in a staggered stance. Always keep back heel lifted and weight on toe. Weight should be centered evenly between both feet. Place hands on hips or out to sides for balance. Keep eyeline and chin lifted. Lower back knee down toward floor then push back up using the front heel and gluteal. Repeat dipping back knee down and up 10x. Switch to other side.

Nutrition Tip:
Try replacements for high calorie foods that taste good and satisfy your cravings but don't have as many calories. Examples include eating frozen yogurt instead of ice cream, using low fat sour cream and salad dressings. Don't deny yourself the good tastes but find substitutes that will allow you to eat less calories with the same amount of pleasure.

Experience Good Thoughts:
"Health is the greatest gift, contentment the greatest wealth, faithfulness the best relationship."

—The Buddha

Think Golf:
Women take more golf lessons than men do. The National Golf Foundation reports that 35% of female golfers compared with only 14% of male golfers are currently taking lessons.

Make Me Smile:
Ever notice how an avid golfer gives directions? It sounds something like this, "Sure, I can give you directions to the shopping center. It's about a par 4 away from here straight through the next light."

WEDNESDAY

Name: PRE-ROUND WARMUP: WRIST ROLLS

Goal: Loosen up tight joints and small muscles of elbows, wrists, hands and fingers before round; prevent injury.

Explanation:

Stand with hands in front of chest, bent arms and backs of hands touching. Roll the wrists one way and notice how backs of hands and base of palms roll around each other constantly touching. Then reverse the circle feeling a slight warmth and stretch to the wrist and forearm area. Repeat rolls 10x each direction. Be careful not to force the stretch or press too hard.

Nutrition Tip:
White bread expands your waist! Researchers at Tufts University found that people who ate the most white bread daily (2-4 slices) saw their waistlines widen three times as much as people who did not. This was true even when the same amount of calories was consumed. Why? Because simple carbs like white bread break down quickly and produce high levels of blood sugar. Your body can't use all of it at once so it stores it as fat. Choose 100% whole wheat bread, which breaks down into blood sugar slowly.

Experience Good Thoughts:
There is tremendous happiness in making others happy, despite our own situations. Shared grief is half the sorrow, but happiness when shared, is doubled. If you want to feel rich, just count all the things you have that money can't buy. "Today is a gift, that's why it is called the present."

Think Golf:
Of the 26 million golfers in the United States, only 20 percent maintain a handicap. The average handicap is 19-20.

Make Me Smile:
At my last lesson the pro explained the different shots. "If it goes right," he said, "it's called a slice. If it goes left, it's a hook." "And, for you," he added, "if it goes straight, it's a miracle!"

THURSDAY

Name: YOGA/STRETCH: KNEELING ONE ARM ROTATION
Goal: Stretch spine from head to tail bone as well as hip shifting mobility; open chest muscles to aid in turn.

Explanation:

Similar to Yoga Spread Out- Start kneeling on all fours. Hands are shoulder width apart, knees are hip width apart. Place left hand directly under face and rotate right arm up toward sky. Eyes follow hand and back will rotate along with hips shifting at end of movement to allow more range of motion. Repeat 5 times on same side then repeat. Exhale on rotation upwards.

Nutrition Tip:
It's been proven that one or two drinks a day may increase the "good" cholesterol (HDL) in your body and have cognitive benefits as well. Women especially seem to lower their risk of experiencing problems with their mental abilities later in life when they drink low levels of alcohol. But don't overdo it. Drinking more than a couple can lead to high blood pressure and contribute to heart disease and strokes. Don't try to rationalize more alcohol because of its health benefits because the opposite holds true when a person drinks too much.

Experience Good Thoughts:
People will forget what you said . . .
People will forget what you did . . .
But people will NEVER forget how you made them feel.

Think Golf:
The most popular states for golf travel are Florida, North Carolina, California and Arizona. Golfers spend over $26 billion on golf travel, most of which goes to transportation, hotel and eating.

Make Me Smile:
Bounces can be explained in two ways. They are either unfair or they bounced just the way you meant it to go.

FRIDAY

Name: PILATES: TEASER I

Goal: Increase complete core stabilization, trunk control and balance so crucial for generating clubhead speed while maintaining balance.

Explanation:

Lie on back with spine imprinted into floor and legs bent with feet flat on floor hip distance apart and arms overhead. Inhale slide shoulder blades down back and reach arms toward ceiling. Exhale flexing upper spine and rolling up to balanced position right behind sit bones. Arms point diagonally toward toes sitting in a "V" position. Inhale bring arms overhead without moving ribcage. Exhale initiate movement rolling hipbones back down to floor followed sequentially by spine to beginning. Repeat 5x.

Nutrition Tip:

Don't skip your salad before dinner. People who start their dinners with a low-calorie green salad eat less overall during their meals. Keep the salad to about 100 calories by using alternatives for salad dressing such as lemon juice or vinegar mixed with a small amount of olive oil. It's a healthier combination and will curb your appetite.

Experience Good Thoughts:

"The indispensable first step to getting the things you want out of life is this: decide what you want."
—Ben Stein

Think Golf:

Relaxing your arms and letting them hang down in front of you before addressing the ball is part of a pre-shot routine that will help to maintain consistent and solid shots.

Make Me Smile:

I guess I'll never be a good golfer. Experience in other sports has shown me that I'm just not meant to be good at aiming. The last time I went fishing, I missed the lake when I tried to cast the line into the water.

SATURDAY/SUNDAY

GOLFING DAYS ARE GOOD FOR YOUR HEALTH

REFLECTING ON THE PAST WEEK:

What was your basic attitude? Were you a positive thinker or did you need an "attitude adjustment?" Are you having success with eating healthier and doing your exercise program? How do you feel physically? If you went golfing, write down any comments that might be helpful later in improving your game. Remember, that laughter is the best medicine in the face of adversity. Are you seeing the lighter side of life?

The exercise that helped me the most this week was on page:

_____

My nutritional habits this week were:

_____

What made me smile this week?

_____

_____

Looking back at my golf week:
      My Score: _____ What did I do right? _____

_____

      What could I do to improve?

_____

_____

Goals for next week: _____

_____

MONDAY

Name: TOWEL: LYING HAMSTRING
Goal: Stretch hamstrings, which help to prevent imbalances and tightening of low back muscles resulting in injury.

Explanation:

Lie on back with legs outstretched. Hold onto ends of towel with both hands. Bend right leg into chest and wrap towel around bottom of lifted foot. Straighten right leg toward ceiling feeling a stretch down entire back of leg. Toes will flex toward body pushing heel toward sky. Pause slightly then return to bent. Repeat 5 times with same leg then switch. Do not force a stretch. Focus on exhaling during the exertion of the stretch.

Nutrition Tip:
Selenium is a trace mineral that the body requires in small amounts. Brazil nuts, tuna, eggs, wheat germ, turkey and baked ham are all good sources of selenium. But be careful to not overdo it. Most people get enough of this mineral through food and do not need a supplement. Too much selenium can be toxic.

Experience Good Thoughts:
"Far and away the best prize that life has to offer is the chance to work hard at work worth doing."

—Theodore Roosevelt, 26th President

Think Golf:
Have you ever hit the ball only to have it go violently to the right? That common shot is called a "shank" and usually happens when a player stands too close to the ball or reaches forward through impact.

Make Me Smile:
A novice golfer goes out with his friend and after 9 holes he asked his friend, "Do you think I'm the worst golfer you've ever played with?" "No," his friend replied, "but I have seen places today that I didn't know were even on this course!"

TUESDAY

Name: HEAVY BALL: PUSHUP W/CLOCK WALK

Goal: Promote total body stability and balance while strengthening chest and shoulder girdle for power and control during swing.

Explanation:

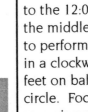

Start in plank position with feet on top of ball. Pretend body is a hand of a clock and is pointing to the 12:00 with ball and feet in the middle of clockface. Goal is to perform 12 pushups moving in a clockwise position keeping feet on ball finishing a complete circle. Focus on balance and engaging abdominals through-out movement. One rotation is enough!

Nutrition Tip:
Listen up, cherry lovers. Not only do cherries taste great but research has also shown that Montmorency tart cherries may relieve the pain of arthritis and gout and help fight cancer and heart disease. They contain those incredibly healthful, antioxidants.

Experience Good Thoughts:
"Wise men talk because they have something to say; fools talk because they have to say something."

—Plato

Think Golf:
If you hit the "sweet spot" on the clubface, you are most assuredly going to hit a ball that flies straight, high and far. The sweet spot is the center of the clubface.

Make Me Smile:
A bum asked a passerby for $2.00. The man asked if he would buy alcohol with it. The bum assures him he wouldn't. The man asked if he was a gambler. The bum said, "Absolutely not, sir." Finally, the man asked if he would spend the money on green fees. The bum said that he didn't even play golf. Then the man said to the bum, "Will you please come home with me so I can show my wife what happens to a man who doesn't drink, gamble, or play golf?"

WEDNESDAY

Name: YOGA/STRETCH: HALF MOON

Goal: Promote balance while stretching hamstrings and enhancing focus on a task.

Explanation:

Bend over and place right hand approximately one foot in front of right foot. Shift your weight to the right leg. Lift your left leg and left arm off floor and reach toward sky with both. Keep gaze toward right hand. Try to straighten all 4 limbs. Hold for 10 seconds with focus on slow breathing.

Nutrition Tip:

Store bananas at room temperature. If you want them to ripen faster, place them in the sun. Never store bananas in the refrigerator because they will decay from the inside. And they won't ripen but will turn black in the refrigerator.

Experience Good Thoughts:

"We tend to get what we expect."

—Norman Vincent Peale

Think Golf:

Although we sometimes get anxious to get the putting started, never drop or slam the flagstick on the green. The green surface is delicate and can easily dent. Gently place it on or near the fringe, out of view, if possible.

Make Me Smile:

Always feel good about how your game is going. Remember that no matter how bad you are playing, it is always possible to play worse.

THURSDAY

Name: CARDIO: CYCLING

Goal: Increase cardiovascular endurance and stamina for the 4+ hours of golf; enhance concentration and focus; improve coordination, balance and rhythm.

Explanation:

Bicycle riding is a safe way to increase cardiovascular health without impact to the joints of the ankles, knees, hips, and spine. Know how to ride a bike? Just ride! Wear a helmet and take some water. Enjoy the scenery! Try to ride a bike 3x a week for 30 minute duration.

Nutrition Tip:
Apricots, mangoes, carrots, pineapples and tomatoes are loaded with Vitamin A. So what's Vitamin A good for? Healthy skin and hair and Vitamin A is necessary for proper bone growth and tooth development.

Experience Good Thoughts:
"The path to success is to take massive, determined action."
—Anthony Robbins, Author & Speaker

Think Golf:
If playing in a mixed group, don't assume the man should always drive the cart. Any of the host players should drive the cart because they know the layout of the course better. Having a member of the club, whether a man or a woman, drive the cart helps to move play along at a faster pace.

Make Me Smile:
They say everything happens in threes. So when you shoot four bad shots in a row, be careful about thinking your next shot will be great. It could be that you have actually just begun a new group of three.

FRIDAY

Name: BIG BALL: LATERAL SIDE BEND W/LET GO

Goal: Increase ability to side bend with control and balance.

Explanation:

Stand with feet hip distance apart and ball overhead. Maintain even amount of weight in both heels. Lean to one side without shifting hips. Take top arm away for a moment to add a challenge to shoulders and forearms. Return arm to ball and stand back to center. Repeat each side 5x. Inhale on the way down, exhale on return to center.

Nutrition Tip:
Pineapples, fresh kiwi, and papaya contain a protein-splitting enzyme. This substance makes the fruit easy to digest and when cooked with meat it makes it more tender. If the fruit is cooked like all canned and other processed fruit, this enzyme is no longer active. So buy fresh fruits to preserve the benefits of this specialized enzyme.

Experience Good Thoughts:
"It is a fine thing to have ability, but the ability to discover ability in others is the true test."

—Elbert Hubbard, Author & Publisher

Think Golf:
The old cliché, "Drive for show, putt for dough" came about because players discovered the extreme importance of accurate putting. Practicing distance and direction in your putts can cut several strokes off your score.

Make Me Smile:
If ranting and raving after a bad shot had any effect on the direction or distance of a ball, most players would be much better at the game.

SATURDAY/SUNDAY

GOLFING DAYS ARE GOOD FOR YOUR HEALTH

REFLECTING ON THE PAST WEEK:

What was your basic attitude? Were you a positive thinker or did you need an "attitude adjustment?" Are you having success with eating healthier and doing your exercise program? How do you feel physically? If you went golfing, write down any comments that might be helpful later in improving your game. Remember, that laughter is the best medicine in the face of adversity. Are you seeing the lighter side of life?

The exercise that helped me the most this week was on page:

_____

My nutritional habits this week were:

_____

What made me smile this week?

_____

_____

Looking back at my golf week:
        My Score: _____ What did I do right? _____

_____

_____

        What could I do to improve?

_____

_____

Goals for next week: _____

_____

_____

MONDAY

Name: PILATES: TWIST (WINDMILL)

Goal: Strengthen entire shoulder girdle, core, hips, and inner/outer thigh muscles aiding in stability consistency throughout swing.

Explanation:

Start in pushup plank position with feet and hands hip distance apart. Inhale to prepare. As you exhale, turn feet onto sides with toes pointing right. Lift up right arm in the air straight to sky. Balance is centered on left hand and between both feet. Pause. Inhale return to center. Repeat each side 8x with control. Focus on maintaining alignment through spine, hips and legs.

Nutrition Tip:

Sweet potatoes are a good source of protein, fiber, beta carotene, Vitamin C, folate and calcium. Contrary to their name, sweet potatoes are not really potatoes. They are roots. Though white potatoes contain much more niacin, sweet potatoes are overall more nutritious. Store sweet potatoes in a cool, dry pantry not in the refrigerator, where they can lose their taste.

Experience Good Thoughts:

"Discipline is the foundation upon which all success is built. Lack of discipline inevitably leads to failure."

—Jim Rohn, American Businessman & Author

Think Golf:

Practice turning by placing a club behind your neck and make slow turns from one side to the other for more flexibility. This will help you in your swing to make a full shoulder turn. When you are finishing your swing, let the natural motion of your follow-through bring you to a position where your right shoulder is pointing at your target.

Make Me Smile:

It becomes much easier to make a 30-foot putt when you're already on your 8th shot!

TUESDAY

Name: HEAVY BALL: FORWARD LUNGE W/ ROTATION

Goal: Lower body strength with spinal stability and rotational core strength.

Explanation:

Stand with feet together and ball in bent arms in front of chest. Lunge right foot forward dipping left knee towards floor. Outstretch arms forward as you step forward. While pausing at bottom, rotate arms, ball, and torso together to the right. Return ball back to front and push off front foot back to start position. Ball then comes back into chest. Alternate lunging legs 20x focusing on correct form.

Nutrition Tip:
Sunflower seeds are a natural source of Vitamin E and linoleic acid. Low Vitamin E levels are associated with angina. Increasing linoleic acid decreases both total and LDL cholesterol. Sunflower seeds have also been used in the form of tea to remove mucus accumulation and to cure prostate problems.

Experience Good Thoughts:
"Education is the ability to listen to almost anything without losing your temper or your self-confidence."

—Robert Frost

Think Golf:
A low score is what golf is all about. So when you play, use the clubs that work best for you. Don't worry about what you should use from the tee or from the rough. If you want to use an iron from the tee and feel more comfortable swinging it, then do it. The goal is to get the lowest score possible playing by the rules.

Make Me Smile:
What common characteristic in scoring proves that golf is really a child's game? Answer: Golfers and young children can't count past 5.

WEDNESDAY

Name: PRE-ROUND WARMUP: SQUAT W/CLUB

Goal: Prepare body for round; decrease risk of injury by loosening up muscles in low back, hips, and legs.

Explanation:

Stand with feet hip distance apart holding ends of club in both hands with arms straight in front of chest. Inhale as you sit back into a squat position keeping weight mostly in heels and maintaining spine angle. Exhale squeeze through gluteals and back of legs pushing back to standing start position. Club remains in front of body and does not drop. Complete 10 repetitions.

Nutrition Tip:

Although it is high in fats and sugar, chocolate also boasts heart-healthy flavonoids. Flavonoids are protective antioxidants, and early research indicates that cocoa with flavonoids can help increase blood flow in the brain and the extremities. Chocolate has chemicals like those in red wine and green tea that help improve circulation and cut blood pressure.

Experience Good Thoughts:

"The best portion of a good man's life: his little, nameless, unremembered acts of kindness and love."

—William Wordsworth

Think Golf:

It is usually better to keep the pin in the cup when you are hitting from a little off the green, especially if it is a downhill shot. The pin will act as a stop and will be of help more times than not. Leaving the pin in may even stop your ball near the hole instead of letting the ball roll past quickly.

Make Me Smile:

If golf is a scientific game with principles of physics and mathematics influencing every shot, then hitting a tree or landing in a water hazard is simply bad luck.

THURSDAY

Name: HEAVY BALL: PLANK W/FEET ON BALL

Goal: Promote total body stability and balance.

Explanation:

Place both hands directly under shoulders in pushup position and place feet on top of ball. Feet may be pointed with tops of feet resting on ball or flexed balanced on toes. Maintain egular breathing engaging chest and entire midsection. Goal is to be able to hold position for 30 seconds. Extra challenge: lift one foot slightly off ball.

Nutrition Tip:
Lemons have several health benefits such as: they are antiseptic; they are one of the most highly alkalinizing foods; they destroy microbes and create germ invulnerability; they are good at retaining calcium in the body; and they are soothing for sore throats. They may be sour in taste but they are sweet for the body.

Experience Good Thoughts:
"There are three ways to get something done: do it yourself, hire someone to do it, or ask your kids NOT to do it."

—Malcolm L. Kushner

Think Golf:
Flexibility is key to a better swing. Try not to straighten your right leg as you turn back. Keep your right knee slightly bended throughout the swing to give you more support as you turn back.

Make Me Smile:
You can tell you've been golfing too much when you feel the need to mark everything you pick up on the floor.

FRIDAY

Name: YOGA/STRETCH: HALF WALL STRETCH
Goal: Lengthen spine; stretch shoulders, hamstrings, and calves.

Explanation:

Place your hands on a wall, shoulder width apart at shoulder height. Step back until your arms are completely straight keeping your feet directly under your hips. Keep your back straight as you bend forward allowing your head to drop below your elbows. Take several breaths then walk toward the wall to release the pose.

Nutrition Tip:

A little stiff in the joints? Glucosamine Sulfate is a natural compound formed within the body that plays a role in proper formation of cartilage. Because of this, it is sold as a supplement to decrease the pain associated with osteoarthritis. Studies exist showing that Glucosamine is effective in alleviating pain in the majority of people with this disease. However, the time it takes to work differs from immediate to 6 months.

Experience Good Thoughts:

"It's easy to make a buck. It's a lot tougher to make a difference."

—Tom Brokaw

Think Golf:

Today with water conservation as an important issue in many areas, golf courses are a prime target for criticism. So when you wake up in the morning and see it raining, you can complain because the weather is rainy or you can be thankful that the fairways are getting watered for free!

Make Me Smile:

Out of the mouths of babes! A bedtime prayer: Dear God, Is it true that my daddy won't go to Heaven if he uses his golf words in the house?

SATURDAY/SUNDAY

GOLFING DAYS ARE GOOD FOR YOUR HEALTH

REFLECTING ON THE PAST WEEK:

What was your basic attitude? Were you a positive thinker or did you need an "attitude adjustment?" Are you having success with eating healthier and doing your exercise program? How do you feel physically? If you went golfing, write down any comments that might be helpful later in improving your game. Remember, that laughter is the best medicine in the face of adversity. Are you seeing the lighter side of life?

The exercise that helped me the most this week was on page:

_____

My nutritional habits this week were:

_____

What made me smile this week?

_____

_____

Looking back at my golf week:
    My Score: _____ What did I do right? _____

_____

_____

    What could I do to improve?

_____

_____

Goals for next week: _____

_____

_____

MONDAY

Name: DB STRENGTH: DUMBBELL BICEP HAMMER CURL

Goal: Strengthen arm muscles for endurance and club control.

Explanation:

Stand tall with feet hip distance apart. Hold a 5-10-15lb dumbbell in each hand with arms straight to sides with palms facing inward. Curl dumbbells up to chest/shoulder area keeping torso erect. Lower dumbbells to starting position. Repeat 10-15 repetitions in sets of 3. at a controlled speed. Do not sway body.

Nutrition Tip:

Adding grapefruit to your daily diet may help you to lose more weight. Scientists believe this is due to the fruit's ability to lower insulin levels, which results in the body processing energy more efficiently.

Experience Good Thoughts:

"It is the peculiar quality of a fool to perceive the faults of others and to forget his own."

—Cicero, Roman Orator

Think Golf:

A player may not use the handle of a putter to knock the ball into the hole or to push it in billiards style. The ball must be struck with the clubhead or the player receives a penalty. USGA Rule #14

Make Me Smile:

"If there's a golf course in heaven I hope it's like Augusta National. I just don't want an early tee time!"

—Gary Player

TUESDAY

Name: BIG BALL: SEATED HIP TILTS
Goal: Increase muscle control of midsection and hips with focus on balance.

Explanation:

Sit on ball with feet hip distance apart and directly under knees. Place hands on ribcage with thumbs facing up to help stabilize and ensure no movement of upper body. Find "neutral spine" and placement of hips. Inhale. Exhale and pull belly button into spine which tilts hip bones backwards. Inhale tilt hips forward. Repeat F & B 20x. Using muscles on side of torso directly under ribcage, tilt hips right and left repeating 20x. Use control of breath and muscles to control body, not momentum.

Nutrition Tip:
To help stabilize your blood sugar, instead of just eating an apple, slice it and dip it into peanut butter or you can put it on top of a veggie burger for zip in flavor! Always think — carb-protein-fat!

Experience Good Thoughts:
"The less you open your heart to others, the more your heart suffers."
—Deepak Chopra, M.D. & Author

Think Golf:
Golf has been played almost everywhere — even on the moon. During his 1971 lunar mission, astronaut Alan Shepard shot a golf ball several hundred yards across the surface of the moon using a 6 iron. Nearly the whole world was watching.

Make Me Smile:
"Tom, do you think my game is getting better?" asked his novice golfer wife looking for moral support. Trying to be tactful, he replies, "It sure is, honey! You're missing the ball much closer than before."

WEDNESDAY

Name: YOGA/STRETCH: TRIANGLE
Goal: Challenge side-bending and flexibility of hamstrings simultaneously, thus reducing strain of low back during swing.

Explanation:

Stand tall with feet a lot wider than hip distance apart. Turn right foot to right. Arms out to sides parallel with floor. Inhale and reach right arm out over right foot bending at the waist and reaching hand to foot. Allow right hand to rest on right ankle while left arm reaches toward the sky. Turn head to look at left arm. Squeeze all muscles tight while still lengthening through joints. Hold for approximately 10 seconds. Switch sides.

Nutrition Tip:
Did you know that ONE glass of water stopped midnight hunger pangs for almost 100% of the dieters in a University of Washington study. So, if you're one of the thousands of people who wake up at night and get something to eat or drink, try drinking a glass of water before you go to bed.

Experience Good Thoughts:
"As irrigators lead water where they want, as archers make their arrows straight, as carpenters carve wood, the wise shape their minds."

—The Buddha

Think Golf:
A good sand wedge shot never strikes the ball directly. It should slice into the sand just under the ball. This throws up a dynamic spray of sand and lofts the ball onto the green in a graceful arch.

Make Me Smile:
Tip for Beginning Golfers: When someone asks about your handicap, don't pull out your glass eye.

THURSDAY

Name: DYNAMIC STRETCH: DIAGONAL HAND/TOE REACH

Goal: Stability and strength of spine musculature while arms and legs are moving. Flexibility of hamstrings and shoulders.

Explanation:

Stand with feet together and arms close to ears straight overhead. While maintaining straight spine, kick right leg out in front while reaching down toward toe with left arm. Alternate sides 10x. It is important to keep erect posture and belly button pulled into spine.

Nutrition Tip:
Skipping meals and then consuming sugar can possibly cause hypoglycemia, a blood sugar imbalance whose symptoms include headaches, dizziness, anxiety, trembling and irritability. Sudden changes in blood sugar levels can also trigger hunger — leading to overeating.

Experience Good Thoughts:
"There are only two lasting bequests we can give our children . . . one is roots, the other wings."

—Stephen Covey

Think Golf:
Annika Sorenstam was the source of unending media attention when she played in the 2003 Colonial, an annual PGA event, against male professionals. Sorenstam played a great game, missing the cut by only 4 strokes and showing herself to be a competent and polished player.

Make Me Smile:
"Don't get your knickers in a knot; nothing is solved, and it just makes you walk funny."

—Kathryn Carpenter

FRIDAY

Name: PRE-ROUND WARMUP: RUNNER'S LUNGE/STRETCH

Goal: Elongate hip and hip flexors to reduce tightness while in repeated address position.

Explanation:

Begin kneeling on all fours. Step your left foot forward between your hands. Left ankle/knee/hip will form a 90 degree angle. Curl toes of back foot under pushing heel away from body. Lean body forward edging right thigh toward floor. Advanced: Put both elbows on floor inside of left foot. Repeat with right leg.

Nutrition Tip:
Is chicken soup really good for a cold? Researchers say the Vitamin B6 and protein in chicken can help boost the immune system. When you add carrots, diced tomatoes, and leafy greens you also get beta-carotene and Vitamin C. All good for your health.

Experience Good Thoughts:
"The virtue of man ought to be measured, not by his extraordinary exertions, but by his everyday conduct."

—Blaise Pascal, French Scientist

Think Golf:
A good golf swing requires follow-through since this ensures maximum acceleration of the clubface at impact. However, overemphasizing the follow-through may cause you to open the clubface and slice the shot. Keep in mind that there is nothing you can do to influence the flight of the ball once you have struck it.

Make Me Smile:
The fun way to stay healthy — Walk to the liquor store (exercise), Put lime in your Corona (fruit), add celery to your Bloody Mary (veggies), drink on the patio (fresh air), feel good, tell jokes and laugh (eliminate stress) and then pass out (rest)!

SATURDAY/SUNDAY

GOLFING DAYS ARE GOOD FOR YOUR HEALTH

REFLECTING ON THE PAST WEEK:

What was your basic attitude? Were you a positive thinker or did you need an "attitude adjustment?" Are you having success with eating healthier and doing your exercise program? How do you feel physically? If you went golfing, write down any comments that might be helpful later in improving your game. Remember, that laughter is the best medicine in the face of adversity. Are you seeing the lighter side of life?

The exercise that helped me the most this week was on page:

_____

My nutritional habits this week were:

_____

What made me smile this week?

_____

_____

Looking back at my golf week:
　　　My Score: _____ What did I do right? _____

_____

_____

　　　What could I do to improve?

_____

_____

Goals for next week: _____

_____

_____

MONDAY

Name: YOGA/STRETCH: LYING PIGEON
Goal: Open and increase range of motion in low back, hips, and groin allowing for maximal power in swing and less risk of injury.

Explanation:

Lie on your back with knees bent and feet flat on floor. Cross right ankle over left knee pointing right knee out to side. Reach hands around left thigh and pull legs off floor and knees toward chest. Relax the head. For added stretch, head may be lifted reaching chin toward legs with control. Hold 10 seconds and switch sides..

Nutrition Tip:
Apples are good for so many different things. Did you know that the tannins in apple juice are believed to help keep your gums healthy? Apples are also know to lower cholesterol, improve bowel function, and reduce risk of stroke, prostate cancer, type II diabetes and asthma.

Experience Good Thoughts:
"In the long run, we shape our lives, and we shape ourselves. The process never ends until we die. And the choices we make are ultimately our responsibility."
—Eleanor Roosevelt, Former First Lady

Think Golf:
Since there was no machinery available to cut fairways and greens, many early golf courses in Scotland and England relied on rabbits to keep the grass short. The rabbits did such a great job that some courses kept this way of maintenance long into the 20th century.

Make Me Smile:
We know we should all get more exercise but sometimes we just don't have enough time. The good news is there are some exercises you might already be doing, such as bending over backwards, jumping on the bandwagon, running around in circles, and even possibly climbing the ladder of success.

TUESDAY

Name: PILATES: HALF ROLL BACK

Goal: Target control of the abdominals and hip flexors throughout slower movement while maintaining spine angle in flexed position.

Explanation:

Sit tall with knees bent, legs together and feet flat on mat. Arms are reaching overhead. Inhale to prepare. Exhale and roll back behind tail bone starting with pelvis. Roll back only as far as abdominals can stay activated with feet still flat on floor. Spine will be rounded with chin down. Inhale and roll back up to seated starting position. Complete 10 repetitions with control and focus on breathing.

Nutrition Tip:

Bananas contain Vitamin A and C, folate, magnesium, calcium, and potassium. Many of these help regulate the heartbeat. Bananas are also high in antioxidants that neutralize disease-causing free radicals. New evidence finds that bananas may also help to reduce the risk of kidney cancer.

Experience Good Thoughts:

"It is understanding that gives us an ability to have peace. When we understand the other fellow's viewpoint, and he understands ours, then we can sit down and work out our differences."

—Harry S. Truman, 33rd President

Think Golf:

Don't try to lift a shot with your swing. If you do, you'll likely hit a bad slice and end up searching for your ball in the woods. The loft of the clubface is meant to do the lifting, and you can trust it to get your ball airborne.

Make Me Smile:

Overheard on a golf course: "I know I have flabby thighs, but I'm lucky that my stomach covers them."

WEDNESDAY

Name: DB STRENGTH: TRIANGLE RAISES

Goal: Increase upper body strength and power; reinforce stabilization of shoulder girdle as well as total back for consistent swing.

Explanation:

Stand with feet hip distance apart holding 3-5-8lb dumbbells in hands with palms facing outer thighs. Inhale lift arms straight out to side always keeping palms down. Exhale move arms parallel to floor directly in front of chest keeping arms straight. Inhale lower down to front of thighs. Exhale repeat "triangle" in reverse (front-side-down) alternating breaths. Repeat lifting sequence 5-10x each way. Do not allow body to sway or move during exercise.

Nutrition Tip:
Keep tabs on your calcium intake. Women should try to get 1,000 to 1,200 mg. a day. Low-fat cheese and yogurt are good choices. But if you don't like dairy products, eat calcium-fortified foods such as orange juice and cereal.

Experience Good Thoughts:
"Old friends pass away, new friends appear. It is just like the days. An old day passes, a new day arrives. The important thing is to make it meaningful; a meaningful friend — or a meaningful day."   —The Dalai Lama

Think Golf:
It is wise to use your time on the driving range. Set reasonable goals and try to achieve them. It is important to hit practice shots the same way you would hit them on the course. Then you'll develop muscle memory and you won't have to think about the mechanics of the swing when you're on the course.

Make Me Smile:
Two women were ready to tee off at their country club when one asked, "Before we start playing, are we going to play men's rules today — OR — does every shot count?"

THURSDAY

Name: BIG BALL: LYING HIP ROTATION STRETCH
Goal: Stretch low back muscles used in rotation for prevention of injury.

Explanation:

Lie on floor with legs draped over ball. Ball should be close to hips. Arms outstretched to side, rotate hips and legs back and forth over ball. This is a stretch, not a strengthening exercise. Repeat 10x each side. Focus on relaxed breath.

Nutrition Tip:
A heart-healthy diet is low in saturated fats such as butter and fatty meats, refined carbs and sugar, and high in whole grains, leafy greens and good fats such as the omega-3 fatty acids found in fish and nuts.

Experience Good Thoughts:
"Be happy in the moment, that's enough. Each moment is all we need, not more."
—Mother Teresa

Think Golf:
Not hitting your drive far enough? Using some of our stretching and strengthening exercises will give you more distance. You need strengthening of the core muscles of the torso combined with stretching of the legs, hips and shoulders. Work to develop the proper muscles used in the golf swing.

Make Me Smile:
I always wondered where the safest place to be is when you call up the foursome behind you on a par three. After careful consideration I realized it would be right next to the hole!

FRIDAY

Name: HEAVY BALL: FIGURE 8

Goal: Improve and reinforce spinal, shoulder, and trunk stability which are so crucial to a consistent swing.

Explanation:

Stand with feet hip distance apart and ball held out chest height with straight arms. Trace a sideways "figure 8" in the air 10x one direction maintaining good form. Then repeat 10x the opposite direction.

Nutrition Tip:

Melons are a good source of potassium, Vitamins A & B, and beta-carotene. They are also composed of distilled water that contains the best mineral elements. So not only are they refreshing but they are also really good for you. Eat them alone in chunks as a snack.

Experience Good Thoughts:

"You'll have time to rest when you're dead."

—Robert De Niro, Actor

Think Golf:

When striving for greater distance, don't let your ambition cause you to overswing. Increasing the arc of your swing can create more clubhead speed and produce a longer shot. However, an over-rotated backswing will throw you off balance, causing you to hook or slice, and may actually reduce distance. Take the clubhead back only as far as you can comfortably turn your shoulders with balance.

Make Me Smile:

A parishioner who loved to golf asked his priest, "Father, is it a sin to play golf on Sunday?" The priest put his hand on the man's shoulder and said, "I've seen you play golf and it's a sin ANY day."

SATURDAY/SUNDAY

GOLFING DAYS ARE GOOD FOR YOUR HEALTH

REFLECTING ON THE PAST WEEK:

What was your basic attitude? Were you a positive thinker or did you need an "attitude adjustment?" Are you having success with eating healthier and doing your exercise program? How do you feel physically? If you went golfing, write down any comments that might be helpful later in improving your game. Remember, that laughter is the best medicine in the face of adversity. Are you seeing the lighter side of life?

The exercise that helped me the most this week was on page:

_____

My nutritional habits this week were:

_____

What made me smile this week?

_____

_____

Looking back at my golf week:
    My Score: _____ What did I do right? _____

_____

_____

    What could I do to improve?

_____

_____

Goals for next week: _____

_____

_____

MONDAY

Name: DYNAMIC STRETCH: GOLF SWING
Goal: Increase circulation and comfortable rotation while in compromised spine angle during swing.

Explanation:

Stand in address position. Go through motions of golf swing allowing the arms to flail and open to increase turn and open chest. Keep arms straight during movement.

Nutrition Tip:
The best time to go grocery shopping is AFTER you have eaten. You'll be less likely to buy snack and impulse foods. And, if you take a list with you, it will help you to buy only what you need. Spontaneous buying leads to spontaneous eating.

Experience Good Thoughts:
"It isn't a calamity to die with dreams unfulfilled, but it is a calamity not to dream."
—Benjamin E. Mays, Educator & Clergyman

Think Golf:
Hitting your caddie with the ball is not just bad form, it's also a violation of the rules for which you'll be assessed a two stroke penalty. Then, consequently, you'll have to play the ball from where it lies. USGA Rule #19

Make Me Smile:
Golf is a lot like taxes. You spend your whole life driving for the green and you always end up in the hole.

TUESDAY

Name: PRE-ROUND WARMUP: SIDE STRETCH

Goal: Loosen and relax side muscles for smoother, more powerful swing.

Explanation:

Begin standing with club overhead. Perform a slightly inward pull of the abdominals to help support spine. Cross your right leg in front of your left leg. Then slowly lean to the right until you feel a gentle stretch. Don't slouch…lift and separate through the ribcage. Hold for about 10 seconds. Repeat with other leg 3 times.

Nutrition Tip:

Beet greens are delicious in salads and high in Vitamin A, iron, and calcium, while the roots are rich in iron, potassium, niacin, copper and Vitamin C. Most of us discard the greens, but they can provide the fundamentals of a salad without having to use lettuce.

Experience Good Thoughts:

"There are three ingredients in the good life: learning, earning, and yearning."

—Christopher Morley

Think Golf:

"Golf is a game where guts, stick-to-itiveness and blind devotion will net you absolutely nothing but an ulcer."

—Tommy Bolt

Make Me Smile:

After playing a particularly bad round of golf, the duffer asked his partner what the appropriate gift would be to give to his caddie. His partner responded, "How about your clubs!"

WEDNESDAY

Name: **STRENGTH: TENNIS BALL (STRESS BALL) SQUEEZES**
Goal: To grip club consistently without slipping or releasing by strengthening key small muscles in hands and arms.

Explanation:

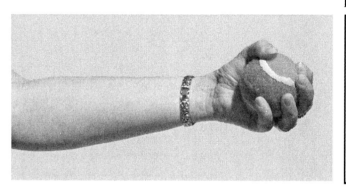

Get your hands on a tennis ball or stress ball and simply squeeze and release, emphasizing a firm grip. Begin with just a few repetitions in each hand being careful not to overwork the small muscles. Squeeze, release, rotate, re-grip, squeeze again. Switch hands.

Nutrition Tip:
Love deviled eggs? Try filling the white halves with guacamole mixed with mayo instead of the yolk. This healthy combination gives about 80 mg. of potassium per tablespoon.

Experience Good Thoughts:
"Patience and perseverance have a magical effect before which difficulties disappear and obstacles vanish."

—John Quincy Adams, 6th President

Think Golf:
The leading cause of golf injuries is repetitive stress of practice and play. During a typical round of golf, a golfer walks approximately 4-5 miles, takes about 100 swings, leans over 30-40 putts, and bends down 40-50 times. Hmmmmm......now do you think conditioning may help?

Make Me Smile:
After observing his partner play all day the player finally challenges him and says, "Hey, I don't like the way you've been cheating on this round." His partner looked at him expectantly and replied, "Well, if you know a better way, I'd certainly be glad to hear it."

THURSDAY

Name: BIG BALL: REVERSE CRUNCH
Goal: Strengthen abdominal area and aid in pelvic control for stability throughout swing.

Explanation:

Lie on your back with legs in the air and ball between your ankles. Tail bone is on the floor with abdominals pulled into spine and hands face down at sides. Contract your abdominals, exhale, and draw hip bones toward your ribcage slowly rolling tailbone slightly up and ball off floor. This is a very subtle movement. Focus on using your muscles to lift, not momentum. Pause at top and return to floor. Complete 15-20 repetitions.

Nutrition Tip:
Avocados contain more magnesium than most of the fruit we eat on a regular basis. Magnesium is important because it plays a role in the production of energy and in muscle contraction and relaxation.

Experience Good Thoughts:
"When it's all over, it's not who you were — it's whether you made a difference."
—Bob Dole

Think Golf:
Swing smooth, not hard. Never try to hammer the ball. Instead, think of the ball as a single point along the arc of a fluid swing that begins well before and flows well past the point of impact. Swing as if the ball isn't even there, not like you're trying to smash it.

Make Me Smile:
A novice golfer asked her husband to comment on her new golf clothes. "Honey, what kind of shoes do you think I should wear with my new clothes?" Knowing the fate of her game, her husband replied, "How about a nice set of waders?"

FRIDAY

Name: TOWEL STRETCH: LYING OUTER HIP/LOW BACK

Goal: Stretch outer thigh musculature helping to prevent imbalances and tightening of low back muscles resulting in injury; enhances rotational flexibility.

Explanation:

Lie on back with left leg outstretched on floor. Extend right leg straight to ceiling with wrapped towel around foot. Hold onto ends of towel with left hand only while right arm extends shoulder height to right on floor for support. Slowly pull ends of towel toward left side of body allowing leg to drop across torso and rest on floor. A stretch will be felt across outside of right hip and low back. Pause slightly then return leg toward ceiling. Repeat 5 times with same leg then switch. Do not force a stretch. Focus on exhaling during the exertion of the stretch.

Nutrition Tip:

If you see these additives on food labels, try to avoid them. Bromated vegetable oil (BVO), monosodium glutamate (MSG), saccharin, sodium nitrate and nitrite, sulfites, butylated hydroxytoluene (BHT), and sulfur dioxide.

Experience Good Thoughts:

"Our greatest glory is not in never falling, but in rising every time we fall."

—Confucius

Think Golf:

Shinnecock Hills Golf Club in Southampton, New York, is considered to be the birthplace of women's golf. It was founded in 1891 and broke the tradition by being the first to include women as members.

Make Me Smile:

"I really want to make this shot," said a golfer to his partner. "My mother-in-law is sitting on the clubhouse patio." His partner responded, "Don't be ridiculous. It's way over 300 yards. You couldn't possibly hit her from here!"

SATURDAY/SUNDAY

GOLFING DAYS ARE GOOD FOR YOUR HEALTH

REFLECTING ON THE PAST WEEK:

What was your basic attitude? Were you a positive thinker or did you need an "attitude adjustment?" Are you having success with eating healthier and doing your exercise program? How do you feel physically? If you went golfing, write down any comments that might be helpful later in improving your game. Remember, that laughter is the best medicine in the face of adversity. Are you seeing the lighter side of life?

The exercise that helped me the most this week was on page:

_____

My nutritional habits this week were:

_____

What made me smile this week?

_____

_____

Looking back at my golf week:
     My Score: _____ What did I do right? _____

_____

     What could I do to improve?

_____

_____

Goals for next week: _____

_____

_____

MONDAY

Name: DYNAMIC STRETCH: SHOULDERS FORWARD/BACK

Goal: Release tension and increase circulation around shoulder joints for better and unhindered movement during swing.

Explanation:

Stand with feet hip distance apart, palms facing toward outer thighs. Inhale, squeeze shoulder blades together and stick out chest. Exhale, reversing the movement squeezing shoulders and chest forward and lengthening across midback. Repeat 30x with control. Arms and hands will rotate slightly around legs.

Nutrition Tip:
Some natural substances are said to support mental health but you should always consult your health care professional before using natural remedies. For depression, PMS and/or menopause try these: B vitamins, calcium, flaxseed oil, magnesium, primrose oil, and St. John's Wort.

Experience Good Thoughts:
"Plan for the future, because that is where you are going to spend the rest of your life."

—Mark Twain

Think Golf:
When your ball ends up in an unplayable lie, it is usually best to take advantage of the rules of golf allowing you to drop the ball in exchange for a penalty stroke. Trying to play the ball where it is may make you end up with disastrous results.

Make Me Smile:
You know you're an obsessed golfers when your philosophy is: Give me a set of clubs, a great golf course to play, and a beautiful woman -- and let's go golfing. She can keep score.

TUESDAY

Name: YOGA/STRETCH: WARRIOR I
Goal: Increase strength, balance, and flexibility in legs as well as focus on breath to calm mind.

Explanation:

Stand in lunge position with right foot forward with weight on toward heel and left foot back on ball of foot. Maintain balance and center of gravity between both feet. Raise arms over head palms facing each other. Lift eye line toward hands and head slightly back. Squeeze muscles throughout body in lifted fashion. Hold 10 seconds then repeat other side.

Nutrition Tip:
Beans are not only good for you but they're a great addition to soups. They are inexpensive, low in fat, and rich in protein, iron, folic acid, and fiber. Pinto, black, navy, kidney and garbanzo beans are packed with healthy nutrients. If you don't like beans as an individual side dish, eat them in a tortilla with salsa.

Experience Good Thoughts:
"Coming together is a beginning, staying together is progress, and working together is success."

—Henry Ford

Think Golf:
Be sure the grips on your clubs are in good condition. If they are worn, ragged, or slippery, you are likely to hold the club too tight, resulting in undesirable shots. A relaxed grip can increase your distance and improve your score.

Make Me Smile:
Golf is the only game where the ball may not lie well, but the players sure do. Oh — how disappointing! Golf is promoted as a game of integrity, isn't it?

WEDNESDAY

Name: STRENGTH: PUSHUP MEDIUM

Goal: Increase base strength of chest and shoulders with focus on shoulder stability aid in less breakdown at top of swing.

Explanation:

Start in basic pushup position. Whether knees remain down or up, there should be a straight line between head, shoulders, spine, hips, and knees. Place hands directly under shoulders and sternum between thumbs. Keeping spine and abdominals tight, lower body straight down to the floor by bending at elbows and return to straight arms. Repeat 10x for 3 sets. Inhale as you lower down, exhale on the return push back up.

Nutrition Tip:

The old stand by – an orange – is rich in Vitamin C, folic acid and fiber. Cut one in wedges for easy to eat snacks or squeeze them for fresh juice. You can add them to a fruit salad or slice them thin and place them around your plate at dinner for a festive look and a juicy end to a good meal.

Experience Good Thoughts:

"There are two big forces at work, external and internal. We have very little control over external forces such as tornados, earthquakes, floods, disasters, illness, and pain. What really matters is internal force. How do I respond to those disasters? Over that I have complete control."

—Leo Buscaglia

Think Golf:

Since the clubface is the only thing that will contact the ball, line it up to the target first. Then take a proper stance with feet and shoulders parallel to the intended flight of the ball.

Make Me Smile:

A golfer posed a question to his club pro, "Did you know you make more money than the President?" "Why shouldn't I?" replied the pro. "I'm a better golfer than he is."

THURSDAY

Name: BIG BALL: TOY SOLDIER
Goal: Enhance coordination of arms and legs while stabilizing torso.

Explanation:

Lie on floor with arms and legs in the air with ball balancing between toes and fingertips. Keep abdominals engaged pulling belly button to spine. Inhale removing opposite arm and leg away from ball. Take R arm overhead and L leg the other way. Keep both limbs an inch off floor. Exhale and return arm and leg back to ball. Repeat 10x each side.

Nutrition Tip:
Once thought to be just a pleasant drink, teas have been found to contain chemicals that may protect our arteries and reduce the risk of cancer. They have other helpful properties too. If you're feeling a little stressed, try some natural relaxants. Chamomile, jasmine, and peppermint teas are known to settle you down.

Experience Good Thoughts:
"Destiny is not a matter of chance, but of choice. Not something to wish for, but to attain."

—William Jennings Bryan

Think Golf:
Bobby Jones invited the world's best amateurs and professionals to compete in a tournament on his new Augusta National Course in the spring of 1934. That was the beginning of the Masters! Horton Smith was the first winner.

Make Me Smile:
The hysterical mom screamed into the phone, "Doctor, I'm at the golf course and my baby just swallowed a tee." "I'm on my way. I'll be there in just a few minutes," said the doctor. "But what should I do until you get here?" cried the frantic mom. "Practice your putting!"

FRIDAY

Name: PILATES: SPINE TWIST

Goal: Aid in muscle isolation when in backswing; stabilize pelvis while rotating trunk with control.

Explanation:

Sit tall with legs outstretched with feet slightly wider than hips. Arms reach out shoulder height to sides with palms down. Inhale to prepare. Exhale for 3 counts while rotating spine. Rotate slightly more on each breath to maximum. Inhale return to center lengthening through spine. Repeat same movement each side 3-5X.

Nutrition Tip:

Be sure to get enough calcium. Calcium helps regulate your heartbeat, clot your blood, and even burn fat. If you don't get enough calcium, your body draws it from your bones, which in time will weaken them. Here's a list of foods high in calcium. Skim milk, non-fat plain yogurt, dark greens such as kale and broccoli, almonds, dried figs, oranges, canned sardines and salmon, cottage cheese, non-fat sour cream, and fortified cereals. Vitamin D (sunshine) aids the body in absorbing calcium. High fiber foods interfere with calcium absorption so try to eat them separately.

Experience Good Thoughts:

The Bible says, "Love must be completely sincere. Hate what is evil, hold on to what is good."

—Romans 12: 9

Think Golf:

The tournament purses earned by professional golfers 50 years ago were quite small compared to those today. Ben Hogan's best year netted him $42,000. Jack Nicklaus earned approximately $250,000 in the 1970s. Today, winners are rewarded upwards of $10 million annually.

Make Me Smile:

How bad is your game??? My game is so-o-o bad that I just had to have my ball retriever re-gripped!

SATURDAY/SUNDAY

GOLFING DAYS ARE GOOD FOR YOUR HEALTH

REFLECTING ON THE PAST WEEK:

What was your basic attitude? Were you a positive thinker or did you need an "attitude adjustment?" Are you having success with eating healthier and doing your exercise program? How do you feel physically? If you went golfing, write down any comments that might be helpful later in improving your game. Remember, that laughter is the best medicine in the face of adversity. Are you seeing the lighter side of life?

The exercise that helped me the most this week was on page:

_____

My nutritional habits this week were:

_____

What made me smile this week?

_____

_____

Looking back at my golf week:
     My Score: _____ What did I do right? _____

_____

_____

     What could I do to improve?

_____

_____

Goals for next week: _____

_____

_____

MONDAY

Name: PRE-ROUND WARMUP: CHEST/SHOULDER STRETCH WITH WALL

Goal: Aid in maximal turn in backswing by opening up chest and front shoulder muscles.

Explanation:

Stand at a corner wall. Place left hand on the wall, keeping arm parallel with floor and arm straight. Slowly turn your body and feet to the right away from the hand on wall. Focus on lifting through the spine. Exhale as you gently push against the wall and turn more. Hold for 10 seconds each side.

Nutrition Tip:
Drink your water! Even MILD dehydration will slow one's metabolism as much as 3%. Lack of water is the primary reason for daytime fatigue.

Experience Good Thoughts:
"The best time to plant a tree was 20 years ago. The second best time is NOW."
—Chinese Proverb

Think Golf:
Most golfers have been told to "keep your head down" by someone offering good advice. Instead of concentrating on keeping your head down, try to keep it level. Some head motion in your swing is inevitable and necessary. Keeping your head down may cause a reverse weight shift.

Make Me Smile:
Getting a little frustrated with his swing the golfer finally asks the pro at his club for help. After watching him hit a few balls the pro says, "I see what your problem is. You're not addressing the ball correctly." The irritated player looked at him and replied, "Well I think I've been courteous to the thing long enough."

TUESDAY

Name: **YOGA/STRETCH: KNEELING WRIST EXTENSION**

Goal: Promote elasticity in wrists for greater club control and accuracy; loosen up wrist and forearm muscles for better support during cocking and uncocking swing movements.

Explanation:

Kneel on all fours with knees and hands body width apart. Place palms on floor with fingers spread wide. Shift body weight slightly forward over hands pressing ends of fingers into the floor. Hold for 5 seconds then release and repeat 3x. Do not force stretch.

Nutrition Tip:
Super-potency vitamins are unnecessary because our bodies can only absorb a certain amount of each. Taking supplements with meals and buying chelated and time-released varieties that are easier to digest will get more of the ingredients into our system.

Experience Good Thoughts:
"Nurture great thoughts for you cannot go higher than your thoughts."
—Benjamin Disraeli

Think Golf:
Vijay Singh has a name that is truly appropriate. "Vijay" is a hindi word translated into English as "victory" – a recognized testament to his achievements.

Make Me Smile:
Two golfers go out to play a round and the first player takes out a brand new ball and places it on the tee. His first shot lands right in the water hazard. So, he reaches into his bag and takes out another brand new ball. This time he slices it smack into a wooded area. Huffing and angry, he stomps back to his bag and takes out another brand new ball. Finally, his partner says to him, "I see that you're losing a lot of brand new balls. Why don't you use some old ones until you're hitting a little better." The player looks up and replies, "I don't own any old balls!"

WEDNESDAY

Name: DB STRENGTH: TAKE AWAY SQUAT II

Goal: Mimic the golf swing from takeaway through impact adding outside resistance to the body to overload the muscles used; promotes muscle memory.

Explanation:

Start with 3-5-8lb weight in right hand in top swing position. Lower right elbows onto right hip, shift body weight to left, keeping hand with weight back. Repeat 20-30x.

Nutrition Tip:

Millions of Americans have tried a vegetarian diet and many of them find it to be beneficial and nutritious. Studies have shown that people who get more of their daily calories from plant sources have a lower risk for heart disease and lower cholesterol levels. Just don't smother them with butter or cheese sauces. Darn!

Experience Good Thoughts:

"Nothing is particularly hard if you divide it into small jobs."

—Henry Ford

Think Golf:

What a way to go! Singer, actor and comedian Bing Crosby was an avid golfer. He played his last round in Spain on October 14, 1977 where he suffered a massive heart attack and died just after finishing 18 holes.

Make Me Smile:

A large golf store hired a golf professional to give lessons. Two women walked up to the pro and he said to one of them, "Are you here to learn how to play golf?" "Oh, no," she replied. "My friend is the one who's interested in learning. I learned yesterday."

THURSDAY

Name: HEAVY BALL: FORWARD LUNGE ROTATE & FLEX
Goal: Lower body strength with spinal stability and rotational core strength.

Explanation:

Stand with feet together and gall in bent arms in front of chest. Lunge right foot forward dipping left knee toward floor. Outstretch arms diagonally over right knee bending forward to touch ball to floor on outside of foot. Push off front foot back to starting position. Ball then comes back to chest. Spine will round forward slightly during lunge, but focus on engaging abdominals to support joints.

Nutrition Tip:
Try to stave off the flu the natural way. Eat right by being sure to get ample amounts of fruits and veggies. Bump up your Vitamin C supplement. Drink plenty of water. Remember to exercise because exercise helps build your immune system. Wash your hands often. Get lots of fresh air and sufficient rest.

Experience Good Thoughts:
"As I grow older, I pay less attention to what men say. I just watch what they do."
—Andrew Carnegie

Think Golf:
If a player fails to mark the position of the ball before lifting it or moves the ball in any other manner such as rolling it with a club, a penalty of one stroke is incurred.

Make Me Smile:
Did you ever think about why there are 18 holes on a golf course? It's because that's how long it took the Scotch players (the ones who invented the game) to finish their bottle of whiskey.

FRIDAY

Name: CARDIO: HIKING

Goal: Increase cardiovascular endurance and stamina for the 4+ hours of golf; enhance concentration and focus; improve coordination, balance and rhythm.

Explanation:

Hiking is similar to regular walking, but on uneven surfaces. Hiking can be through hills and valleys, on dirt or rocky paths. Wear hiking boots or durable treaded sneakers. Always take water with you and watch where you step. Enjoy nature and allow your hike to relieve some stress. Hikes can be quick (30min) or many hours or days.

Nutrition Tip:
A new study in Cancer Epidemiology Biomarkers & Prevention found that eating at least 35 servings of fruits and vegetables a week can cut the risk of developing hormone-stimulated breast cancer tumors by a third in postmenopausal women. Leafy greens and colorful vegetables are especially good cancer fighters.

Experience Good Thoughts:
"Every day, think as you wake up, today I am fortunate to be alive. I have a precious human life. I am not going to waste it. I am going to use all my energies to develop myself, to expand my heart out to others, to achieve enlightenment for the benefit of all beings. I am going to have kind thoughts towards others. I am not going to get angry or think badly about others. I am going to benefit others as much as I can."
—The Dalai Lama

Think Golf:
When you pick up your ball from the green or the cup, bend with your knees rather than your back. Using your leg muscles will spare potential injury to your back.

Make Me Smile:
Barometer for knowing when it's too wet to play golf — your cart capsizes.

SATURDAY/SUNDAY

GOLFING DAYS ARE GOOD FOR YOUR HEALTH

REFLECTING ON THE PAST WEEK:

What was your basic attitude? Were you a positive thinker or did you need an "attitude adjustment?" Are you having success with eating healthier and doing your exercise program? How do you feel physically? If you went golfing, write down any comments that might be helpful later in improving your game. Remember, that laughter is the best medicine in the face of adversity. Are you seeing the lighter side of life?

The exercise that helped me the most this week was on page:
_____

My nutritional habits this week were:
_____

What made me smile this week?
_____
_____

Looking back at my golf week:
       My Score: _____ What did I do right? _____
_____
_____

       What could I do to improve?
_____
_____

Goals for next week: _____
_____
_____

MONDAY

Name: PILATES: SWIMMING

Goal: Challenge coordination, balance and rhythm while strengthening ability to separate torso from limbs for more body awareness.

Explanation:

Lie face down with arms and legs outstretched hip and shoulder width apart. Inhale to prepare. As you exhale, maintain your back and pelvis in place while reaching your arms and legs slightly off floor. Inhale 5 counts while swimming arms and legs straight up and down in flutters. Then exhale 5 counts performing the same move. Continue the reciprocal swim action through 5 sets of inhales and exhales. Relax.

Nutrition Tip:
Lentils are a very healthy choice when making soup. Add some onions, carrots, and celery to the mix. For a more filling meal, cook some brown or long-grain rice and pour the lentil soup over it. Or you can cook think spaghetti and mix it with the soup.

Experience Good Thoughts:
"As human beings, our greatness lies not so much in being able to remake the world as in being able to remake ourselves."

—Mahatma Gandhi

Think Golf:
Playing golf for prizes or for fun is playing by the rules. If you are not playing by the Rules of Golf, you are not playing the game of golf. If you choose not to count all of your strokes, you are not playing golf by the rules. If you choose to take "gimmies," you are not playing golf by the rules.

Make Me Smile:
In a teaching session the golf pro said to his student, "Now just go through the motions of your swing without hitting the ball." The student looked at him and said, "What kind of teacher are you? That's exactly what I'm trying to overcome."

TUESDAY

Name: STRENGTH: SQUAT TURN LUNGE
Goal: Improve coordination, balance, and lower body strength.

Explanation:

Stand with feet slightly wider than hips. Squat down. As you stand back up pivot on feet turning to the right and sink body down into a lunge dipping back knee down. As you push back up, turn back to front and sit down into squat again. Repeat entire sequence to the left side. Each turn Front-left-front-right is one repetition. Complete 10 repetitions.

Nutrition Tip:
Injuries require larger amounts of protein, Vitamins A and C, and zinc for the healing process. Help your body and eat foods rich in these nutrients for a faster recovery.

Experience Good Thoughts:
"I am beginning to learn that it is the sweet, simple things of life, which are the real ones after all."
—Laura Ingalls Wilder

Think Golf:
Do you know where the term "bogey" came from? It is derived from Colonel Bogey, a British fictional character described as steady but not very bright. His attempts as "The Bogeyman" to play professional tournament golf were highlighted in a comical way by author, George Plimpton.

Make Me Smile:
As a beginner golfer, John was excitedly anticipating a better round. He remembered his pre-swing routine, getting in his proper stance, and visualizing the shot he was about to make. All of a sudden, a voice on the loudspeaker from the clubhouse, announces, "Will the gentleman on the ladies tee back up to the men's tee, please?" John stood there, ready to make his stroke, when the loud announcement was repeated. Irritated now, John lost his concentration, broke his stance, and turned to the clubhouse. In his loudest voice, John responded, "Would the announcer in the clubhouse please shut up and let me play my SECOND shot!"

WEDNESDAY

Name: YOGA/STRETCH: KNEELING WRIST FLEXION

Goal: Promote elasticity in wrists for greater club control and accuracy; loosen up wrist and forearm muscles for better support during cocking and uncocking swing movements.

Explanation:

Kneel on all fours with knees and hands body width apart. Press the back of the hands to the floor spreading the fingers wide. The palms will be up and fingers pointing toward knees. Hold four five seconds then release. Repeat 3 times. Do not force stretch or put too much weight into hands.

Nutrition Tip:
According to recent USDA surveys, most Americans intake of Vitamin B-6 was below the RDA. Get your B-6 from Vitamin-fortified cereals, prunes, and breads.

Experience Good Thoughts:
"Love all. Trust a few. Do wrong to none."

—William Shakespeare

Think Golf:
When hitting a ball into a high wind, concentrate on fundamentals and swing very easy. A well-hit ball has less spin and more flight giving the shot greater distance.

Make Me Smile:
A guy who loved golf was stranded on a deserted island for several years when one day he noticed something approaching on the water. He finally recognized it as a raft and soon a beautiful blonde wearing a wet suit walks up to him and asks, "When was the last time you had a cigarette?' "Many years ago," he answered. So she unzips her suit and pulls out a waterproof container filled with cigarettes. Then she asked when the last time was that he had a drink. He replied, "More years than I'd like to remember." And she unzips her suit a little more and pulls out a flask of rum. By now he is ecstatic enjoying his smoke and drink. Finally she asks, "When was the last time you played around?" All smiles he replied, "I can't believe you have a set of clubs in there too!"

THURSDAY

Name: BIG BALL: ABDOMINAL CURL

Goal: Promote spinal stability and strengthen torso for power transfer and prevent back injury.

Explanation:

Lie face up on big ball with feet hip width apart and low back resting on top of ball. Body should be parallel to ground. Place hands under base of head for support and contract abdominals bringing upper body closer to sky in crunch motion. Keep abdominals and gluteals engaged at all times. Repeat 3 sets of 10-15 reps.

Nutrition Tip:

Vitamin B-1 is most commonly known as thiamin and is required for the cells in our body to produce the enzymes that break down carbohydrates. As with all B complex vitamins, thiamin helps to reduce stress as it increases the body's immune system and makes it more resistant to infections. Food sources for Vitamin B-1 include organ meats, whole grain cereals, wheat germ, and brewer's yeast — not a very appetizing list. Stick with the whole grain cereals!

Experience Good Thoughts:

"The glory of friendship is not in the outstretched hand, not the kindly smile nor the joy of companionship; it is the spiritual inspiration that comes to one when he discovers that someone else believes in him and is willing to trust him."

—Ralph Waldo Emerson

Think Golf:

USGA Rule #25 states that if your ball lands in a tree stump, the ball cannot be retrieved and dropped without a penalty stroke unless the stump is scheduled to be removed and has been declared "ground under repair."

Make Me Smile:

How long a minute is depends on how far you are from the clubhouse when you need a restroom.

FRIDAY

Name: HEAVY BALL: FORWARD LUNGE BALL OUT-IN
Goal: Lower body strength with spinal stability and core strength.

Explanation:

Stand with feet together and ball in bent arms in front of chest. Lunge right foot forward dipping left knee towards floor. Outstretch arms forward. Pause in this position slightly then push body back to start position by pushing off front heel not toe. Ball then comes back into chest. Alternate lunging legs 20x focusing on erect back and even amount of weight distributed between both feet.

Nutrition Tip:
Eat watermelon as a snack. It's an excellent source of Vitamin C and carotenoids. It's refreshing and low in calories. And if you have a hard time drinking enough water in a day, eating watermelon will help to get the water you need while enjoying a great taste.

Experience Good Thoughts:
"Ninety-nine percent of failures come from people who have the habit of making excuses."

—George Washington Carver

Think Golf:
Do you know who the "Father of Modern Golf Architecture" is? His name is Robert Trent Jones and he designed more than 500 courses across the United States and in 34 other countries.

Make Me Smile:
Living on earth can be expensive, especially if you like to play golf at resort-type courses. But remember, you get a free trip around the sun every year at no additional cost.

SATURDAY/SUNDAY

GOLFING DAYS ARE GOOD FOR YOUR HEALTH

REFLECTING ON THE PAST WEEK:

What was your basic attitude? Were you a positive thinker or did you need an "attitude adjustment?" Are you having success with eating healthier and doing your exercise program? How do you feel physically? If you went golfing, write down any comments that might be helpful later in improving your game. Remember, that laughter is the best medicine in the face of adversity. Are you seeing the lighter side of life?

The exercise that helped me the most this week was on page:

_____

My nutritional habits this week were:

_____

What made me smile this week?

_____

_____

Looking back at my golf week:
    My Score: _____ What did I do right? _____

_____

_____

    What could I do to improve?

_____

_____

Goals for next week: _____

_____

_____

MONDAY

Name: YOGA/STRETCH: SPREAD-OUT HAND TO FLOOR TWIST

Goal: Stretch spine from head to tail bone as well as hip shifting mobility; open chest muscles to aid in turn.

Explanation:

Stand with feet wider than hips. Feet turned parallel to front. Inhale to prepare. Exhale and hinge at hips bringing both hands to floor. Legs remain straight. Lift right arm to sky twisting spine. Eyes follow hand allowing neck, entire spine and hips to turn toward the right. Hold for 5 seconds and repeat on other side.

Nutrition Tip:

Our bodies need 15 minerals that help to regulate cell function. The three major minerals are calcium, phosphorus, and magnesium. Amounts needed for most of these minerals are quite small and excessive amounts can be toxic. So check before taking supplements of these.

Experience Good Thoughts:

"The person who gets the farthest is generally the one who is willing to do and dare. The sure-thing boat never gets far from shore."

—Dale Carnegie

Think Golf:

Wanna play a different golf game? RABBIT: A round of Rabbit starts with the "rabbit on the loose." The first player to win a hole is said to "hold the rabbit." When another player wins a hole, the rabbit is on the loose again. Any player holding the rabbit on either the 9th or 18th hole WINS.

Make Me Smile:

"I owe a lot to my parents, especially to my mother and father."

—Golfer Greg Norman (July, 2001)

TUESDAY

Name: STRENGTH: SQUAT NARROW

Goal: Enhance lower body muscular strength and endurance for better base of support throughout swing.

Explanation:

Stand tall with feet together and arms straight down to sides. Inhale as you bend knees sitting hips back as if to sit down on a chair. Weight remains mostly in heels and knees squeeze toward each other. Arms raise forward and parallel with floor for better balance. Keep abdominals held in tight and engaged. Exhale as you return to standing, pushing through heels and squeezing gluteals. Repeat 10-20x.

Nutrition Tip:
How can a person get enough Vitamin B-12? Meat is the greatest source for Vitamin B-12. Meat includes fish and poultry as well. Liver has a very generous supply of the vitamin. If you're not a meat eater, many foods are fortified with Vitamin B-12 including a large group of cereals.

Experience Good Thoughts:
"Confidence comes not from always being right but from not fearing to be wrong."
—Peter T. McIntyre

Think Golf:
A player has not made a stroke unless he begins his downswing. If he stops his downswing voluntarily, then it is not considered a stroke.

Make Me Smile:
This story has been passed down for years — Did you hear about the golfer who was sentenced to death by hanging? He was so obsessed with golf that he asked if he could take a few practice swings first!

WEDNESDAY

Name: PRE-ROUND WARMUP: WIDE SQUAT

Goal: Loosen up muscles around hips and legs to prepare for round of golf; help to prevent injury.

Explanation:

Stand tall with feet slightly wider than hips and toes aiming outward at 45-degree angles. Inhale lowering buttocks and hips down and back as if to sit. Knees should stay still and weight remains mostly in heels. Feel stretch in inner thighs and tops of thighs. Pause slightly at bottom. Exhale squeezing buttocks and push through heels to stand up. Repeat 10-15x with focus on strong hips without pressure in knees.

Nutrition Tip:
Remember what your mother told you — You are what you eat! Ouch!

Experience Good Thoughts:
"I like living. I have sometimes been wildly, despairingly, acutely miserable, racked with sorrow, but through it all, I still know quite certainly that just to be alive is a grand thing."

—Agatha Christie

Think Golf:
Play this golf game! A SCRAMBLE is commonly used for group outings and amateur or corporate tournaments. Foursomes usually comprise the teams, with each team starting simultaneously on a different hole (shotgun start). In a scramble, each team member hits a tee shot and the best ball is selected. The other team members move their ball to the selected drive and all play a second shot from that location. The best second shot is selected and the procedure repeats itself until one team member holes out. Long ball hitters are an advantage off the tee, but short game skills are essential for the team to post a competitive score.

Make Me Smile:
The easiest way to be good at golf is to be bad with numbers.

THURSDAY

Name: **YOGA/STRETCH: BIRDWINGS**

Goal: Improve shoulder turn; increase range of motion around shoulders; promote better posture.

Explanation:

Stand with elbows at 90 degrees palms facing up and out to sides of body. Elbows are "sticking" to ribs. Inhale externally rotating arms outward sticking chest out slightly and shoulder blades slightly squeezing together. Exhale brings arms to crossed position in front of body. Elbows will still stay in tight. Shoulder blades will slightly "flare" outward imposing a stretch under them. Repeat process 10x alternating crossing hands in front of body.

Nutrition Tip:

Drink your water! A drop in body water can trigger fuzzy short-term memory, trouble with basic math, and difficulty focusing on the computer screen or on a printed page.

Experience Good Thoughts:

"Everything that irritates us about others can lead us to an understanding of ourselves."

—Carl Jung, Swiss Psychiatrist

Think Golf:

Ever notice that the people who are late to the tee are often much more cheerful than the players who have to wait for them? Be prompt to the tee so everyone can have a better time.

Make Me Smile:

Bears have been known to appear on golf courses. Golfers are advised to wear little bells on their clothing to alert but not startle unsuspecting bears and to carry pepper spray in case the need arises to defend yourself. Black bears don't bother golfers but grizzly bears are dangerous. Golfers can determine the difference by the kind of droppings on the course. Black bear droppings contain berries and fur from small animals. Grizzly bear droppings contain little bells and smell like pepper spray!

FRIDAY

Name: HEAVY BALL: PUSHUPS W/FEET ON BALL
Goal: Improve core balance while strengthening chest and shoulder girdle for power and control during swing.

Explanation:

Start in plank position. Place feet on top of ball either pointed or flexed. Maintain straight plank body and balance on ball. Perform as many pushups with correct form as possible. Inhale down and exhale up. 10-20 repetitions is the goal.

Nutrition Tip:
When eating out, ask for dressings and sauces on the side. You'll use considerably less than if you have the restaurant pour it on and mix it for you.

Experience Good Thoughts:
"When you're finished changing, you're finished."

—Ben Franklin

Think Golf:
Play Ready-Golf! Efficiency is key for the golfers behind you. Walk at a steady pace and be ready to hit when it is your turn. Don't hold things up with too many practice shots.

Make Me Smile:
A newly retired guy was given a set of golf clubs as a parting gift from his co-workers. Not knowing anything about the game, he decided to take a few lessons from the local pro. At his first lesson, the pro said, "Just hit the ball toward the flag on the green up ahead so I can get a feel for your swing." The novice teed up and hit the ball onto the green where it landed about 6 inches from the hole. "Now what?" he said waiting for the next instruction. The pro was speechless but finally said, "The object of the game is to hit the ball into the hole." "Great, now you tell me!" said the disappointed beginner.

SATURDAY/SUNDAY

GOLFING DAYS ARE GOOD FOR YOUR HEALTH

REFLECTING ON THE PAST WEEK:

What was your basic attitude? Were you a positive thinker or did you need an "attitude adjustment?" Are you having success with eating healthier and doing your exercise program? How do you feel physically? If you went golfing, write down any comments that might be helpful later in improving your game. Remember, that laughter is the best medicine in the face of adversity. Are you seeing the lighter side of life?

The exercise that helped me the most this week was on page:

_____

My nutritional habits this week were:

_____

What made me smile this week?

_____

_____

Looking back at my golf week:
    My Score: _____ What did I do right? _____

_____

_____

    What could I do to improve?

_____

_____

Goals for next week: _____

_____

_____

MONDAY

Name: STRENGTH: FRONT SQUAT-NARROW
Goal: Strengthen lower body for good base of support for swing; focus on inner thigh muscles.

Explanation:

Similar to medium squat, but with feet together throughout movement. Squat down and up with emphasis on sitting back as far as possible keeping weight in heels and arms forward. Repeat 10-20x.

Nutrition Tip:
Buy whole grain bread. It's higher in fiber and has more vitamins and minerals than regular wheat bread. It has a firmer consistency and tastes good too!

Experience Good Thoughts:
"People of humor are always to some degree people of genius."
—Samuel Taylor Coleridge, Poet

Think Golf:
Even the pros don't hit great shots every time. Annika Sorenstam, LPGA Touring Pro, admits, "Disaster is a very common thing on the golf course. You've just got to learn to deal with it." So forget about your terrible shots and move on. Try to duplicate your great shots over and over. Part of a healthy mental game is to keep a positive outlook and continue to visualize great shots.

Make Me Smile:
Golfers will try just about anything to improve their game. Sometimes new techniques work and sometimes they don't. This cliché says it all. Any great change in your technique will work for a maximum of one day and a minimum of "not at all."

TUESDAY

Name: **PILATES: NECK PULL**
Goal: Strengthen entire trunk musculature while stabilizing the pelvis and systematically strengthening and stretching hip flexors.

Explanation:

Lie on your back with legs extended straight and feet flexed hip distance apart. Hands are placed behind ears with elbows wide. Inhale, lengthening back of neck and dropping chin to look at feet lifting upper back off floor. Exhale and continue rolling spine off floor sequentially through while keeping upper spine flexed and rounded ending with face and chest aiming parallel with legs. Inhale return to sitting tall and spine straight. Exhale sliding shoulder blades down spine rolling spine back down to mat one vertebrae at a time to rest in starting position on floor. Focus on pulling abdominals into spine at all times. Complete 10 controlled repetitions.

Nutrition Tip:
Magnesium is an important mineral needed by the body. It is found mainly inside muscles, soft tissues and bone, and functions in many enzyme processes. Eat nuts, legumes, whole grains and green vegetables to get your daily requirement of magnesium.

Experience Good Thoughts:
"If you can't laugh at yourself, then who can you laugh at?"   —Tiger Woods

Think Golf:
The old adage that 90% of putts left short don't go in says it all. Being able to putt for correct distance is the single most important technique for lowering your putting strokes.

Make Me Smile:
Golf was once a rich man's sport, but now there are millions of poor players!

WEDNESDAY

Name: CARDIO: SWIMMING

Goal: Increase cardiovascular endurance and stamina for the 4+ hours of golf; enhance concentration and focus; improve coordination, balance and rhythm.

Explanation:

There are many different types of swimming. You don't have to know an exact technique to reap the benefits of swimming. Just jump in a pool move however you can back and forth across the pool. To increase endurance, don't hurry, rush, or panic. Relax and calmly swim. You do not even have to put your head in the water if you are a beginner. Practice swimming 3x a week for 30 minutes each time. Focus on deep breaths, relaxed facial muscles, and positive thinking.

Nutrition Tip:
Garlic helps to reduce high blood pressure, cholesterol, and dangerous blood clotting. It fights potent carcinogens and helps to strengthen the immune system. So sprinkle that garlic powder generously when cooking. Eat fresh parsley to reduce the odor in your breath from garlic.

Experience Good Thoughts:
"Science may have found a cure for most evils; but it has found no remedy for the worst of them all — the apathy of human beings."

—Helen Keller

Think Golf:
Knowing the swing weight of your club is as indispensable to playing good golf as knowing the temperature of the grass in the fairway. However, having your clubs custom fitted by a professional whose job it is to know about the swing weight of your clubs is a necessity to playing your best golf.

Make Me Smile:
When walking down the fairway, looking for your ball, you can assume that — Any ball you can see in the rough from fifty yards away is definitely not yours.

THURSDAY

Name: YOGA/STRETCH: STANDING WRIST FLEXION

Goal: Promote elasticity in wrists for greater club control and accuracy; loosen up wrist and forearm muscles for better support during cocking and uncocking swing movements.

Explanation:

Stand with right arms outstretched directly in front of chest palm down. Reach left hand out and hold on to right fingers. Gently pull right fingers and palm toward toward inside of wrist as if in a cupping position. The resistance that the left hand provides on the back of the right hand will create a stretch in the back of the wrist and forearm. Hold for 5 seconds then switch arms. Repeat each arm 3x. Do not force stretch!

Nutrition Tip:

Butter or margarine? It really doesn't matter. Nutritionists used to prefer margarine until they discovered that trans fats are just as unhealthy as the saturated fat in butter. Very small amounts of either are fine. Some believe butter is natural and therefore a better choice.

Experience Good Thoughts:

"Have a heart that never hardens, and a temper that never tires, and a touch that never hurts."   —Charles Dickens, Author

Think Golf:

Using a regulation ball is imperative. And there are many kinds of balls that make magnificent claims about their capability. For most golfers, though, the difference between a one-dollar ball and a three-dollar ball is two dollars.

Make Me Smile:

This story has been passed down for years – Did you hear about the golfer who was sentenced to death by hanging? He was so obsessed with golf that he asked if he could take a few practice swings first!

FRIDAY

Name: STRENGTH: STATIC LUNGE BALANCE

Goal: Enhance lower body strength and endurance with extra focus on balance.

Explanation:

Start with arms out to the sides parallel with floor to aid in balance. Place feet in wide staggered stance: left foot firmly in front with most of the weight on heel, while right foot is behind body with only ball and toes of foot on floor. Weight and body should be centered between both feet. Inhale as you lower right knee down about two inches from floor, then on exhale lift back up. Repeat same leg position 10-15x. Then repeat other side. Keep eye line lifted and chin up looking forward.

Nutrition Tip:

Eggplant is a powerful antioxidant and boosts immunity by stimulating activity of protective enzymes. A delicious way to eat eggplant is to cut it in half, then cut in slices. Place on paper towels to drain for a few minutes. Dip in beaten egg and dredge in flour or seasoned bread crumbs. Fry breaded slices in hot olive oil for about 5 minutes on each side. Drain thoroughly before eating.

Experience Good Thoughts:

"When you get to the end of your rope, tie a knot and hang on."
—Franklin D. Roosevelt, 26th President

Think Golf:

Counting on your opponent to inform you when he breaks a rule is like expecting him to make fun of his haircut. Except for Bobby Jones, who lost the U.S. Open by one stroke because he admitted to making the ball move and took a penalty stroke. No officials or spectators in the area saw the ball move. Integrity is paramount!

Make Me Smile:

99.99% of all matter is empty space, but that .01% will stop a golf ball dead.

SATURDAY/SUNDAY

GOLFING DAYS ARE GOOD FOR YOUR HEALTH

REFLECTING ON THE PAST WEEK:

What was your basic attitude? Were you a positive thinker or did you need an "attitude adjustment?" Are you having success with eating healthier and doing your exercise program? How do you feel physically? If you went golfing, write down any comments that might be helpful later in improving your game. Remember, that laughter is the best medicine in the face of adversity. Are you seeing the lighter side of life?

The exercise that helped me the most this week was on page:

_____

My nutritional habits this week were:

_____

What made me smile this week?

_____

_____

Looking back at my golf week:

    My Score: _____ What did I do right? _____

_____

    What could I do to improve?

_____

_____

Goals for next week: _____

_____

_____

MONDAY

Name: HEAVY BALL: FIGURE 8 KNEES UP
Goal: Warm up powerhouse muscles and joints of low back, hips, and knees; strengthen torso; coordination and balance.

Explanation:

Stand tall with feet hip distance apart. Hold ball with bent arms in front of chest. Lift alternating legs and trace ball in a figure 8 pattern under lifted leg. Repeat 10x one direction (inside out) then change directions (outside in). Focus on keeping chest open and lifted while lifting knees higher.

Nutrition Tip:
If you are trying to lessen your appetite, eat fruit 20 minutes before a main meal. And remember, eat to live; don't live to eat.

Experience Good Thoughts:
"Courtesy is the one coin you can never have too much of or be stingy with."
—John Wanamaker, American Merchant

Think Golf:
When you're having a exceptionally good round, keep your emotions under control. As the pressure builds to continue your low score, try to keep everything in perspective. Slow your thought process down and think clearly about your next shot. This will help to keep your swing fluid and your timing in sync. Your head controls your fine motor skills, which are required in pitching, chipping and putting.

Make Me Smile:
You played a hard round and the rough was almost like a hazard. You congratulated yourself for a round well played – under the circumstances, even though your score was several shots higher than your usual game. You're posting your score at the clubhouse. Then you find out --The rough will be mowed tomorrow!

TUESDAY

Name: PRE-ROUND WARMUP: SEATED TWIST IN CART

Goal: Prepare and "repair" spine before, during, and after round; increase spinal and shoulder rotation.

Explanation:

Sit tall in cart with feet together. Reach back to cart pole with right hand and place left hand on seat rail. Inhale to prepare. Exhale sitting taller and turn upper body toward right as hip remain still and quiet. Repeat five times each side (moving to driver's seat). Focus on breath and lifting of the spine away from hips.

Nutrition Tip:
If you love beef, you don't have to give it up. Just be sure to buy the leanest cuts such as eye of round cuts, ribeye, flank steak, sirloin steak, rump roast, tenderloin, or extra-lean ground beef.

Experience Good Thoughts:
"A true friend is someone who thinks that you are a good egg even though he knows that you are slightly cracked."
—Bernard Meltzer, American Law Professor

Think Golf:
Bobby Jones once said, "Not every hole is meant to be birdied." And that should be one of the guiding principles in your golf game. Maybe you can get on every green in regulation but it's the short game that tests your skill. Remember that your main opponent is yourself and golf is meant to be fun. Do your best. Let it happen.

Make Me Smile:
Confidence fades away in the presence of water.

WEDNESDAY

Name: HEAVY BALL: FOLLOW THROUGH IN THIRDS

Goal: Promote muscle memory in torso for follow through; enhance stability and posture.

Explanation:

Stand in address position with ball in hands in place of club. Inhale. Exhale and move ball 1/3 into follow through. Inhale return to address. Repeat to 2/3, then to the top of follow through. Sequence of thirds will be repeated 5x. Focus on spinal placement and abdominal strength. Exercise should mimic golf swing as much as possible.

Nutrition Tip:
Good overall health means being physically, mentally and emotionally healthy. Keep calories from fat to 20 percent or less of your total caloric intake. Maintain a healthy weight by eating right and exercising regularly. Men between the ages of 31 and 50 who are moderately active should eat a maximum of 2,400 to 2,600 calories a day. Women in the same stats should eat a maximum of 2,000 calories a day. Avoid salt and refined sugars as much as possible.

Experience Good Thoughts:
"You are not here merely to make a living. You are here in order to enable the world to live more simply, with greater vision, with a finer spirit of hope and achievement. You are here to enrich the world, and you impoverish yourself if you forget the errand."   —Woodrow Wilson, 28th President

Think Golf:
Remember that every hole is a new experience. It's always different and each one offers a unique challenge. Don't miss the moment by falling prey to either an adrenaline rush if you're having a great round or to despair if you're shooting less than stellar shots. Slow down. Be patient. Take your time.

Make Me Smile:
Psychologists say 1 out of every 4 golfers is obsessed with the game. Check 3 of your friends. If they play for recreation, you're it!

THURSDAY

Name: YOGA/STRETCH: WARRIOR II
Goal: Increase strength, balance, and flexibility in legs as well as focus on breath to calm mind.

Explanation:

Start in Warrior I position with right foot forward and left foot back on ball of foot. Turn left foot outward flat and open arms parallel with floor so chest faces left. Palms face down. Hold strong in this position for 10 seconds. Repeat other side.

Nutrition Tip:
Worried about heart disease, high blood pressure, and cancer? Reduce your risk by eating a high fiber diet. You can only get fiber from eating plant foods, such as fruits, vegetables, and whole grains. Most adults only eat about half the recommended amount of fiber each day. Eating a leafy green salad with your meals will help boost fiber intake and lessen the amount of food you eat at your main meal.

Experience Good Thoughts:
"Your children need your "presence" more than your "presents."
—Jesse Jackson, Civil Rights Leader

Think Golf:
Roger Maltbie, past PGA player and NBC golf commentator, believes in the synergy of the body and mind when playing golf. In his words, "The most important thing is to develop a pre-shot routine and make that a habit. If you do the same thing over and over in a robotic fashion, your body will have a very difficult time discerning the difference between a pressure situation and being on the driving range."

Make Me Smile:
A woman married to a golf nut was talking to her oldest daughter about when her time comes to die. "When I die, bury me on the golf course," she said. "Then I'll be sure your dad will visit me."

FRIDAY

Name: **PILATES: LEG PULL FRONT**
Goal: Reinforce spinal, shoulder and pelvic stability; increase coordination.

Explanation:

Start in pushup position with legs straight. Inhale lifting one foot off floor in flexed position. Exhale and further flex the supporting foot while pointing the foot that is lifted. Repeat 5x then return foot down and repeat other side. Focus on maintaining straight body alignment throughout entire movement.

Nutrition Tip:

Omega-3 fatty acids, found in oily fish such as mackerel, salmon, tuna and herring, help prevent blood clots from forming, which ultimately reduces the risk of heart disease. You get more benefit from eating the fish itself than from taking fish oil supplements.

Experience Good Thoughts:

"Good fortune is what happens when opportunity meets with planning."

—Thomas Edison

Think Golf:

Watching the flight of your ball will help you know what to do to improve. Two factors apply in determining the direction of the ball: the angle of the clubface at impact and the path of the clubhead relative to the target line. If you are aware of these, you are on your way to consistently hitting better shots.

Make Me Smile:

For men, similar rules and form apply when golfing or using a public restroom such as: Use a loose grip at all times; keep your head down; be quiet while others are preparing to go and keep correct form — back straight, knees bent and feet shoulder width apart.

SATURDAY/SUNDAY

GOLFING DAYS ARE GOOD FOR YOUR HEALTH

REFLECTING ON THE PAST WEEK:

What was your basic attitude? Were you a positive thinker or did you need an "attitude adjustment?" Are you having success with eating healthier and doing your exercise program? How do you feel physically? If you went golfing, write down any comments that might be helpful later in improving your game. Remember, that laughter is the best medicine in the face of adversity. Are you seeing the lighter side of life?

The exercise that helped me the most this week was on page:

_____

My nutritional habits this week were:

_____

What made me smile this week?

_____

_____

Looking back at my golf week:
     My Score: _____ What did I do right? _____

_____

_____

     What could I do to improve?

_____

_____

Goals for next week: _____

_____

_____

MONDAY

Name: DB STRENGTH: TWISTER

Goal: Promote spinal dynamic flexibility and power for turn while keeping legs and hips quiet.

Explanation:

Stand in address position with 10-15-20lb dumbbell held in both hands against sternum. Head looking at ball. Rotate only trunk back and forth quickly in short arc. Focus on stabilizing with legs and gluteals while trying to increase shoulder turn. Repeat 50x. Breathe and maintain good posture with activated abdominals.

Nutrition Tip:
Cantaloupe is not only refreshing but it's really good for you. Did you know that a quarter of a melon will supply your body with almost as much Vitamin A and C as most people need in a whole day?

Experience Good Thoughts:
"We are what we repeatedly do; excellence, then, is not an act but a habit."
—Aristotle, Greek Philosopher

Think Golf:
Having a through swing is a necessity for good distance and direction. Consistently returning the clubshaft and front arm to their original angle at impact will help you to score your best. Focus on your downswing and follow-through.

Make Me Smile:
After a long day on the course, the frustrated golfer looked at his caddie and said, "You are absolutely the worst caddie in the world." The caddie calmly replied, "I don't think so. That would be too much of a coincidence!"

TUESDAY

Name: HEAVY BALL: FIGURE 8 THROUGH KNEES

Goal: Warm up powerhouse muscles and joints of low back, hips, and knees; strengthen torso; coordination and balance.

Explanation:

Stand with feet slightly wider than hip distance apart. Holding ball with bent arms in front of chest, squat down placing weight mostly in heels. Figure 8 ball around knees 10x one direction then switch directions. Focus on bending from hips and knees remaining in squat. Keep head and shoulders higher than hips and abdominals tight.

Nutrition Tip:
Peppers are high in Vitamin C, bioflavonoids, and Vitamin A, and contain folic acid, potassium, and niacin. They also inhibit cancer–causing agents during digestion. Try to find new ways to incorporate peppers into your meals.

Experience Good Thoughts:
"The journey of a thousand miles must begin with a single step."   —Lao Tzu

Think Golf:
Watching the pros play in tournaments can bring to light some important swing techniques that have the capacity to improve your game. Walking from hole to hole taking in their stance, swing, follow-through, attitude, focus and disposition can be the start of a better game for you. Professional Tournaments are played all year round in every area of the country. If you have never been a spectator at a live PGA event, treat yourself to one this year.

Make Me Smile:
A blonde calls a golf course and asks, "Can you tell me how long it takes to play 9 holes?" The receptionist replies, "Just a minute." "Thank you," the blonde says, and hangs up.

WEDNESDAY

Name: CARDIO: DANCING

Goal: Increase cardiovascular endurance and stamina for the 4+ hours of golf; enhance concentration and focus; improve coordination, balance and rhythm.

Explanation:

Can't dance? Sure you can! Dancing to any upbeat tune is a great way to expend some pent up energy, increase rhythm, and let off some steam. Put some music on and let the body go! Want to burn more calories? Get the arms and legs moving wildly over head and out to the sides. Try some claps and leg kicks too. Dance for 30 minutes.....or dance the night away.

Nutrition Tip:
Vegetables that grow above ground such as cabbage, broccoli and brussel sprouts have fiber, slow-release energy, and no fat. They are considered to be anti-cancer foods.

Experience Good Thoughts:
"Give me six hours to chop down a tree and I will spend the first four sharpening the axe."

—Abraham Lincoln, 16th President

Think Golf:
Solid, steady shots start with a consistent pre-shot routine. Whether it's a practice swing, a relaxation thought, a yardage and wind check, a last look at the target, or getting your stance just right — if you do the same thing before each and every swing, your body and mind will know what's coming and you'll be able to depend on your mind to reproduce the shots you want it to remember.

Make Me Smile:
The golf course has a way of diminishing your self-confidence. I start out the round feeling like Tiger Woods and after playing 18 holes, the course has whipped me into Winnie the Pooh!

THURSDAY

Name: PILATES: ONE LEG KICK
Goal: Emphasize shoulder and pelvic stabilization while strengthening hamstrings for better muscular balance for swing.

Explanation:

Lie on floor face down with upper body propped up on elbows and legs straight, squeezed together, toes pointed. Inhale to prepare. Exhale as one knee bends and pulses twice kicking heel toward buttocks. (First pulse: point, second pulse: flex foot) Inhale to return pointed foot back down. Repeat alternating legs. Complete 5-8 repetitions with each leg. Focus on maintaining spine angle and tightening hamstrings for power.

Nutrition Tip:
Drinking 1 or 2 glasses of red wine a day may reduce heart disease. Red wine has flavonoids which is good for cholesterol. It is best with foods containing B vitamins. An interesting note is that all alcohol raises the "good" cholesterol in our bodies, but white wine, liquor & beer are nutritionally lacking and not as healthy.

Experience Good Thoughts:
"I dream my painting and then paint my dream."

—Vincent Van Gogh

Think Golf:
When you're in the sand, your first thought is just to get the heck out. Many times that lack of planning leads to a backswing that is too short and results in a stroke that doesn't have the power to lift the ball out of the sand. Keep your head out of the sand and take the time to plan your shot.

Make Me Smile:
On the course a golfer saw another player put three golf balls in his pocket. He walked up to him and asked, "What's in your pocket?" The golfer answered, "Golf balls." The other player asked, "Is that anything like tennis elbow?"

FRIDAY

Name: YOGA/STRETCH: SPIDER

Goal: Increase flexibility and elasticity in inner thighs; help to prevent injury.

Explanation:

Stand with feet wider than hip distance apart and toes aiming outward at 45 degree angle. Squat down keeping weight in heels and rest elbows on thighs. Try to hold position for approximately 10-15 seconds then repeat. For extra stretch, place hands on floor inside feet and prop elbows on inside of knees. Breath slowly through stretch allowing muscles to "give in" to gravity and experience full stretch.

Nutrition Tip:

Eating at restaurants a lot? Here are some suggestions for healthy eating when you dine out. Try a veggie pizza, pasta and vegetables with marinara sauce, veggie wrap, vegetable soup, or salads. If you stay away from cream sauces and soups and replace French fries with salad, you'll add nutritious foods to your quick meals.

Experience Good Thoughts:

"You give but little when you give of your possessions. It is when you give of yourself that you truly give."

—Kahlil Gibran

Think Golf:

Keeping your spine angle from your waist to your neck steady helps to maintain consistent shots. If you move that angle up or down during your swing, you'll be prone to erratic shots.

Make Me Smile:

Gerald Ford on his improving game: "I know I'm getting better at golf because I'm hitting fewer spectators."

SATURDAY/SUNDAY

GOLFING DAYS ARE GOOD FOR YOUR HEALTH

REFLECTING ON THE PAST WEEK:

What was your basic attitude? Were you a positive thinker or did you need an "attitude adjustment?" Are you having success with eating healthier and doing your exercise program? How do you feel physically? If you went golfing, write down any comments that might be helpful later in improving your game. Remember, that laughter is the best medicine in the face of adversity. Are you seeing the lighter side of life?

The exercise that helped me the most this week was on page:

_____

My nutritional habits this week were:

_____

What made me smile this week?

_____

_____

Looking back at my golf week:
       My Score: _____ What did I do right? _____

_____

_____

       What could I do to improve?

_____

_____

Goals for next week: _____

_____

_____

MONDAY

Name: DB STRENGTH: TAKEAWAY SQUAT III
Goal: Mimic golf swing from top swing through impact adding resistance outside the body; promote muscle memory.

Explanation:

In wide stance, hold 3-5-8lb weight in right hand, same arm in top position. Bring right elbow past right hip, shift body weight to left keeping hand with weight back. At the impact position, bring weight down across, and bending knees, reach across left foot. Repeat 20-30x with control.

Nutrition Tip:
Grill fruits or vegetables for a different taste. Wrap them in aluminum foil or use skewers. Pieces of pineapple, yellow squash, eggplant, nectarines, zucchini, cherry tomatoes, onions, and mushrooms work especially good on the grill.

Experience Good Thoughts:
"I have yet to find the man, however exalted his station, who did not do better work and put forth greater effort under a spirit of approval than under a spirit of criticism."
—Charles Schwab, Businessman

Think Golf:
When you walk up to a hole, survey the shot, estimating yardage and any hazards. Then decide on the club to use and pull it out of the bag. Don't rush to pull a club out first and then try to decide if it's the right one. Chances are that you'll use the club in your hands even if you don't think it's the best for that shot.

Make Me Smile:
Golfer's prayer: Lord, grant that my ball lie in green pastures and stay out of still waters.

TUESDAY

Name: DYNAMIC STRETCH: STANDING CHEST OPENER

Goal: Open chest and ribcage for better posture at address and ability to maintain spine angle throughout swing to increase accuracy.

Explanation:

Stand with your feet in address position. Clasp hands behind your back opening up chest cavity. Slowly bend over from waist allowing arms to follow and point up toward sky. Hold belly button in to support spine and keep knees bent. Allow head to hang looking back through knees. Slowly roll back up to standing with head being last to roll. Repeat 3 times.

Nutrition Tip:

Choose a sweet potato instead of a white one. Sweet potatoes are nutritional greats, one of the best vegetables you can eat and are loaded with potassium, Vitamin C, fiber and carotenoids. Add applesauce instead of butter for flavor and moisture.

Experience Good Thoughts:

"One word frees us of all the weight and pain of life: That word is love."

—Sophocles, Greek Tragic Dramatist

Think Golf:

When you're setting up to use your driver, be sure your hands are under your head and not extended too far away from your body. This will help you to make solid contact and start with better tee shots.

Make Me Smile:

An old duffer was playing golf with his friends when his second shot left him with a thirty-foot putt. Thinking no-one would believe he could make the putt, he offers a bet. "I have a dollar bill that says I can make this putt. Will anyone bet me on that?" His friends all agreed and the old duffer missed the putt by 15 feet. All of the guys came up to collect their money from the bet and the old golfer pulls out a dollar bill that had the words "I can make this putt" written on it. He grinned from ear to ear since he had literally won the bet.

WEDNESDAY

Name: BIG BALL: DIAGONAL LIFT W/LEG LIFT

Goal: Promote balance and posture; increase coordination and control in different planes of motion.

Explanation:

Stand tall holding ball in front of body and feet hip distance apart. Inhale to prepare. Exhale shifting weight on to right foot. Simultaneously, lift leg leg straight out to side while lifting ball straight over head. Ball will be at same angle as body and ears right between elbows at top. Lift and lower 10x one side then switch legs.

Nutrition Tip:

Do you like fresh herbs? Optimum conditions for drying and maintaining flavor are temperatures above 85 degrees and humidity below 60%. Tie herbs in bunches with cotton string and place upside-down in a large paper bag pierced with air holes. Tie the bag and hang it with the leaves facing downward in a warm, airy place. The bag keeps light out, retaining the flavor of the leaves and catches any seeds that may fall.

Experience Good Thoughts:

"The Dictionary is the only place that success comes before work. Hard work is the price we must pay for success. I think you can accomplish anything if you're willing to pay the price."
—Vince Lombardi

Think Golf:

Youngsters and women with small hands might find that the interlock grip helps them to hold the club better. Place your little finger of your right hand between the index and second fingers of your left hand when you grip the club. This locks your fingers together and helps to have better control of the club.

Make Me Smile:

What's my handicap? Let's see. I think it might be my woods, my irons and even my putter!

THURSDAY

Name: HEAVY BALL: FEET ON BALL PLANK
Goal: Promote stability and posture control throughout joints of body from ankles to shoulders.

Explanation:

Kneel on all fours with heavy ball behind feet. Lift body into pushup position, then slowly lift one foot then the other onto ball. Toes may be pointed or flexed. Body should maintain flat back. Evenly disperse weight between hands and feet. Hold with controlled breathing for 10-30 seconds.

Nutrition Tip:
If you have trouble drinking as much water as is recommended, try squeezing a piece of lemon (about 1/8 of a whole lemon) into the water. Not only does it give it a refreshing and flavorful taste but it also adds some vitamins to your daily diet.

Experience Good Thoughts:
"Teachers open the door but YOU must walk through it yourself."
—Chinese Proverb

Think Golf:
If your ball lands on a dirt road, try to glide the ball off without making a divot. Take a wide backswing, hit the ball, and graze the top of the road with your club. The ball will fly low and run.

Make Me Smile:
Two friends went out to play golf and decided they would play completely by the rules that day. During the game, one player's ball landed on the cart path. He picked up the ball ready to get relief when his partner said, "I thought we agreed not to improve our lie." The player tried to explain that this relief was within the rules but his partner would not allow him to move the ball. So the player went to the cart to get a club. He took a few practice swings, hitting the pavement each time, scraping his club so hard it sent sparks flying. Finally, he took his shot. The ball took off and landed just a few feet from the pin. "Great shot!" his friend exclaimed. "What club did you use?" The player answered with a grin on his face, "YOUR 7 iron!!!!"

FRIDAY

Name: YOGA/STRETCH: DOWNWARD FACING PUPPY

Goal: Stretch and strengthen back muscles while opening chest and ribcage for better turn capability during swing.

Explanation:

Kneel on all fours similar to cat/cow pose. Inhale pulling belly button into spine and sit back onto heels. Keep palms on floor and allow head to fall between elbows. Exhale and bring body back up to kneeling position. Repeat 10x.

Nutrition Tip:
TOTAL cereal has it all. It supplies your body with 100% of the recommended daily requirement for vitamins and minerals while adding only 100 calories to your diet.

Experience Good Thoughts:
"Wherever life takes us, there are always moments of wonder."
—Jimmy Carter, 39th President

Think Golf:
Accuracy is always more important than distance when you're playing any course. Striking the ball on center with good tempo is better than hitting a ball at high speed off center.

Make Me Smile:
A pastor, a doctor and an engineer were behind a particularly slow foursome. "What's with these guys? They're so slow," the engineer says. The doctor replies, "I don't know, but they're pretty pathetic players too." The pastor sees the greens keeper coming and decides to ask about them. The greens keeper says, "That's a group of blind firefighters. They lost their sight saving our clubhouse from a fire so we let them play free anytime." The pastor compassionately says that he would pray for them. The doctor says he's going to check some ophthalmologist friends to see if anyone can help them. And the engineer blurts out, "Why can't they just play at night!"

SATURDAY/SUNDAY

GOLFING DAYS ARE GOOD FOR YOUR HEALTH

REFLECTING ON THE PAST WEEK:

What was your basic attitude? Were you a positive thinker or did you need an "attitude adjustment?" Are you having success with eating healthier and doing your exercise program? How do you feel physically? If you went golfing, write down any comments that might be helpful later in improving your game. Remember, that laughter is the best medicine in the face of adversity. Are you seeing the lighter side of life?

The exercise that helped me the most this week was on page:

_____

My nutritional habits this week were:

_____

What made me smile this week?

_____

_____

Looking back at my golf week:
       My Score: _____ What did I do right? _____

_____

_____

       What could I do to improve?

_____

_____

Goals for next week: _____

_____

_____

MONDAY

Name: HEAVY BALL: PLANK W/HANDS ON BALL
Goal: Promote total body stability and balance.

Explanation:

Place both hands on ball: thumbs facing forward and fingertips aiming downward. Lift into plank position with legs straight and feet together. Maintain regular breathing engaging chest and entire midsection. Goal is to be able to hold position for 30 seconds. Extra challenge: lift one foot off floor

Nutrition Tip:
Preliminary research indicates that 64+ oz. of water a day could significantly ease problems for up to 80% of those suffering with back and joint pain.

Experience Good Thoughts:
"Love is supreme and unconditional; like is nice but limited."
—Duke Ellington, Jazz Composer & Pianist

Think Golf:
Approximately 1/3 of all professional golfers are playing injured at one time or another. 80% of those injuries are back related.

Make Me Smile:
Moses, Jesus and God are playing golf. Moses starts – hits his drive and it lands in the water. Moses raises his club and the water parts so he can play his ball. Next Jesus goes up to the tee, hits a great drive and his ball lands in the water. He walks up to the pond, walks on the water till he finds his ball, then chips it up onto the green. God is up next and whacks the ball from the tee. His ball heads for the water but lands on a lily pad. A large bullfrog snatched the ball and within seconds an eagle swoops down, grabs the frog with the ball in his mouth, and flies away. Just as they're passing over the green, the frog squeals with fright and drops the ball. It lands on the green and bounces right into the hole for a hole-in-one. Moses looks at Jesus and says, "I just hate playing with your dad."

TUESDAY

Name: **DB STRENGTH: FINISH SQUAT I**
Goal: Mimic golf swing from impact through follow through/finish adding resistance outside the body; promote muscle memory through repetition.

Explanation:

In wide stance, hold 3-5-8lb weight in LEFT hand. From impact position, follow through with left hand to balance finish position. Keep right shoulder down and flip right heel over. Repeat 20-30x focusing on balance and posture.

Nutrition Tip:
Use herbs, spices, and lemon juice for flavoring instead of salt. You'll be surprised how much salt you can reduce from your diet by making simple substitutions that taste good, wake up your taste buds, and are better for your health.

Experience Good Thoughts:
"It's always worthwhile to make others aware of their worth."   —Malcolm Forbes

Think Golf:
Don't be afraid to bend down to read the green before your putt. Cup your hands over the sides of your eyes and face. This will help you to concentrate on your line and will assist in keeping surrounding distractions from ruining your focus.

Make Me Smile:
The persistent golfer just keeps trying. He hits his ball and watches as it slices to the right and goes right through an open window. Knowing that he'd never find it, he takes out another ball and continues to play. On the fourth hole, a police officer comes up to him and says, "Are you the guy who hit a golf ball through that window back there?" "Yep, that's me," he replied. "Well, says the officer, it hit a dog who ran out in the street and a driver swerving to miss the dog ran into a house and three people are now in the hospital. All that because you sliced the ball." "I feel terrible," he says, "Is there anything I can do?" The officer thought for a minute and replied, "Why don't you try keeping your head down and close up your stance a little."

WEDNESDAY

Name: BIG BALL: DIAGONAL WOODCHOP
Goal: Enhance total body flexibility in all planes of motion; increase rhythm and coordination in timed movement.

Explanation:

Stand tall with feet slightly wider than hip distance apart. Hold ball directly in front of chest with straight arms. Inhale and reach ball to top left corner over shoulder slightly raising up on right toe. Exhale pulling ball down toward right ankle. Legs will bend into a slight lunge lifting left heel off floor. Focus on good form and rhythm. Repeat 10x on one side, Then switch to other side.

Nutrition Tip:
The following foods can be combined to make up a complete protein:
Rice Pudding, Corn and Lima Beans, Cereal with Milk, Macaroni and Cheese, Cheese Sandwich, Pasta with Tomato Sauce and Parmesan Cheese, Baked Potato with Yogurt, Split-pea Soup with Whole-Grain Crackers.

Experience Good Thoughts:
Love is a word we use freely but the Bible describes the enormity of the word "love" so much more completely. I Corinthians 13:4-7 says, "Love is patient and kind; it is not jealous or conceited or proud; love is not ill-mannered or selfish or irritable; love does not keep a record of wrongs; love is not happy with evil, but is happy with the truth. Love never gives up; and its faith, hope, and patience never fail.

Think Golf:
Keep your hands on the club throughout the swing in the same way you gripped it during your set-up. Moving your hands during the swing can lead to unwanted shots.

Make Me Smile:
"The ardent golfer would play Mount Everest if somebody would put a flagstick on top."
—Pete Dye

THURSDAY

Name: STRENGTH: SUPERMAN

Goal: Increase strength and endurance of low back musculature and gluteals to help prevent injury.

Explanation:

Lie face down on floor with arms and legs straight out. Inhale. As you exhale lift both arms and legs high as if flying. Head should be slightly lifted. Hold abdominals tight. Reach toes back and arms forward as far as possible. Hold for approximately 5-10 seconds. Then relax. Repeat 5x.

Nutrition Tip:
Research has found that the combination of iron and calcium offers the most benefit for bone health. Iron works better in your body if you take about 800 to 1,200 mg. of calcium a day.

Experience Good Thoughts:
"The reason why worry kills more people than work is that more people worry than work."

—Robert Frost, Poet

Think Golf:
"Golf is a game in which one endeavors to control a ball with implements ill adapted for the purpose."

—Woodrow Wilson, 28th President

Make Me Smile:
Golf is like middle age because at this time of life you really do have to play it as it lies. You don't have the opportunity to start all over. The most you can get is a mulligan. If it's an unplayable lie, everyone sympathizes, but you still have to take a penalty. On the other hand, golf and midlife also offer another chance. No matter how badly you hit one ball, you can still hit a stellar shot the next time. Of course, you can always screw up the next shot too!

FRIDAY

Name: YOGA/STRETCH: WARRIOR III
Goal: Increase strength, balance, and flexibility in legs as well as focus on breath to calm mind.

Explanation:

Step the right leg forward with arms overhead palms facing each other. Keep hands to left foot in one straight line. Begin to balance on right leg bringing arms forward and left leg back parallel to floor. Hold balance for 10 seconds. Slowly return back to both legs. Repeat balancing on other leg.

Nutrition Tip:
A mineral involved in the body's healing process, sense of taste, growth and sexual maturing, and part of many enzymes that regulate metabolism, zinc is important to the body's function. However, too much zinc can be harmful to the body and interfere with the way the body uses other essential minerals. So get enough but not too much by eating meat, liver, eggs, and seafood (especially oysters).

Experience Good Thoughts:
"I do not think there is any other quality so essential to success of any kind as the quality of perseverance. It overcomes almost everything, even nature."
—John D. Rockefeller

Think Golf:
Imagine the ball in flight straight down the fairway or rolling directly into the hole. Visualize the perfect shot. Jack Nicklaus said, "I never hit a shot, not even in practice, without having a very sharp in-focus picture of it in my head."

Make Me Smile:
Golf is a game invented by the same people who think the noise that comes out of a bagpipe is music!

SATURDAY/SUNDAY

GOLFING DAYS ARE GOOD FOR YOUR HEALTH

REFLECTING ON THE PAST WEEK:

What was your basic attitude? Were you a positive thinker or did you need an "attitude adjustment?" Are you having success with eating healthier and doing your exercise program? How do you feel physically? If you went golfing, write down any comments that might be helpful later in improving your game. Remember, that laughter is the best medicine in the face of adversity. Are you seeing the lighter side of life?

The exercise that helped me the most this week was on page:
_____

My nutritional habits this week were:
_____

What made me smile this week?
_____
_____

Looking back at my golf week:
    My Score: _____ What did I do right? _____
_____
_____

    What could I do to improve?
_____
_____

Goals for next week: _____
_____
_____

EPILOGUE

Mindi: Well, Mary Ann, after almost a whole year of working on this project, we're finally finished. It feels good to complete such a huge undertaking. Just like one of our messages in the book says: Follow-through is a key ingredient to success.

Mary Ann: You're right, Mindi. I remember that there were times when both of us wanted to just quit. It always seemed as though there was too much to do, and it was hard to see the light at the end of the tunnel. But now that we've finished, I'm sure we both feel satisfied about following through and being able to get our message out.

Mindi: You know, I know about the fitness and nutrition portions of this book. I live them every day. I work out with my clients and teach classes all week. But I really opened my mind to the other sections. I think I have a better outlook on my golf game and my life since I've been paying more attention to the mental and spiritual elements of our message.

Mary Ann: I'm just the opposite. I was always pretty aware of the mental and spiritual sides and don't take my game too seriously. I'm not a club thrower or pouter. Sure, I'd like to have a lower handicap, but I don't beat myself up over the double and triple bogeys I often get. I definitely needed more concentration on the physical part of my game and lifestyle. And, that's the part of the book I've been focusing on.

Mindi: Do you see a difference in your game since you've been exercising and eating healthier?

Mary Ann: I really do. I have greater stamina to walk the course, and my drives go farther, too. Your fitness program has done wonders for me, and since we started on this project together my handicap has come down several points. I can truly thank you for making exercising and fitness more fun and less work. I do my exercising in about 10 minutes a day. Who can't find that little bit of time to devote to a healthier body?

Mindi: I'm so glad you have benefited from our project. I have, too. I spend a lot of time outdoors, both golfing and exercising. But I've started to look at things a little more closely and have become more aware of my surroundings. I'm letting my senses come alive, and that leads me to thoughts and places

I had never been before. Another benefit of that seems to be that I'm much more focused on success in all areas of my life now.

Mary Ann: I think this lesson in "synergy" really works! We've learned that although the word "synergy" is not used often, when practiced it actually can produce an enormous impact on everyday life. Each of us concentrated on the parts we needed to develop, while also reinforcing the elements that we already were aware of. In the end, I feel better physically and emotionally, and my game has improved, too. As we noticed, when two or more things work together, the results can be astonishing.

Mindi: Yes, it's really amazing how this all fits together—like a big, human puzzle. We all know that we have to nourish the physical, mental and spiritual parts of our being. But actually doing it can seem like a monumental task. What both of us found out is that by feeding each element for a few minutes every day, we were able to improve our chances for success in the end. It wasn't nearly as difficult reaching our goal, working on it one day at a time.

Mary Ann: Well, we started out with an idea, developed it, put many months of hard work into it, tried to stay positive and laugh at ourselves when we'd get too serious about it all—and finally we have a finished product that we can be proud of. And we used a simple format to make it easy to follow and make progress. I know I'm eating healthier, thinking healthier, and feeling healthier.

Mindi: Me, too. And I'm excited about the way we were able to do this for ourselves and for others. Being able to turn just one page a day and incorporate those tips and elements into your life a little at a time really works. It breaks down the enormity of getting yourself into an overall healthier state into an attainable task.

Mary Ann: Now it's time to ask our readers some questions. Look over the pages where you recorded your scores and observations.

> ➢ Has your golf game improved?
> ➢ Has the fitness regimen helped to strengthen your muscles and allow you more flexibility?
> ➢ Are your drives going farther?
> ➢ Are you thinking in a more success-oriented frame of mind, positive in most situations, and consistently considerate of others?
> ➢ Have you benefited from the nutrition information, found yourself laughing at the jokes, and improved your game by using some of the golf tips?

Mindi: We hope this book has offered you new hope for attaining your goals and has proven to you that great things can be accomplished if you do just one small action every day. So turn back to page 1 now and start over. It's another year, and that means lots more opportunities to become a better YOU! And, if you'd rather have a live demonstration of the exercises, go to www.fitforgolfusa.com and order my DVDs. You'll find all of the exercises in this book on the DVDs.

BIOGRAPHIES OF AUTHORS

MINDI BOYSEN, LWMC, CGFP

Mindi Boysen, Certified Golf Fitness Specialist, is a recognized professional with a degree in education and 13 years of experience in the fitness industry. She is also a nationally Certified Lifestyle/Weight Management Consultant, Personal Trainer, and Group Fitness Instructor who specializes in functional, pilates-based training.

Her professional experience includes six years on the faculty at Indiana/Purdue University as a Physical Education Instructor, where she received the IUPUI Teacher Excellence & Recognition Award in 2000. Mindi has taught pilates and sports conditioning at several golf clubs, and now manages her own lifestyle coaching business teaching clients the best way to keep their bodies strong and healthy while preventing damage or injury to muscles.

Mindi coaches health-conscious golfers of all skill levels. From players on the PGA Tour to recreational golfers, she teaches fitness techniques designed to improve both a player's golf game and overall health. Her format includes strengthening of the specific muscle groups used in the golf swing, flexibility exercises, and reinforcement of balance and stability movements.

Her series of three DVDs, Fit For Golf/Fit For Life, have been in demand with golf enthusiasts around the country. The popularity of her first DVD triggered her decision to build on her philosophy: "A fit golfer is a better golfer." Each DVD takes beginners and skilled golfers alike to higher levels of golf fitness. Her careful choice of exercises helps to prevent back and joint damage related to swinging a club. These videos contain effective pre-game workouts that require very little time or space and produce the best results with the least amount of effort. Learn more about Mindi and her DVDs by visiting her website at www.fitforgolfusa.com.

Mindi won the 1998 Ms. Indy Lightweight Bodybuilding and Ms. Fitness Indiana State championships. Since then, she has taught numerous classes ranging from Yoga and Kickboxing to Seniors Stability/Balance and Obstacle Course Training. Mindi's love of fitness, coupled with her love of golf, has been instrumental in the development of this book.

MARY ANN SOUTER

Mary Ann Souter is an independent marketing consultant and freelance writer and is currently working with the Arizona Women's Golf Association, the second largest women's golf association in the nation. She contributes to the success of the organization by composing their monthly newsletter, writing press releases and articles, visiting golf groups, developing membership materials, and seeking promotional opportunities. Through her affiliation with the AWGA, she has come to understand the importance of the synergistic relationship among body, mind, and spirit as a vital component for a player to reach his or her full potential in golf. The philosophy that "golf is more than swinging a club" has become apparent as she works in the golf industry and strives to improve her own golf game.

Her published materials include numerous cover stories for M.D. NEWS, as well as frequent articles in health and sports publications such as Arizona Golfer, Golf Today, World Golf, Golf the Desert, Health & Lifestyles and AZ Health magazines. In addition, she has contributed to several local periodicals and newspapers.

Mary Ann has extensive experience in the areas of research and writing, which has been exhibited in a variety of settings and locations around the country. During her tenure with non-profit organizations such as the Arthritis Foundation and RSVP program for senior citizens, she wrote advertising materials and newsletters for their membership. She was editor of the Business Quarterly, a city government newsletter. In the late 1990s she added financial communications to her work history, writing press releases, company overviews and annual reports for an investor relations firm. Most recently, her experience has incorporated health-related articles on the subjects of chiropractic care, natural health supplements, and laser vision correction. Her work has included promotional pieces, technical explanations of products and procedures, and human interest stories about physicians and their practices.

The development of this book has called upon Mary Ann's talents and positive attitude to provide information and inspiration that will help everyday golfers as well as skilled golfers play their best game. Having faced many humbling moments on the golf course has allowed her to experience, first-hand, the need for a synergistic approach to golf. Her ability to provide useful facts in a reader-friendly format has attracted readers nationwide to her style of presentation.

INDEX

CARDIO

CHEST

CLUB CONTROL/ACCURACY

FLEXIBILITY

LOW BACK

STRENGTH